TŪRANGA WAEWAE

TŪRANGA WAE WAE

Identity & Belonging in Aotearoa New Zealand

SECOND EDITION

Edited by Ella Kahu, Te Rā Moriarty,
Helen Dollery & Richard Shaw

MASSEY UNIVERSITY PRESS

Contents

7   KUPU MĀORI/GLOSSARY

13   INTRODUCTION:
*Ella Kahu, Te Rā Moriarty,
Helen Dollery and Richard Shaw*

PART ONE: FACES OF AOTEAROA NEW ZEALAND

22   FACES:
Introduction
Richard Shaw

25   CHAPTER ONE:
Identity and citizenship
Laying the foundations
Ella Kahu

40   CHAPTER TWO:
Tangata whenua
Māori, identity and belonging
Te Rā Moriarty

59   CHAPTER THREE:
Aotearoa's ever-changing face
Diversity as an unfinished project
*Trudie Cain and
Tracey Nicholls*

PART TWO: VOICES OF AOTEAROA NEW ZEALAND

82   VOICES:
Introduction
Trudie Cain and Ella Kahu

86   CHAPTER FOUR:
Voices in the House
Political representation and participation
Richard Shaw

107   CHAPTER FIVE:
Shout it out
Participation and protest in public life
Ella Kahu

128   CHAPTER SIX:
Voicing cultural rights
Arts, identity and belonging
Rand Hazou and Trudie Cain

PART THREE: PLACES IN AOTEAROA NEW ZEALAND

152   PLACES:
Introduction
*Trudie Cain and
Juliana Mansvelt*

156 CHAPTER SEVEN:
Physical places
Home as place
Trudie Cain and Juliana Mansvelt

177 CHAPTER EIGHT:
Institutional places
The university
Richard Shaw and Matt Russell

200 CHAPTER NINE:
Digital places
Identity, participation and power
Stella Pennell

PART FOUR: STORIES OF AOTEAROA NEW ZEALAND

224 STORIES:
Introduction
Ella Kahu

228 CHAPTER TEN:
We're all equal here
Ideals of equality
David Littlewood

247 CHAPTER ELEVEN:
Clean and green
A myth that matters
Juliana Mansvelt

268 CHAPTER TWELVE:
Anzac
'Lest we forget' or 'Best we forget'?
Helen Dollery and Carl Bradley

295 CONCLUSION:
Identity and belonging in Aotearoa New Zealand
Richard Shaw

305 ABOUT THE CONTRIBUTORS

309 ACKNOWLEDGEMENTS

310 INDEX

Kupu Māori / Glossary

WORD OR PHRASE	DESCRIPTION
ahikā	Continued occupation; describes the home people of marae/hapū/iwi
Aotearoa	The Māori name of New Zealand
aroha	Love
atua	Māori deities of the natural world
awa	Ancestral river; a river
hā	Breath; essence
hāora	Oxygen
hapū	Consists of a number of whānau sharing descent from a common ancestor; the primary political unit in traditional Māori society; to be pregnant; to be conceived
haukāinga	Local people of the marae; home
hauora	Health; vitality; wellbeing
Hawaiki	Distant homeland; an origin point
He Whakaputanga o te Rangatiratanga o Nu Tireni	The Declaration of Independence
heke	To descend; to journey; painted panels in a wharenui representing an ancestor's ribs
hīkoi	To walk; also adopted for the act of protest marches
Hineahuone	The original human ancestor; the original female ancestor
Hine-te-Aparangi/Kura-mārō-tini	The names of the ancestors credited with naming Aotearoa
hui	To meet; to gather; a meeting or gathering
iwi	A large group of people sharing a common ancestry and associated with a distinct territory; bone
kai	Food; to eat; to consume
kaimoana	Food from the ocean
kāinga	Home; village; settlement

kaitaka	Traditional cloak adorned with tāniko patterns
kaitiakitanga/ kaitiekitanga	Guardianship; stewardship; the act and responsibility of looking after land; resources and people
karakia	Ritual chant; an incantation
kaupapa	Project; initiative; activity; theme
kawa	Marae protocol; customs of the marae
kāwanatanga	Governance
korowai	A cloak made from flax fibre and decorated with tassels
koru	Spiral motif integral in Māori art, based on the silver fern frond; symbolises creation and how life changes yet stays the same
kotahitanga	Unity
kōwhaiwhai	Painted scroll ornamentation, commonly used on meeting-house rafters
mana	Authority; control; influence; prestige; power; spiritual gift; spiritual authority and power
mana atua	Strength and prestige drawn from the deities and our responsibility to those connections
mana motuhake	Independence; self-determination
mana tangata	Strength and prestige of people alive today and our responsibilities to each other
mana tūpuna	Strength and prestige drawn from our ancestors and our responsibilities to them
mana whenua	Strength drawn from ancestral lands; our responsibility to protect those lands
manaaki/ manaakitanga	To look after; to care for; to be hospitable; to elevate the mana of another
manawa	Heart
mangōpare	A pattern representing the hammerhead shark seen in the painted panels inside of a wharenui
manuhiri/ manuwhiri	Guests; visitors
Māori/māori	Indigenous person to Aotearoa; normal; native flora and fauna
marae	Centre of a Māori community; the tūrangawaewae of a Māori person or people
Māui Pōtiki/Māui Tikitiki a Taranga	Ancestor
maunga	Ancestral mountain; a mountain
Maungapōhatu	A mountain in Te Urewera

mauri	Life principle; life force; the energy of life
mihimihi	A greeting which introduces the speaker and their connections to others
muka	Fine processed flax fibre used for making clothing
Mumuwhango	A female atua of the forest
Murirangawhenua	Ancestor; the kuia (grandmother) of Māui
Ngā Kete o Te Wānanga	Three baskets of knowledge, obtained by Tāne-mahuta (or Tāwhaki, depending on iwi narrative) for humankind to use
ngā matatini Māori	Māori diverse realities
oranga	Life; health; wellbeing; sustenance
pā	Village; fort; city
Pākehā	Originally used for people from Britain and Europe; a New Zealander with ancestry to those places
Papatūānuku	Female origin; Earth Mother
pepeha	A form of words linking a person ancestrally with the communities and physical features of a particular landscape (mountains, rivers and oceans)
pōhiri/pōwhiri	Ceremony of welcome; to welcome
poupou	An upright carving often depicting an ancestor
pūhoro	Tāmoko design on the legs
pūrākau	Ancient narrative; story
rāhui	Temporary ban or restriction on an area or resource
rangatira	Chief; leader
rangatiratanga	Chieftainship; authority; independence
Ranginui	Original male ancestor; Sky Father
rauponga	Carving pattern consisting of bold spiral
Rongo	Child of Ranginui and Papatūānuku; the deity of peace and cultivation
rongoā	Medicine; remedy
roto	Inside of something; a lake
rūnanga	A high council or legislative assembly called to discuss matters of significant concern to an iwi or community
tāhuhu	Ridge pole of a wharenui representing an ancestor's spine
Takaparawhau/ Bastion Point	A marae site in Tāmaki Makaurau. It was marked for development, which led to a 506-day protest occupation that started in 1977
tāmoko	Māori tattooing

Tāmaki Makaurau	Auckland
Tāne-mahuta	Child of Ranginui and Papatūānuku; deity with authority over the forests and birds
tangata/tāngata	Person/people
tangata whenua	Indigenous people of the land
tangata tiriti	Non-Māori New Zealanders
tangihanga	Weeping; funeral; rites for the dead
tāniko	To finger weave; embroider; a patterned border for cloaks
taonga	A treasure; something cherished; something valued
tapu	Restriction; sacred; prohibited
tauā	War party, army
Tāwhirimātea	Child of Ranginui and Papatūānuku; deity with authority over the winds, clouds, rain, snow and storms
te ao Māori	The Māori world including the Māori language, rituals, processes, practices, sites of importance, and ties to whānau, hapū and iwi
Te Ao Mārama	The world of light and understanding
Te Hiku o Te Ika	Northern regions of Te Ika a Māui
Te Ika a Māui	The fish of Māui; the North Island of Aotearoa New Zealand
Te Kore	The time of great potential; the nothing; the void
Te Pō	The time of activation; the night; gestation period
Te Punga a Māui/ Rakiura	Stewart Island
Te Reinga	The northernmost tip of Te Ika a Māui
te reo Māori	The Māori language
Te Taitokerau	The northern region of Te Ika a Māui
Te Tauihu o Te Waka a Māui	The northern region of the South Island of New Zealand
Te Tiriti o Waitangi	The Māori-language version, and most signed version, of the Treaty of Waitangi
Te Upoko o Te Ika a Māui	The southern region of the North Island of New Zealand
Te Waka a Māui	The vessel of Māui; the South Island of New Zealand
te whaiao	Birth canal; the world of light; entry point to Te Ao Mārama
tikanga	Protocol; practices; the appropriate way things are done
tino rangatiratanga	Absolute authority and independence; the right to self-determination

toa	Warrior; brave man
Tūmatauenga	Child of Ranginui and Papatūānuku; deity of conflict, defence and humanity
tūpāpaku	The body of the deceased
tupua/tipua	Supernatural
tupuna/tūpuna	Ancestors
tukutuku	Lattice work decorating the inner walls of a wharenui
tūrangawaewae	Place of belonging where we draw our strength from; 'standing' place
urupā	Burial ground; cemetery
wāhi tapu	A sacred place or site; a place subject to restriction on access or use
waho	Outside of something
wai	Water
waimāori	Fresh water
waiora	Life-giving waters; health
wānanga	Place of higher learning; to discuss; to deliberate and consider
whakapapa	Ancestry; genealogy
whakatauākī	A proverbial expression where the author is known
whakataukī	A proverbial expression
whānau	Family; close kinship group; to be born
whanaunga	A relation
whanaungatanga	Relationships
whare	House; building; residence; habitation
wharekai	Dining hall
wharenui/whare tūpuna/tīpuna whare	Main house of the marae; ancestral house
whare wānanga	Place of higher learning
whenua	Land; soil; placenta
wiri	The shaking movement of hands during waiata to demonstrate an affinity with nature

This glossary was compiled for the first edition of the book by Margaret Forster, Te Rina Warren and Veronica Tawhai. Additions for the second edition were made by Te Rā Moriarty. A small number of definitions were sourced from two online sites: the Māori Dictionary (https://maoridictionary.co.nz) and the Ngata Dictionary (https://www.teaching.co.nz/ngata).

Introduction

*Ella Kahu, Te Rā Moriarty,
Helen Dollery and Richard Shaw*

This book explores identity, belonging and citizenship in Aotearoa New Zealand. At the individual level it explores some of the threads that comprise our personal identities and the relationships we have with others which help shape a sense of self, while at the broader societal level it critically examines some of those things said to define New Zealand's national identity.

It was once suggested that the English spend little time reflecting on what it means to be English 'because it is so simply and obviously a fact' (Barker, 1948, p. 195). The same can be said of us here in Aotearoa New Zealand. Except that it isn't that simple, of course: what it means to be a New Zealander or to be in this place (and these are not necessarily the same things) may be quite different for different people. Understanding this, and the complexity of the social world and our place in it, requires reflection, a capacity to ask questions of things that are often taken for granted, and a willingness to be open to alternative ways of seeing things. These are what this book intends to do: to probe, prompt and encourage you to reflect on aspects of your own sense of self, and of the ways in which we collectively make sense of who we are, which might otherwise continue to enjoy the status of received wisdom.

It would be difficult to overstate the importance of understanding the diversity of people, and of appreciating others' ways of being and doing at this point in place and time. So many of the large challenges facing Aotearoa New Zealand and the world are grounded in issues of identity, such as the material consequences of political polarisation, the increasing divide between the haves and the have-nots, the nefarious effects of social media, and the myriad public health and other issues thrown up by the global Covid-19 pandemic.

Some of those challenges have very sharp edges indeed. Following the Christchurch mosque attacks in 2019, the New Zealand government set up a Royal Commission of Inquiry to investigate what happened, and, more importantly, to look at how such terrible events could be prevented in the future. A key finding was the need to improve social cohesion — defined by the Commission as that state of social affairs in which all people have a sense of belonging, social inclusion, participation, recognition and legitimacy (Royal Commission of Inquiry into the terrorist attack on Christchurch masjidain on 15 March 2019, 2020). The Commission's definition reflects many of the key ideas of this book (as outlined in

Chapter 1). A better understanding of oneself, and from that a better understanding of what it means to be a citizen of this place, are both essential to the tasks ahead. To put this a little differently: it is hard to think of a time when the matters addressed in this book were more urgent and of greater importance than they are right now.

Structure of the book

Following the introduction, the book is arranged in four parts, each of which opens with a short discussion in which the central questions and issues pursued in the subsequent chapters — what we call a 'conceptual template' — are set out. The other core feature of the publication is that each substantive chapter is preceded by 'He tirohanga Māori: A Māori perspective', written by Te Rā Moriarty, and a whakataukī or whakatauākī, a relevant Māori proverb. What Te Rā gifts readers of the book through these reflections is a series of thoughtful, informative perspectives on the topics of the chapters themselves: put side by side, his words and those of the chapters' various authors comprise a nuanced, comprehensive appreciation of the matters that are at the heart of this book.

The chapters

Part 1, 'Faces of Aotearoa New Zealand', sets the scene by exploring both the rapidly changing demographic composition of our population, and several other ways in which the individual and the collective faces of New Zealand are altering. It examines some of the diverse identities that make up Aotearoa New Zealand. The central theme is that the use of the singular category 'citizen' masks what is, increasingly, a rich, messy and tremendously diverse national population.

Ella Kahu gets things started in Chapter 1, in which she introduces, defines and illustrates the core ideas running through the book. An awful lot has been written about the concepts of identity and citizenship, in particular, and the core purpose of Ella's chapter is to provide a clear explanation of the ways in which we work with those terms in this book.

In Chapter 2, Te Rā Moriarty offers a Māori perspective on notions of identity, belonging and citizenship. Drawing on sacred stories, and Māori experiences of colonisation, one of the important things Te Rā does is gently show us that the range of intellectual tools we can use to make sense of things such as identity, belonging and citizenship is probably greater than many of us are aware.

Trudie Cain and Tracey Nicholls explore the shifting face(s) of Aotearoa New Zealand through the lens of demography and identity, in Chapter 3. Inevitably, they cannot cover each and every important dimension of these changes in full detail; what they do provide, though, is an intricate portrait of a country in which ethnicity, age, and sexuality and gender identity — and the intersections of these — all feature.

Part 2, 'Voices of Aotearoa New Zealand', explores some of the ways in which we give voice, individually or as part of a group, to our views, fears, hopes and aspirations. This section is explicitly about participation — how people express their points of view and seek to have them acknowledged as legitimate contributions to public debate; it has to do with how people's identities are expressed and heard. Richard Shaw, in Chapter 4, explores the ways in which people seek to express their voice through formal parliamentary politics, but he also suggests that choosing not to engage with politics is a legitimate expression of voice (albeit one with potentially disturbing consequences). In Chapter 5, Ella Kahu looks at participation outside of Parliament, exploring what motivates people to protest using two case studies to illustrate the impacts of voice on identity. In Chapter 6, Rand Hazou and Trudie Cain consider the role of the arts in both representing (including through protest) and constructing identity.

The penultimate section, Part 3, 'Places in Aotearoa New Zealand', explores the ways in which our identity is connected to places of significance to us, and examines how both tacit and explicit conventions, norms and rules structure relationships between people in these places. Beyond the level of the individual, our encounters with others in these contexts also have implications for notions of citizenship. Some places comprise environments in which the communities we belong to (or to which we aspire to belong) come together; others can provide a refuge and disengagement from such collective interactions. Trudie Cain and Juliana Mansvelt begin this section with a chapter in which they explore different understandings of home as a place of significance. In Chapter 8, Richard Shaw and Matt Russell examine the tacit and explicit 'rules of the game' that structure relationships within universities, while, in Chapter 9, Stella Pennell looks at the relationship between people's sense of self and their engagement with the digital world.

The chapters comprising Part 4, 'Stories of Aotearoa New Zealand', critically engage with three of the major narratives told in this country as a way of asserting national identity. The narratives we examine — which are about inequality, the environment and Anzac — are examples of the ways in which national narratives convey powerful messages about what it means to be in and of this country. In so doing, they can shape both our individual and collective (or national) senses of who we are. Clearly, each has elements of truth; equally, each tells only a partial story, and masks both the lived experiences of some members of our society and competing accounts of the way things are.

David Littlewood begins this process in Chapter 10 by examining the origins, evolution and accuracy of the idea that New Zealand is a society where everyone is treated equally. In doing so, he highlights the complex links between equality of opportunity and equality of outcome. In the following chapter, Juliana Mansvelt examines another story we like to tell — that New Zealand is clean and green. After tracing the history of the story, including its links to the '100% Pure' sloganeering of Brand New Zealand, Juliana puts our environment under the microscope to reveal a very different image of New Zealand. In Chapter 12, Helen Dollery and Carl Bradley turn our attention to the Anzac story, which talks of New Zealand's national identity being founded on the shores of Gallipoli. They explore the origins of the narrative, and then broaden the lens to focus on different views of war, and to highlight some of the groups in our society whose experiences of war are missing from the Anzac story.

In the concluding piece, Richard Shaw offers some final thoughts on the issues and debates raised throughout the book. Stepping back from the detail of earlier chapters, he reflects on the magnitude of what is presently happening in Aotearoa New Zealand, on the long-term challenges and opportunities these trends present, and on how we might as a national community react to the sorts of changes discussed in this book.

The choice of topics

Finally, a word or two on our choice of topics. Deciding what we were going to focus on was no easy matter. For every choice we made, others were forgone. Given the amount of time many of us spend in sports clubs, charitable organisations or churches, for example, Part 3 could happily have included chapters on each of these places. And in Part 4 we might well have chosen other narratives — that this is a great place to raise kids, perhaps, or that farming is the backbone of the nation, or that New Zealand is now a bicultural nation — each of which contains elements of truth while also obscuring inconvenient facts. In the end, we stand by our choices, but in future editions of the book we may well take the opportunity to explore these alternatives.

Several reasons lie behind our decision to dedicate a chapter to Māori ethnicity and to incorporate Te Rā's 'He tirohanga Māori'. First, Chapter 2 serves as a specific study of how and why ethnicity is important to all of us; Te Rā introduces us to terms and concepts in the context of tangata whenua, but many of these have analogues in other ethnic contexts. That said, the voice of Māori — which, as

Mason Durie (2003) has shown us, is not one but a chorus of voices — is still, even in these purportedly post-Treaty settlement times, often silenced.

Māori imagery and symbolism are important elements in our collective identity, and central to the way we represent — and overtly market — ourselves as a nation to others. Indeed, we have used a Māori term in the title of this publication (one which was gifted to the course of university study to which this publication is attached by Massey University's Māori Language Advisory Group), and for many it would be inconceivable that an All Black test could start without a haka. Yet Māori views on, and understandings of, citizenship are not as widely understood as they should be. Our choices, therefore, are explicitly intended to showcase Māori — although this is not to deny other ethnicities, including Pākehā; indeed, the entire book comprises an extended invitation not only to learn about others' ways of doing and being, but also to reflect on the ethnic and other bases of your own sense of self.

We are mindful that our decision may trigger calls for a different sort of coverage. For instance, some might argue that a chapter on Māori should be complemented with one on Pākehā (or, depending on your linguistic preferences, European New Zealanders). As editors, that is not a view we share. Rather, our position is that — with the exception of Chapter 2 and the 'He tirohanga Māori' — the bulk of this book is framed by a Pākehā/European New Zealander lens. It may not be obvious at first sight because — to reiterate the point made by Barker (1948) at the beginning of this introduction — for many of us this is what is natural and therefore taken for granted, but both the content of each other chapter, and the cultural frameworks within which those chapters' authors work, are predominantly non-Māori. Seen in this way, a single chapter on te ao Māori in a book numbering 12 substantive chapters seems, if anything, insufficient rather than overly generous.

How to use this book

At several points in each chapter, you will find a QR code and URL that will take you to a video or a piece of text that offers further information. As well as these links there will be a further QR code and URL at the very end of each chapter. Scan the code or insert the URL into your browser, whereupon you will be taken to an interview with someone who knows a good deal about the topic, as well as a series of suggestions about other online resources. Taking time to browse through these links will help you make sense of the material covered in the chapter. Here is a complete list of all the chapter webpages:

Visit the Tūrangawaewae website for more online resources:
http://turangawaewae.massey.ac.nz/index_ed2.html

You will also see that every chapter concludes with an extensive list of references. Of course this is an academic convention, and we wouldn't expect you to go to all of them. But among these titles there are some that we do urge you to read as they will deepen your knowledge and thinking. Each chapter, therefore, also ends with a 'further reading' list.

References

Barker, E. (1948). *National character and the factors in its formation* (4th ed.). Methuen & Co.

Durie, M. (2003). *Ngā kāhui pou: Launching Māori futures*. Huia.

Royal Commission of Inquiry into the terrorist attack on Christchurch masjidain on 15 March 2019. (2020). *Ko tō tātou kāinga tēnei*. https://christchurchattack.royalcommission.nz

PART ONE:
FACES OF AOTEAROA
NEW ZEALAND

Faces
Introduction

Richard Shaw

Welcome to the first of the four parts — faces, voices, places and stories — comprising this book. Each begins with one of these brief discussions, the purpose of which is to introduce the conceptual template that gives shape to the individual chapters within it. Think of this short piece, then, as a sort of map designed to guide both the structure of each subsequent chapter and your engagement with it.

About Part 1

Let me borrow (and in so doing possibly butcher) a metaphor from art to explain the specifics of Part 1 and its three constituent chapters. The diversity that now characterises this country — ethnic, linguistic, religious, familial and so on — is so pronounced that we need many colours to paint its portrait. In this context, the fundamental purposes of Part 1 are (a) to define, in Chapter 1, the core terms and concepts we will be using throughout the book, and (b) to provide a sense — through Chapters 2 and 3 — of the breadth, depth and richness of the people of Aotearoa New Zealand, by examining some of the different demographic characteristics of those who live here. Starting with the first peoples of Aotearoa New Zealand, we then look at the changing ethnic composition of the population, and, consistent with the points Ella makes in Chapter 1, we will also acknowledge other identities, such as age, gender and sexuality. Put these and other identity threads together — as occurs in Chapters 2 and 3 — and you will begin to develop a sharper sense of the ways in which the collective face of Aotearoa New Zealand is changing.

Chapter 1 is something of a scene-setting chapter, and its primary job is to clarify the meanings of a series of terms that you will encounter throughout the rest of the book. However, the conceptual template for the two other chapters in Part 1 has four elements:

1. We examine the shifting patterns of identity in Aotearoa New Zealand in the twenty-first century, and take a close look at the ways in which the profile of the population is evolving.
2. We also explore some of the ways in which our identity threads intersect with wider social, political and other forces to continuously shape and reshape our personal sense of self and our understandings of national identity.
3. We assess some of the ways in which identity is expressed (through, for instance, rituals, symbols and art).
4. Finally, we consider some of the present and future consequences and challenges of the changing face of Aotearoa New Zealand. We analyse what the demographic and other trends explored in Part 1 mean to different groups, and look at some of the reactions to those developments.

Overview of chapters

Ella Kahu begins Chapter 1 with a deceptively simple question: Who are you? It's a question that is harder to answer than you might initially think, partly because our sense of self comprises many different aspects, changes over time, and is shaped by the different contexts through which we move in the course of our lives. Nonetheless, in a publication about identity and belonging we need a common language: the purpose of Ella's chapter, therefore, is to introduce, define and illustrate the core ideas that form the foundation of this book. In it she introduces the notion of identity threads (the different strands that make up our identity), and explains the interaction between these and the various contexts in which we live. Ella also explores some of the competing understandings of the term 'citizenship', and illustrates how citizenship status can work to either include or exclude people from their communities.

In Chapter 2, Te Rā Moriarty introduces historical and contemporary understandings of identity, belonging and citizenship that are particular to Māori. The chapter is a detailed exploration of the ways in which these conceptions are shaped by the contextually specific experiences of a particular ethnic group (albeit one containing, as he points out, diverse realities). Among other things, Te Rā provides insights into notions of identity, belonging and citizenship that are indigenous to Aotearoa New Zealand. In doing so, he reminds us of the dissonant chord that can be struck when Māori understandings of such notions are placed alongside those that emerge from different cultural contexts. Neither is more nor less correct: the point to be made is that what makes sense (and is perhaps taken for granted) by some is far from obvious for others.

In the third chapter of Part 1, 'Aotearoa New Zealand's ever-changing face', Trudie Cain and Tracey Nicholls explore the contested, shifting and changing face of citizenship in this country. Focusing on broad demographic developments, Chapter 3 explores how three significant identity threads — ethnicity, sexuality and age — influence our sense of self and shape our interactions with others. The chapter highlights how context is dynamic, insofar as the changing patterns of age and ethnicity in New Zealand, along with evolving understandings of sexuality and gender identities, affect all those who live here. Trudie and Tracey work through some of the consequences these seismic shifts are having for what counts as identity and citizenship at the individual and societal levels. What they offer is a portrait of a country that is quite different from that which existed only a few short decades ago.

Conclusion

Part 1 provides a context for the rest of the book. As such, its most important jobs are to provide you with some definitional certainty and to sketch, albeit at a necessarily broad level, the rich and varied nature of the individual and collective identities that comprise Aotearoa New Zealand. A third and somewhat less overt aim is to invite you to begin (or perhaps to continue) the process of challenging or reappraising your own assumptions about what it means to be in and of this country.

A fourth objective is to encourage you to think about what the term 'citizen' means in the context of the country that begins to emerge from the following three chapters. 'Citizen' is a unitary category (in formal terms, at least — you either are one or you are not), but the word masks a wide range of different identities: what it means to be a New Zealander will differ, and often quite significantly, from one person to another. There is no one template for being a citizen of — or indeed a visitor to, or a migrant or refugee in — this place. The face of Aotearoa New Zealand is far more colourful and diverse than it was not so terribly long ago. These developments, and the profound consequences they are having for the ways in which we make sense of who we are as people and as a nation, are the focus of the chapters you are about to read. And, indeed, this colourful picture provides the backdrop to the rest of the book.

01.
Identity and citizenship
Laying the foundations

Ella Kahu

Waiho i te toipoto, kaua i te toiroa.
Let us keep close together, not far apart.

Introduction

The purpose of this first chapter is to introduce, define and illustrate the core ideas that form the foundation of this book. Much has been written and there are many debates around the concepts of identity and citizenship, so it is essential that we start with a clear explanation of the meanings we have chosen to work with. Many (but by no means all) of the key ideas are encapsulated in Figure 1 (overleaf), which depicts the self as an individual to the left, and the self as a citizen, a member of a community, to the right.

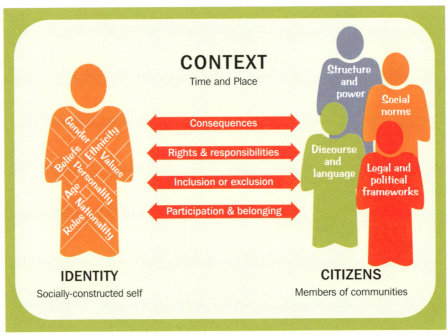

Figure 1. Identity and citizenship

Identity

Who are you? How would you answer that question? You might talk about your personality and say 'I am shy', meaning this is how I usually behave in certain situations. Or you might talk about a biological attribute and say 'I am 58'. Or you might talk about a role you have, 'I am a student', or even a belief, such as 'I am an atheist'. These answers all reflect different aspects of your identity that together form your sense of self. As social science theorist Vivien Burr (2015) explains:

> A person's identity is achieved by a subtle interweaving of many different threads. There is a thread for age, for example they may be a child, a young adult or very old; that of class, depending on their occupation, income and level of education; ethnicity; gender; sexual orientation and so on. All of these, and many more, are woven together to produce the fabric of a person's identity. (pp. 123–124)

In the *Tūrangawaewae* core concepts graphic shown in Figure 1, this idea of identity threads, or multiple identities, is illustrated by the figure of the self on the left. The threads metaphor is useful because it highlights that the whole is more than the sum of the parts, and that identities intersect and interact, as discussed later. Some social scientists distinguish between personal and social identities. Personal identities are those characteristics that make us unique, such as our personality traits, preferences and values, whereas social identities are those identities derived from memberships in broad social groups, such as gender or ethnic categories, and from social roles, such as being a lawyer or a grandparent (Snow & Corrigall-Brown, 2015). However, the distinction between the personal and the social is not clear-cut, and the categories overlap. For instance, someone who is gay may view that as a personal identity, but, in the context of a conversation on homosexual law reform, being gay may function as a social identity — derived from and marking membership of a social group.

In many ways, all identities are social — identity is a way of marking out difference, delineating between 'us' and 'them' (Woodward, 2003). Identities are categories of people. It can even be argued that an identity exists only in comparison to others. For example, Liu et al. (2005) point out that, prior to European arrival, Māori were an iwi (tribal)-based people and the identity of 'Māori' did not yet exist: 'we have no sense of an ethnic self without a contrasting other' (p. 13). We learn about our identities through our encounters and interactions with other people — through personal relationships, through institutions such as schools, workplaces and universities (as Richard and Matt discuss in Chapter 8), and through the vast array of media that depict and construct our social world. We express and present our identities to others in a multitude of ways — through our appearance, through what we say, and through the things that we own and display, the art we create or buy (see Chapter 6 for more on this), the media we choose to consume. Identity is not just within us, it is all around us.

Identity is important. Our identities shape how we experience the world, how the world interacts with us, how we understand what we experience, and the opportunities and challenges we face through life. There are some identities that are particularly central to our sense of self, and to how we are perceived, and even judged, by others, including age, gender, ethnicity, sexuality, class (or socio-economic status) and ability. Within those categories, not all identities are equally valued, and so identity also determines the allocation of social, political and economic power in society, as we will explore when we look at citizenship shortly.

Gender and sexuality are important identity threads. If you'd like to learn more about our diverse rainbow communities, explore the Gender Minorities Aotearoa website: https://genderminorities.com

An important part of appreciating that identity is social — something that occurs between people rather than within people — is understanding that identities are socially constructed, fluid and dynamic. This means that how you experience being male, or Samoan, or 40, or a mother, or retired is dependent on your social context and on the interactions and encounters you have with others, and these are changing all the time.

To illustrate that idea with an example, consider age, an identity thread that on the surface is purely a matter of biology. A person between 13 and 19 years old is a teenager, although the word 'teenager' is a relatively new label. This identity label, this category, what it means to be a teenager, is socially constructed — it depends on when and where you are. Nothing specific happens the day you turn 13. In some societies there is no word or idea that represents adolescence — you are a child and then you are an adult. But in most contemporary Western societies there is a period in between, and this period of adolescence is constructed as one of being impulsive and rebellious, as a period of identity-seeking and developing independence. And that social view of adolescence shapes how the individual experiences being a teenager.

Context is a critical concept here — as shown in Figure 1, everything about identity and citizenship is embedded within the context. At one level, context refers to the immediate physical context — sometimes described as the micro context. This immediate context, such as one's family home (as Trudie and Juliana discuss in Chapter 7) or workplace, is important because different spaces are governed by different rules and norms (an idea we explore in more depth in Part 3 of this book). Those norms then shape how we express and enact our identity. Moreover, different threads of identity become more salient in different contexts — my mother identity is certainly less salient in my workplace than in my home! But context is more than just the physical place.

At another level, the macro context is the broader social, cultural and historical setting. As I alluded to earlier, being a teenager is different in different cultures and in different times. It is different in terms of the opportunities and barriers that exist, and it is different in terms of how one 'should' or 'should not' behave — the norms are different, which impacts on our choices. To give another example, my mother was a stay-at-home mother, and when I had my own children this is what I chose to do — my maternal identity was shaped in part by my encounters within my own childhood home and family. But my decision was not just informed by what I had learned from my mother. She had her children in the United Kingdom in the 1960s, whereas I had mine in Aotearoa New Zealand in the 1990s. Our social, political, cultural and historical contexts were different. Therefore, what it meant to be a mother and how we were supposed to do mothering was different, and this impacted on our individual experiences and identities as mothers — not just in terms of the choices we made, but also in terms of how we felt about those choices and ourselves.

In Figure 1 you will see 'language and discourse' as an influence on us as citizens within communities. Language is a critical part of our context, and shapes us both as citizens and as individuals. The phrase 'stay-at-home mother' did not exist in my mother's time because it was the norm — and it was therefore the easier choice. Now, 28 years after I had my children, that phrase can have a negative connotation, reflecting the shifting social views and norms about what being a mother means, and thereby impacting on the choices that mothers now make.

Another important contribution to the fluidity of our identity is that our identities are not separate and distinct. Coming back to Burr's (2015) metaphor of identity threads, those threads intersect and overlap as is discussed later, and in doing so each influences the others. So, being a mother and the way in which someone enacts their maternal identity will be shaped in part by their other identities, such as ethnicity, values and age. Some identity threads interact more easily than others (depending on the context). For example, in the current cultural context of Aotearoa New Zealand, teenage pregnancy is constructed as a social problem: 'teenager' and 'mother' is a socially undesirable combination of identities. As Wilson and Huntington (2006) point out, 'normative perceptions of motherhood have shifted over the past few decades to position teenage mothers as stigmatised and marginalised' (p. 59). There are other identities that do not easily align with 'mother' as well. In my own research on women's decision-making around family and paid work, first-time mothers talked about the challenge of weaving their existing identity as 'successful woman' in with this new identity of mother (Kahu & Morgan, 2007).

That is the self: a complex, fluid weaving of identities set within an equally complex and fluid context. But if the self is social, then to understand it fully we need to consider how we interact with each other within different communities. The word 'community' stems from the Latin bases of *communitas*, meaning 'the same', and *communis*, meaning 'shared by many'. So a community is a group of people with a common interest or a shared identity thread. Communities can be physical, a geographical area for instance; they can be digital, such as an online support group; and/or they can be social, based on relationships, such as a family. Communities can vary, too, in terms of size, from large, wide communities such as Aotearoa New Zealand, to small, specific communities such as the students in a particular class. Communities are powerful and important to our sense of self, as

Mayo (2008) explains: 'communities are the source of social attachments, create interdependencies, mediate between the individual and the larger society, and sustain the well being of members' (p. 147). So being a member of a community can give people a sense of belonging, an idea we will return to in a moment.

Citizenship

The meaning of the term 'citizenship' is regularly and vigorously debated. Probably the most common understanding of citizenship is as membership of a nation state — holding a passport for a particular country. This is certainly an important definition, not least because of the various rights and responsibilities that flow from citizenship of a nation state like Aotearoa New Zealand (some of which Richard explores in Chapter 4). However, the understanding of citizenship with which we operate in this book is nearer to Turner's (2017) notion of 'social citizenship', which is more closely associated with membership of civil society institutions than it is to either the state or markets.

The various understandings of citizenship are not exclusive, but the point I would like to make here is that when we talk about citizenship we are often talking about membership of (or exclusion from) communities of interest that operate at the sub-state level. Broadly, it can refer to membership of any community — your city, your workplace, your family even. Citizenship is important because it has consequences. It determines material benefits, it fosters a sense of belonging (or a sense of alienation), and it legitimises participation and voice.

Citizenship is about more than just membership of the community, though; it is about the rights and obligations that accompany that membership. The nature of citizenship in any particular community, like identity, is socially constructed, contextual and fluid. Who gets to be a member of a community, as well as the level of rights and obligations that members have, often depends on the identity threads a person has: 'Identity is a fundamental organising principle in the enactment of power, the mobilisation for and the allocation of resources, and a critical marker of inclusion and exclusion' (Liu et al., 2005, p. 15). It also depends on the context — who is a citizen and what that means are different in different communities, and change through time.

As mentioned, the term 'citizenship' is often used specifically in reference to membership of a nation state; nationality is an important thread to most people's identities. At the time of writing, with closed borders and limitations on international movement caused by Covid-19, this is particularly evident. While we are interested in how the individual functions in a range of communities, this book is about identity and citizenship within Aotearoa New Zealand. It is useful, therefore, to use Aotearoa New Zealand as an example community to illustrate the links with identity. Note, however, that everyone who lives here is a member of this community, but not all have a New Zealand passport (they may be permanent residents, temporary visitors or even illegal residents), and therefore are not citizens in the substantive, legal definition of the word. However, in the broader understanding of citizenship as membership of a community, they are citizens, albeit with a different set of rights.

The nature of citizenship is influenced by a range of forces, such as political and legal frameworks, social norms, structures of power, and discourse and language, as shown in the illustration of the book's core concepts in Figure 1. The most tangible of these influences are the political and legal frameworks — the laws of the land. These laws establish, among other things, who counts as a citizen, and which of those citizens have what rights. There are four broad types of citizenship rights: legal rights, such as personal security and access to justice; political rights, such as the rights to vote, to protest and to access information; social rights, such as healthcare, education and welfare; and participatory rights, such as access to jobs and protection from discrimination (Janoski & Gran, 2002).

Not all citizens have access to the same rights, and in part that is determined by their identity. You do not have the right to vote in Aotearoa until you turn 18, for example. In another example, until relatively recently the right to marry was limited to couples of different genders, heterosexual couples — homosexual New Zealanders were denied that right on the basis of their identity. Critically, this type of legal exclusion sent a clear message that a homosexual identity thread was not as valued as a heterosexual identity thread.

Laws exert explicit influences on citizenship, but there are also other less tangible influences, such as social norms and language. For instance, there is a strong discourse (a way of talking about and understanding the world) in New Zealand and most of the Western world these days (i.e. in the current socio-historical context) that paid work is essential — for personal wellbeing and also as a contribution to society. Within this narrative, those who are not in paid work (including beneficiaries, retirees and stay-at-home parents) are seen as a burden — they are not doing their bit for the community. Labels like 'dole-bludger' make this clear. So, while in terms of legal frameworks a person on a benefit may have the same rights as everyone else, the social norms and the way we talk about the world position these identities as lesser citizens. As with the previous example, a significant thread in those people's identity is deemed less valuable, less desirable.

Within the central identity categories — gender, ethnicity, class, sexuality and ability, for instance — some identities are dominant and are deemed to be more valued and desirable than others, which are marginalised and often excluded. In many ways these dominant categories are the norm against which others are measured. For example, as Simone de Beauvoir (1949/1989) pointed out in her classic book *The Second Sex*, male and female are not equal categories: 'man represents both the positive and the neutral, as is indicated by the common use of *man* to designate human beings in general' (p. xxi). The category 'man' becomes the norm against which women are measured, just as heterosexual is the norm against which all other sexualities are measured. These things change through time, of course, and in Chapter 3 Trudie and Tracey explore how changing understandings of sexuality and gender are altering the demographic face of Aotearoa New Zealand.

In some ways, these normative identities are less visible; they are taken for granted. For example, unless stated otherwise a person is assumed to be heterosexual. In other ways, normative identities are more visible. For example, book characters are far more likely to be male — of the top 100 bestselling children's books in New Zealand in 2017, 57 per cent had male-only main characters and just 13 per cent had female-only main characters (Heritage, 2018). In another example, a New Zealand research study found that while Pākehā/ New Zealand Europeans made up 68 per cent of the population, they made up 87 per cent of the people depicted in television advertising (Rubie-Davies et al., 2013). The one exception was government advertising in which Māori and Pasifika were proportionally represented. Unfortunately, this imbalance could also unintentionally reinforce negative stereotypes, as the government campaigns tended to be aimed at reducing negative behaviours, such as drink-driving, gambling, smoking and family violence.

The different valuing of identities is the foundation of prejudice (making assumptions about people based on their group) and discrimination (treating people unfairly based on their identities). It is critical to understand that this is not just about individuals — it is about the social systems. As Johnson (2017) put it: 'The people who get labeled as bigots, misogynists, or homophobes are all following racist, sexist, heterosexist paths of least resistance that are built into the entire society' (p. 76).

Male, white, straight, cisgendered, able-bodied, higher socio-economic status are all markers of privilege — identities that make it easier to walk through the world because they smooth the way and in most contexts do not lead to discrimination. The more of the above threads of identity a person has, the more privileged they

On a Plate

This comic strip by cartoonist Toby Morris was heralded by many as a brilliant explanation of how family background and economic privilege can determine one's opportunities in life. See the full cartoon here: https://www.rnz.co.nz/news/the-wireless/373065/the-pencilsword-on-a-plate.

are. The concept of privilege helps us to recognise that while racism, for example, has serious negative impacts on some people, it also advantages others. Note that I say *easier* to walk through the world, not *easy*. Being part of a privileged group does not necessarily mean life is easy — just that it is easier than for someone of a non-privileged group. Recognising privilege is also not about blaming or shaming people — rather it is about recognising the unearned advantages that the social power structures confer on some people, through the circumstances of their birth.

Many metaphors have been used to explain the concept of privilege, with Peggy McIntosh's (1989) article 'White privilege: unpacking the invisible knapsack' one of the best known. McIntosh observed how difficult people find it to accept or to even see that they have privilege, and so, to address this, she wrote a list of things in her life which she could count on but a woman of colour could not. Examples from the list include 'If a traffic cop pulls me over, I can be sure I haven't been singled out because of my race' and 'I am never asked to speak for all people of my racial group' (p. 11). Other authors have followed, with checklists of the privileges associated with being male, able-bodied, straight and middle-classed.

Earlier, I explained that identities intersect and interact. This is particularly important to understand when thinking about issues of power and oppression. Intersectionality is an idea first developed by Kimberlé Crenshaw (1989), an American lawyer and scholar, in examining the experiences of black women. She highlighted that considering the experiences of just one marginalised identity, black, for example, ignores and distorts the experiences of those who are both black and female: 'the intersectional experience is greater than the sum of racism and sexism' (p. 140). And just as the disadvantages of oppression are compounding, so are the advantages of privilege.

There are two other ideas that link closely to citizenship and identity that need more exploration so we can understand why this all matters: participation, and in particular voice, and belonging. Participation refers to the actions we undertake as members of a community, as active citizens. For example, if the community is the local school your children attend, then your participation includes activities such as helping out at the school fair, attending parent–teacher interviews, and voting in the school's board of trustees elections. Participation encompasses the things we do that contribute to the smooth running of our communities, but it is also how we have a say in how our communities function. So an important part of participation is voice — and not just being able to have a say, but also having our voice listened to, being heard. As British political scientist Richard Bellamy (2008) puts it: 'Those who enjoy a certain status are entitled to participate on an equal basis with their fellow citizens in making the collective decisions that regulate social life' (p. 1).

In the same way that not all citizens have equal rights, not all citizens are able to have an equal say, and not everyone's voice is equally heard. Part of the exclusion and marginalisation of identities that occurs in a community is the silencing of people's voices. Again using the nation state as our example community, Māori have a long history of being silenced in Aotearoa New Zealand — of not being able to participate equally. The obvious example of this is that Māori were long denied equal voting rights, as Richard Shaw discusses in Chapter 4. But the silencing, and therefore the exclusion, of Māori was also evident in other formal and informal social actions, such as the confiscation of Māori land by government and the banning of Māori language in schools. When people are marginalised and their voices are not heard through formal channels, such as voting, they may turn to less formal ways of speaking, such as protest and art, as we discuss in Part 2 of this book. It is unsurprising, then, that we have a long history in Aotearoa New Zealand of Māori protest (Harris, 2004).

Closely linked to participation is the idea of belonging. Belonging is the sense of being an important part of a community — of feeling like a valued member. As illustrated above, different groups of people have been marginalised and excluded in different ways in Aotearoa New Zealand: through being denied equal rights, through social norms and language, through active silencing. In all of these cases, their identity is socially constructed as of less value, as less important. This can have a powerful impact on people's sense of self, and potentially impacts negatively on their sense of belonging in the community of Aotearoa New Zealand. Conversely, participation and belonging have a cyclical relationship. The more someone actively participates (and is allowed and encouraged to participate, and has their voice heard) in a community, the stronger their sense of belonging. And the stronger a person's sense of belonging within a community, the more they are likely to participate in the running and decision-making of that community.

I started with the idea that people come together along shared identity lines to form communities to which people belong. The final piece of the puzzle needed to complete the foundations of this book is the idea of 'collective identity'. Polletta and Jasper (2001) describe collective identity as 'an individual's cognitive, moral and emotional connection with a broader community category, practice or institution' (p. 285). The reciprocal link between citizenship and identity is evident in this definition, and Snow and Corrigall-Brown (2015) make it clearer when they describe collective identity as our 'shared sense of "one-ness" or "we-ness" anchored in real or imagined shared attributes' (p. 175). So our identities bring us together into a community, and at the same time our membership in that community helps shape our individual identities.

KAIKOHE NATIVE SCHOOL CLASSROOM, 1939. NATIVE SCHOOLS PROJECT RECORDS. MSS & ARCHIVES 2008/15, FOLDER 173/1. SPECIAL COLLECTIONS, UNIVERSITY OF AUCKLAND LIBRARIES AND LEARNING SERVICES

Alienation from land and language

Legal frameworks and institutions are a critical part of context. This image depicts students at one of New Zealand's 166 Native Schools (also called 'Māori Schools' after 1947), which were established under the 1867 Native Schools Act. One of the rationales behind this Act was the belief that Māori were best suited for the manual trades. A key priority of the schools was speaking English, with official intolerance of te reo Māori usage hardening as the decades progressed. Students in later years were often physically punished for speaking their first language. Native schools were one attempt to assimilate Māori into Pākehā society, threatening to marginalise indigenous identities to the point of complete erasure. There were still 105 such schools operating in 1969 when it was decided there should only be one state schooling system.

Aotearoa New Zealand as a community therefore has a collective identity. When we talk about New Zealanders being friendly or when we draw on metaphors of 'No. 8 fencing wire', we are drawing on perceived attributes of our collective identity. It does not mean that all New Zealanders are friendly or good at DIY, but nonetheless these ideas form a part of our sense of self. We look more closely at some of the key narratives, the stories we tell, about Aotearoa New Zealand in the final part of this book. A collective identity is as fluid and as socially constructed as a personal identity, and so what it means to be a New Zealander is changing — an idea that resonates throughout this book.

Read more on New Zealand's collective identity here at the Te Ara website: https://teara.govt.nz/en/new-zealand-identity/page-1

These interrelated ideas — identity, citizenship, participation and belonging — form the foundation of this volume. Each section addresses these ideas from a slightly different perspective and, by looking at various identities, events and communities, together the chapters form an understanding of what it means to be of this place, Aotearoa New Zealand, at this time.

Conclusion

Making sense of the complex intersections between these ideas of identity, citizenship, participation and belonging is fundamental to understanding people — and to understanding ourselves. Moreover, in the bigger picture, understanding identity and citizenship is fundamental to many of the large social problems that the world is facing. How countries are responding to the global environmental crisis and to the current pandemic is shaped by understandings of identity and citizenship, for example. Closer to home, debates about the causes and impacts of the housing crisis or about the proper place of Te Tiriti o Waitangi in our system of government are also fundamentally shaped by contrasting understandings of identity. Whichever way you look at it, identity matters.

Making sense of these complex issues requires different intellectual tools, a range of which we will offer you throughout the book. Some are from social scientists, who typically assert the need for greater reflexive identity, 'a greater awareness of how our concepts of ourselves affect our daily lives; from high level political decisions (to go to Iraq) . . . to personal decisions (stance on seabed) . . . to mundane choices (who to invite for dinner, what school for our kids, what music)' (Liu et al., 2005, p. 13). Others are from the disciplines of the humanities, which tend to 'study the meaning-making practices of human culture, past and present, focusing on interpretation and critical evaluation, primarily in terms of the individual response' (Small, 2013, p. 57).

It is our hope that you will draw on these contributions and read this book reflectively. That as you come across different ideas, learn about different identities and hear about different events, you will stop and think about yourself and your place in Aotearoa New Zealand. And that through this process you will gain a better understanding of what it means for each of us to be a citizen of this place and time.

Chapter 1 — Identity and citizenship: Laying the foundations:
http://turangawaewae.massey.ac.nz/ch1.html

Further reading

Beausoleil, E. (2017). Twenty-first-century citizenship: Critical, global, active. In A. Brown & J. Griffiths (Eds.), *The citizen: Past and present* (pp. 25–35). Massey University Press.

Liu, J. H., McCreanor, T., McIntosh, T., & Teaiwa, T. (2005). Introduction: Constructing New Zealand identities. In J. H. Liu, T. McCreanor, T. McIntosh, & T. Teaiwa (Eds.), *New Zealand identities: Departures and destinations* (pp. 11–20). Victoria University Press.

References

Bellamy, R. (2008). *Citizenship: A very short introduction.* Oxford University Press.

Burr, V. (2015). *Social constructionism* (3rd ed.). Routledge.

Crenshaw, K. (1989). Demarginalizing the intersection of race and sex: A Black feminist critique of antidiscrimination doctrine, feminist theory and antiracist politics. *University of Chicago Legal Forum, 1,* 139–167. https://chicagounbound.uchicago.edu/uclf/vol1989/iss1/8

de Beauvoir, S. (1989). *The second sex.* (H. M. Parshley, Trans). Vintage Books. (Original work published 1949).

Harris, A. (2004). *Hīkoi: Forty years of Māori protest.* Huia.

Heritage, E. (2018). Gender (im)balance in NZ children's books. *The Sapling.* https://www.thesapling.co.nz/single-post/2018/03/05/gender-imbalance-in-nz-childrens-books

Janoski, T., & Gran, B. (2002). Political citizenship: Foundations of rights. In E. F. Isin & B. S. Turner (Eds.), *Handbook of citizenship studies* (pp. 13–53). Sage.

Johnson, A. (2017). Privilege, power, difference and us. In M. S. Kimmel & A. L. Ferber (Eds.), *Privilege: A reader* (pp. 69–78). Westview Press.

Kahu, E. R., & Morgan, M. (2007). Weaving cohesive identities: New Zealand women talk as mothers and workers. *Kōtuitui: New Zealand Journal of Social Sciences Online, 2*(2), 55–73.

Liu, J. H., McCreanor, T., McIntosh, T., & Teaiwa, T. (2005). Introduction: Constructing New Zealand identities. In J. H. Liu, T. McCreanor, T. McIntosh, & T. Teaiwa (Eds.), *New Zealand identities: Departures and destinations* (pp. 11–20). Victoria University Press.

Mayo, M. L. (2008). Community. In V. N. Parrillo (Ed.), *Encyclopedia of social problems* (pp. 147–149). Sage.

McIntosh, P. (1989). White privilege: Unpacking the invisible knapsack. *Peace and Freedom,* (July/August), 10–12. https://psychology.umbc.edu/files/2016/10/White-Privilege_McIntosh-1989.pdf

Polletta, F., & Jasper, J. M. (2001). Collective identity and social movements. *Annual Review of Sociology, 27,* 283–305. https://doi.org/10.1146/annurev.soc.27.1.283

Rubie-Davies, C. M., Liu, S., & Lee, K. K. (2013). Watching each other: Portrayals of gender and ethnicity in television advertisements. *The Journal of Social Psychology, 153*(2), 175–195. https://doi.org/10.1080/00224545.2012.717974

Small, H. (2013). *The value of the humanities.* Oxford University Press.

Snow, D. A., & Corrigall-Brown, C. (2015). Collective identity. In J. D. Wright (Ed.), *International encyclopedia of the social and behavioral sciences* (2nd ed., Vol. 4, pp. 174–180). Elsevier.

Turner, B. (2017). Contemporary citizenship: Four types. *Journal of Citizenship and Globalisation Studies, 1*(1), 10–23. https://doi.org/10.21153/jcgs2017vol1no1art1062

Wilson, H., & Huntington, A. (2006). Deviant (m)others: The construction of teenage motherhood in contemporary discourse. *Journal of Social Policy, 35*(1), 59–76. https://doi.org/10.1017/S0047279405009335

Woodward, K. (2003). *Understanding identity.* Arnold.

02.
Tangata whenua
Māori, identity and belonging

Te Rā Moriarty

He kanohi ora nā ngā mātua tūpuna.
A living face of the ancestors.

The above expression is an acknowledgement of those alive today being the living faces of their ancestors; the genealogical result of descent from one ancestor to the next since time immemorial.

Introduction

Koia Te Kore
Koia Te Pō
Koia rā ko Ranginui e tū nei
Koia rā ko Papatūānuku e takoto nei
Heke mai, heke mai, heke mai te ira atua
Ka puta te ira tangata ki te whaiao ki Te Ao Mārama.
Tihei mauri ora!

The above whakapapa, in the form of a karakia, refers to the emergence over aeons of time of the universe, the natural world and the descent of humanity through the metaphorical birthing canal, te whaiao, into the world of light and understanding, Te Ao Mārama, which is the world that is inhabited today. Te Kore can be explained as a void that is also 'a realm of potential being' (Marsden, 2003, p. 20). With this potential for development, Te Kore gave way to Te Pō, a stage of darkness (Te Rangi Hīroa, 1949). This darkness was a gestation period where the sky, Ranginui, and the earth, Papatūānuku, came into existence. From the union of the earth and the sky descend the natural forces of the environment, te ira atua, whence came the human element, te ira tangata (Te Rangi Hīroa, 1949). The phrase 'tihei mauri ora' is often heard at the end of a karakia, and acknowledges the energy of life itself that is contained within every living thing on Earth.

This chapter is arranged into three parts. In the first part, 'Te whaiao ki Te Ao Mārama: Emergence into the world of light', I will present Māori perspectives on the growth of the universe, the natural world and humanity. This will be followed by an explanation of the sources of mana that are inherited from atua, passed to tūpuna, and connected to land, and the importance of mana for people today. The second section, 'Ko te whenua, ko te tangata: Land and people', talks about the early human arrival to Aotearoa from the Pacific, the naming of Aotearoa, the feat of hauling up the land by the tupua Māui Tikitiki a Taranga, and the subsequent names of places derived from that narrative. I will then discuss how connections to the environment are presented through pepeha, the key Māori social structures of whānau, hapū and iwi, preceded by an explanation of the integral Māori place, the marae. The final section, 'He ao ka huri: A world changing', looks at some of the changes over time from the arrival of Pākehā to the present day. He Whakaputanga o te Rangatiratanga o Nu Tireni and Te Tiriti o Waitangi are presented along with the impacts of colonisation on Māori. Māori responses to the Crown are then focused on, leading to an observation of the diverse realities that Māori people experience today.

Te whaiao ki Te Ao Mārama: Emergence into the world of light

Ranginui rāua ko Papatūānuku: The sky and the earth

Many Māori communities throughout Aotearoa acknowledge the union of Ranginui and Papatūānuku as the primal parents of the world that humanity lives in and experiences every day (Mead, 2016). Initially, Rangi and Papa were in a tight embrace encapsulated by aroha. From their relationship came all of the elements that are present on Earth, known as their children, and the atua forces of the planet, which are the developmental energies that environmental realities have come from. This view is expressed in the whakapapa of the tōtara tree, as one example, with the union of Tāne and Mumuwhango, both atua of the forest environment, resulting in the tōtara (Best, 1924). Huirangi Waikerepuru states with reference to the environment that 'Tamanui Te Rā, Papatūānuku, te tai o te moana, te hau e pā mai nei ki ōku pāpāringa; ēnei mea he atua katoa ēnei' (Te Ipukarea, 2017b). I have translated this as 'The sun, the earth, the tide of the ocean, the wind that blows on my cheeks, these are all atua'. Some of these atua are: Tangaroa, the water; Tāne, the trees and the creatures that live off the forest; Tāwhirimātea, the wind and the weather; Tūmatauenga, conflict, strife, defence and debate; Rongo, peace, debate resolution and gardening.

Due to the close embrace Rangi and Papa shared, their children were cramped and living in darkness (Best, 1924). This caused the children to debate how they could alleviate the predicament they found themselves in. As is common in many large whānau, there was some disagreement between the children. However, it was decided that Rangi and Papa should be separated (Best, 1924). This was done through Tāne using his legs to push Rangi and Papa apart, which allowed light to enter into the world, giving way to the phase of the universe that life exists in now, Te Ao Mārama, the world of light.

Hineahuone

From this came the potential for humanity to emerge into the natural world in the form of Hineahuone. The word 'Hine' refers to a female, 'ahu' means to be heaped up, and 'one' is the soil. In order for Hineahuone to develop, Papatūānuku directed her children to a place called Kurawaka, and from there Hineahuone came to be (Royal, 2005b). Through the exchange of hā, Hineahuone came to life (Walker, 1990/2004). The word 'hā' means breath, essence, and through the addition of the word 'ora' we get the word oxygen — hāora (Moorfield, 2021). This 'hā' came from the natural environment and was planted in Hineahuone through the exchange of a hongi with Tāne (Walker, 1990/2004), the atua of the forest, which led to Hineahuone sneezing (tihei), which was the sign that she had a mauri ora, a living energy, inside of her. According to Māori narratives of how humanity came to be, Hineahuone is a phase of development from the natural environment that, over time, has given way to humanity today. As Hineahuone was from the earth, the phrase 'tangata whenua' is used as a word for indigenous people here in Aotearoa and throughout the world (Mead, 2016).

This narrative is just one way that Māori communities interpret and understand the origins of the world. It shows that from a Māori perspective the universe has a whakapapa, a genealogy, acknowledged in this case as emerging with Te Kore, moving into the gestation period of Te Pō, and then the earth and the sky, followed by all life on Earth, including humanity (Te Rangi Hīroa, 1949), residing in Te Ao Mārama today. Therefore, the word 'whakapapa' is used to explain how the world came to be, and how humanity came from the natural world to ancestors, ancestors to their descendants, and current generations to future descendants. This illustrates the critical importance of whakapapa to Māori identity, as it explains our shared connection to the environment and to each other, which influences our responsibilities as citizens of our communities.

Mana

Mana is also a critical concept for te ao Māori that is inherited through our whakapapa. 'Mana' as a word may be defined as authority, control, influence, prestige and power (Williams, n.d.). However, these translations do not capture the depth of mana and its meaning in the Māori world. Looking at mana in the context of mana atua, mana tūpuna, mana whenua and mana tangata makes it easier to understand the importance of mana and how it relates to the natural environment and ourselves as its descendants.

Mana atua is a term that describes the mana of the atua, the developmental energies of the environment. These forces are tapu (Waikerepuru in Te Ipukarea, 2017b), and therefore carry a highly elevated level of mana. Tapu can be defined as a restriction, a sacredness that dictates that tapu things be respected for their mana and that appropriate tikanga be adhered to when dealing with tapu places, people, topics and activities. Mead (2016) states that 'Tapu is everywhere in our world' and 'is inseparable from mana, from our identity as Māori and from our cultural practices' (p. 34). Tikanga refers to all actions that are considered tika, correct, for the occasion. The mana of the atua is paramount and is inherited by our ancestors.

Mana tūpuna is the mana that our ancestors hold through being descendants of the natural world, made up of the atua. This mana also refers to the prestige of the ancestors through their whakapapa and their actions, and is inherited at birth (Mead, 2016). It is through descent from the ancestors that local whānau, hapū and iwi exist as mana whenua in their localised territory. Mana whenua is the mana that communities have through their association over long periods of time to an area that was inhabited by their ancestors (Moorfield, 2021). For humanity, mana can be positively enhanced or negatively affected through one's own actions, and this is evident in how ancestors are discussed, held in reverence and respected by their descendants. Therefore, mana tūpuna is the mana that the ancestors inherit from atua, which is passed to living descendants, those who are alive today, and informs the mana whenua status of whānau, hapū and iwi in their specific regions.

Mana tangata is the mana that people today, as the living faces of the ancestors, are born with. This mana can be affected positively, or negatively, through our own actions (Mead, 2016). It is from the observance of mana that we get an important tikanga, and way of being, known as manaaki or manaakitanga. Manaaki is to 'āki', to encourage and urge on, the mana of somebody. Therefore, manaaki can be explained as the elevation of the mana of another through actions such as supporting people, feeding people, encouraging people, showing aroha and being hospitable (Mead, 2016). In essence, manaaki is about being a good person to others and promoting positive social conditions that inform our duties to each other as citizens.

Ko te whenua, ko te tangata: Land and people

Hawaiki

Having explored the primal and environmental ancestors of Māori, I move now to the arrival of human ancestors to Aotearoa from Hawaiki. Hawaiki is a name that refers to a distant homeland, an origin point, from which ancestral Māori came (Anderson et al., 2014). There can be many Hawaiki throughout the world, and for Māori it will often be a specific island or a cluster of islands, some being located around eastern Polynesia (Anderson et al., 2014). The seeds had already been sown for Māori culture within Hawaiki; Māori people are descendants of the Polynesian islands and brought those cultures here to Aotearoa. Over time, a distinct form of this culture emerged in Aotearoa as a response to the landscape and its climate.

Aotearoa

Aotearoa is the name used commonly for this country, New Zealand. The name came from a voyage of the waka of Kupe, called *Matahourua*, which left land in Hawaiki. Once the waka got close to Aotearoa, a long white cloud was seen from sea. For seafarers, this type of cloud formation, known as an aotea, was a sign that there was land. A wahine on board the waka, Kura-mārō-tini, called out, 'He aotea roa' (Royal, 2005a), translating literally as 'long white cloud'. In some narratives the name was given by the wahine Hine-te-Aparangi (Grace, n.d.). For most iwi in Aotearoa, the waka that the ancestors arrived here on are still used as an identity marker that connects many descendants today. A large number of waka arrived in Aotearoa over a period of centuries. According to Walker (1990/2004), the migration started 'between AD 800 and 900' (p. 28); however, other research suggests the arrival dates were between the 1200s and mid-1300s (Anderson et al., 2014).

Te Ika a Māui and Te Waka a Māui

Widely used names within te reo Māori for the islands of Aotearoa are Te Ika a Māui (North Island, The Fish of Māui) and Te Waka a Māui (South Island, The Vessel of Māui), also called Te Waipounamu (The Waters of Pounamu). Rakiura (Stewart Island) is also referred to as Te Punga o Te Waka a Māui or Te Punga a Māui (The Anchor of the Vessel of Māui). These names are examples of a particular way that ancestors are remembered through pūrākau, ancient narratives, in the landscape.

A version of the narrative of Aotearoa is that Māui Tikitiki a Taranga, also known as Māui Pōtiki (Māui the last-born), and his four older brothers, Māui Mua, Māui Roto, Māui Pae and Māui Taha, set off on their waka one day to go fishing (Bixley et al., 2018). Māui Tikitiki a Taranga encouraged his siblings to go further out into the ocean in the hope that a bigger fish might be caught than previously. It was Māui Tikitiki a Taranga who, using the blood from his nose as a form of bait for his hook, which was made from the jawbone of his kuia, Murirangawhenua, threw his fishing line into the water and hooked a giant fish. Once it was hauled up it was called Te Ika a Māui, representing the North Island, with the waka they fished from representing the South Island.

This is a condensed version of the narrative and may differ from many regional variations; however, what it shows is that Māori people are positioned within the land through narratives of ancestral figures in relation to the environment. This is also a way that individuals and families identify themselves with specific geographical areas. For example, those iwi who inhabit the southern part of Te Ika a Māui are situated in Te Upoko o Te Ika, The Head of the Fish; those who inhabit the middle are situated in Te Puku o Te Ika, The Stomach of the Fish; those who inhabit the northern regions are situated in Te Hiku o Te Ika, The Tail of the Fish; those who inhabit the northern part of Te Waka a Māui are situated in Te Tauihu o Te Waka, The Bow of the Vessel. Therefore, these names are identity markers for Māori communities who descend from the relevant areas and who maintain the existence of the narrative and uphold the mana of the shared ancestor Māui.

Pepeha

Once the many ancestral waka arrived on these shores, the immediate descendants travelled the landscape and intermarried, creating the ancestral links between Māori people today. These links are commonly referred to in the form of pepeha, which is an oral way of connecting oneself to one's waka, environmental features such as maunga (mountains) and awa (rivers), through to the traditional centre of Māori communities, the marae, and to the whānau, hapū and iwi affiliations that inhabit those communities. Therefore, pepeha are the expression of the bonds between humanity and the environment that inform a Māori sense of identity and belonging. While pepeha may follow a standard formula, they are also expressed in varied ways. One form from my iwi is as follows:

Ko Tainui te waka	Tainui is the waka
Ko Whitireia te maunga	Whitireia is the mountain
Ko Parirua, ko Raukawa ngā wai	Parirua and Raukawa are the waters
Ko Takapūwāhia te marae	Takapūwāhia is the marae
Ko Ngāti Toa Rangatira te iwi	Ngāti Toa is the iwi
Ko Ngāti Te Maunu te hapū	Ngāti Te Maunu is the hapū

The above pepeha, and alternative forms of it, are a significant oral expression of identity and belonging for descendants of the iwi Ngāti Toa Rangatira, from the marae Takapūwāhia, and the region in which the marae is located, where the mountain Whitireia stands and the waters of Parirua and Raukawa ebb and flow.

Pepeha are a culturally entrenched way by which Māori people introduce ourselves in a public setting whenever people gather. The utterance of pepeha allows those who hear it to make familial bonds with the speaker if a whakapapa connection is present; the potential outcome is to meet relations descended from the same waka, mountain, waterway, marae, iwi or hapū.

Whānau, hapū and iwi

Traditionally, a Māori community was made up of people descended from a common ancestor. The most intimate group was the whānau, a collection of closely related individuals living together in proximity. The word whānau means 'to be born' (Williams, n.d., p. 487). Whānau were self-sustaining in procuring food (Walker, 1990/2004). There is no clear definition of how big a whānau might be or how close the members connect through their whakapapa; it may consist of those who descend from an ancestor two or three generations prior, but can also be a connection further into the past.

All the closely related whānau made up a hapū. Hapū means to be 'pregnant' (Williams, n.d., p. 36) and, like whānau, isn't strictly confined to a specific number of generations back from the living descendants. The hapū lived closely and worked together to defend the pā, or village, and do the general activities that nourished and sustained the wider community. Building the pā would require great exertion

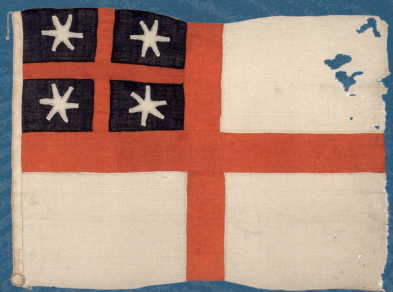

MUSEUM OF NEW ZEALAND TE PAPA TONGAREWA, GH002925

The Empire flexes its muscles

In 1834, rangatira at Waitangi chose the above flag to sail with on trading ships built in Aotearoa. It was chosen out of a selection of three provided by British Resident James Busby (Orange, 2004). In 1835, He Whakaputanga o te Rangatiratanga o Nu Tireni — The Declaration of the Independence of New Zealand — was signed by 34 rangatira, again at Waitangi, with further signatures being collected until 1839 (Orange, 2004). There are four parts of the declaration. The first three contain the following terms that are specific to Māori and relate to notions of citizenship (Warren et al., 2017):

1. Rangatiratanga and whenua rangatira — Independence and independent state;
2. Kīngitanga and mana i te whenua — All sovereign power and authority within the territories of the United Tribes of New Zealand;
3. Rūnanga — Congress at Waitangi in the autumn of each year, for the purposes of framing laws for the dispensation of justice, the preservation of peace and good order, and the regulation of trade (Orange, 2014).

Long march to recognition

In early 1975, the idea was raised of a 'Māori Land March' from Te Hāpua in the Far North to Parliament to focus on landlessness and cultural loss. A meeting of tribal representatives was convened at Māngere marae by the founding president of the Māori Women's Welfare League, Whina Cooper. In her address to the hui, Cooper implied that she was operating under the mantle of great Māori leaders such as James Carroll, Āpirana Ngata and Peter Buck, all of whom she had known. She asserted customary Māori protocol through a 'Memorial of Right', thereby linking the march to a long tradition of earlier petitions to the Crown, especially those by Kings Tāwhiao and Te Rata in 1886 and 1914, respectively.

The Land March combined the forces of Ngā Tamatoa-type radicalism with the wishes and protocols of traditionalist elders, attracting the support of Māori from urban areas and rural marae throughout the country. When it first set off from Te Hāpua on 14 September, there were few on the road, but before long numbers swelled. Marchers sought respect for the communal ownership of tribal lands, believing that the Labour Government's reforms had fallen short. They demanded that 'not one more acre of Maori land' be alienated. As a leaflet entitled 'Why We Protest' explained: 'Land is the very soul of a tribal people . . . [We want] a just society allowing Maoris [sic] to preserve our own social and cultural identity in the last remnants of our tribal estate . . . The alternative is the creation of a landless brown proletariat with no dignity, no mana and no stake in society.'

Five thousand marchers converged on Parliament on 13 October, bearing a petition with 60,000 signatories. Government ministers felt chagrined that the government's extensive consultation procedures and 'progressive' Māori policies and legislation had been rebuked, but, in a sense, the march was not so much about specific land policies or, necessarily, even about land at all. It was a reassertion of autonomist Māori demands and aspirations at a time when the political and social climate was becoming more receptive to them. As one historian later noted, the march represented Māori, at an auspicious moment, 'symbolically reclaiming the tino Rangatiratanga promised by the Treaty of Waitangi'.

of energy, and resources to acquire the materials needed, such as large trees to build the homes and defences. The pā could then house one or many hapū, depending on the size of the area and its fortifications.

Related hapū then made up the iwi. Iwi means 'bone' (Williams, n.d., p. 80), and is the largest of the related kin groups after those who come from the same waka. The iwi inhabited a large area and had multiple pā occupied by the many hapū of the iwi. The iwi came together at times when a greater collective effort was required. For example, in times of large seasonal harvests of fish, a large seine net called a kaharoa was made by joining smaller nets, or sections, together. Each section was made by either whānau or hapū, and once connected created a large net that the iwi used to catch many fish (Fama, 1937). When celebrations occurred, such as a feast, an iwi could muster the huge quantities of food required, and the materials to build the food platforms of the large stage structure called a hākari, which is also the word for feast (Moorfield, 2021). Defensive and reactive warfare could be carried out on an iwi level or a hapū level, depending on the size of the foe. This was due to the communal strength that the iwi could afford in times of need.

Marae

Within te ao Māori the marae is the central location. It is the place that all of the whānau, hapū and iwi can go back to and call their own; it is the tūrangawaewae of a Māori community (Mead, 2016). It consists of a marae ātea, which is the open space of the marae; a wharenui, also called a whare tūpuna or a tīpuna whare; a wharekai; a wharepaku; and possibly other whare used for educational activities or extra sleeping quarters. The wharenui is often named after a prominent ancestor, but may be named after many things; for instance, a migration such as Te Heke Mai Raro of the marae Hongoeka (Hongoeka Marae, 1997).

Many kaupapa take place on the marae, including pōwhiri, hui, celebrations, tangihanga and any activity the haukāinga, the local people, choose. Attention is always given to appropriate protocol, which is upheld as the kawa of the marae (Mead, 2016). The kawa is the way that practices are conducted on the marae, and is specific to region, iwi, hapū and whānau. Therefore, witnessing the kawa in action will look similar on many marae but may also differ.

One of the most widely seen events on a marae is the pōwhiri. A pōwhiri is the traditional practice of welcoming people onto the marae, and follows a sequence of events facilitated by the tangata whenua. They have the authority to run the pōwhiri as they choose, and the kawa of it will be aligned to their area and the whakapapa affiliations that the local people share with other marae.

The tangihanga is the gathering of the community to mourn their dead. When someone dies they are often taken back to the marae and lie in state for a period of time, generally lasting up to three days according to Waikerepuru (Te Ipukarea, 2017a). This gives family members and friends the chance to farewell and pay their respects to the deceased and share in the grief of the occasion. When the tūpāpaku, the body of the deceased, is to be buried, it is taken to the urupā. Each marae will have one or more urupā associated with it where family members will be buried. The urupā is a tapu space, requiring appropriate tikanga to be observed when there and when leaving. For instance, a water source will be placed at the exit point for the purpose of sprinkling on oneself or washing hands to remove the tapu present in the urupā, a place associated with the dead.

Marae are cultural repositories of the tikanga and history of the local people. The marae is the gathering place of the community and stands as a bastion for the protection of local knowledge and customs.

He ao ka huri: A world changing

He Whakaputanga o te Rangatiratanga o Nu Tireni and Te Tiriti o Waitangi

Current realities experienced by Māori people cannot be separated from the history of colonisation in Aotearoa. The arrival of Europeans impacted on te ao Māori in many ways that are impossible to cover in depth in one chapter. However, I will cover the early European arrivals, He Whakaputanga o te Rangatiratanga o Nu Tireni, Te Tiriti o Waitangi, colonisation, land loss and the resistance to it, followed by diverse Māori realities.

The earliest arrival to Aotearoa from Europe was Abel Tasman in 1642, although he did not make landfall, and then James Cook arrived in 1769 (King, 2003). This was followed by sealers, whalers and missionaries in the early nineteenth century. From the late 1700s to the early 1800s Māori were trading internationally and within Aotearoa (King, 2003). Eventually a Crown representative, James Busby, arrived in 1833 (Orange, 2004).

Not long after Busby's arrival, the United Tribes Flag was chosen by Rangatira, and He Whakaputanga o te Rangatiratanga o Nu Tireni was signed, in 1835. Five years after the signing of the Declaration, another document was signed by Māori called Te Tiriti o Waitangi, initially at Waitangi on 6 February 1840 and subsequently throughout Aotearoa (Orange, 2004).

Te Tiriti o Waitangi (1840) is the name for the Māori version, with the English version being the Treaty of Waitangi (1840). The treaties contain a preamble and three written articles, with a fourth oral article included. Importantly, there are key differences between the two versions. The first article of the Māori version, 'Ko te tuatahi', states that the Queen of England will receive 'kāwanatanga', which means 'governorship', of the land. However, this is written as 'sovereignty' in the English version. The second article, 'Ko te tuarua', guarantees 'tino rangatiratanga' to Māori. As we know from He Whakaputanga o te Rangatiratanga o Nu Tireni, the word 'rangatiratanga' was used previously to acknowledge Māori independence. However, in the English version of the Treaty of Waitangi 'tino rangatiratanga' is written as 'exclusive and undisturbed possession' for Māori of their resources. The third article, 'Ko te tuatoru', states that Māori people will be looked after by the Queen, with the word 'tiakina', and that they will receive the same rights as the Queen's British subjects with the words 'ngā tikanga katoa rite tahi ki ana mea'.

The first two articles conflict each other, with the first one giving the Queen rights to govern and the second article agreeing to Māori independence; or, according to Hugh Kawharu (1989), 'the unqualified exercise of their chieftainship' (p. 319). Therefore, due to the 'different understandings' of the Māori and English texts and 'the need to apply the Treaty in contemporary circumstances', Treaty principles have emerged (Te Puni Kōkiri, 2001, p. 74). These are essentially a blend of the two texts, and come from cases that Māori have taken to the courts and the Waitangi Tribunal.

Colonisation and land loss

Following the signing of Te Tiriti o Waitangi, changes to Māori ways of living and authority began to spread across Aotearoa. This is evident, for example, in the vastly reduced size of the land holdings still in Māori ownership, which has plummetted from 100 per cent of Aotearoa prior to the arrival of James Busby to just 5 per cent, 1.4 million hectares, today (Te Puni Kōkiri, 2021). The biggest contributing factors to this loss were the waging of war by the Crown on Māori, the land confiscations that followed and the establishment of the Native Land Court.

Early conflicts between Māori and the Crown occurred in the Wairau region of Te Waipounamu in 1843 and the Wellington region of Te Ika a Māui in 1846 (Collins, 2010). Battles took place in the northern area of Te Ika a Māui from 1845 to 1846, and in Whanganui in 1847 (Belich, 1986/1998). In 1860, war broke out in Taranaki (King, 2003), moved to Waikato in 1863 (Belich, 1986/1998), and then to Tauranga in 1864 (King, 2003). War broke out again in Taranaki from 1865 (Keenan, 2021), with campaigns in the eastern and Bay of Plenty regions of Te Ika a Māui

ARCHIVES NEW ZEALAND TE RUA MAHARA O TE KĀWANATANGA, AAQT 6539 W3537 54 A/54871

New Zealand's passive resisters

The Māori settlement of Parihaka was established in Taranaki by Te Whiti-o-Rongomai and Tohu Kākahi in the late 1860s. After government survey teams moved into the lands north of the Waingongoro River in south Taranaki, the people of Parihaka began a programme of passive resistance in 1879, erecting fences across road lines and ploughing Pākehā farmers' paddocks. So many were arrested and held without trial that an embarrassed government eventually decided on military action. The Armed Constabulary advanced on Parihaka pā in late 1881, part of a combined force of more than 1500. On 5 November the forces surrounded the township and arrested Te Whiti-o-Rongomai and Tohu Kākahi. Over the next few weeks many of the residents were evicted and their houses destroyed. The two chiefs were given an enforced tour of the South Island, designed to demonstrate the advantages and power of Pākehā society. They were returned to Parihaka in 1883. After many years of decline, the village of Parihaka was rejuvenated in the late twentieth century. Since 2006 it has been the venue for the annual Parihaka Peace Festival, which draws visitors from all over New Zealand.

ABRIDGED FROM TE ARA — THE ENCYCLOPEDIA OF NEW ZEALAND

from 1868 to 1872 (Keenan, 2021). The pā of Parihaka in Taranaki was invaded, and its leaders and some of its people taken as prisoners in 1881 (Te Kotahitanga o Te Atiawa, n.d).

Subsequent to these conflicts, large swathes of land were confiscated by the Crown (Keenan, 2021), much of which was subsequently sold to settler farmers, leaving Māori communities with inadequate resources to sustain themselves, leading to starvation and ill-health. Māori were also alienated from land through the Native Land Court: when Māori went to the court to get title for their land they would be left in debt from the process, and then have to use their land to service the debt (Taonui, 2012). The Native Land Court sought to individualise Māori land title that was once held communally (Taonui, 2012). This made it easier for individual title holders to be targetted by land purchasers and for the land blocks to be surveyed and carved up.

As a result, many Māori left their tūrangawaewae to move into towns and cities looking for work to support their whānau. Crown policies during the 1950s and 1960s sought to keep Māori families isolated from other Māori families in urban centres. This was known as 'pepper potting' (Durie, 2019, p. 5). The intention was to assimilate Māori communities into Pākehā society, and had the effect of moving Māori away from each other and their cultural practices (Kingi, 2005). The inevitable consequence of such policies is that traditional whānau, hapū and iwi support bases aren't easily accessible for those living away from the marae, and Māori language and cultural practices are much harder to maintain when living in isolation from one's people.

Protest

Māori communities consistently challenged colonial efforts to take land and to assimilate them into Pākehā society. This was seen in the nineteenth century with the resistance to land sales, the subsequent wars of the nineteenth century outlined above and the passive resistance of Parihaka. The Crown met these actions with legislation such as the Suppression of Rebellion Act 1863 and the Maori Prisoners Trials Act 1879 (Warren et al., 2017). These pieces of legislation unfairly treated Māori by taking land if Māori were opposed to selling, as is the case with the Suppression of Rebellion Act 1863. Those at Parihaka who ploughed settlers' land and erected fences across the path of the coastal road being built by the Constabulary were held indefinitely without trial under the Maori Prisoners Trials Act 1879 (Te Kotahitanga o Te Atiawa, n.d.).

Resistance was also seen with the community of Maungapōhatu in Te Urewera, the establishment of the Māori Women's Welfare League, Ngā Tamatoa, the Land March of 1975, the occupation of Takaparawhau (Bastion Point) and at Raglan, along with the hīkoi protesting the Foreshore and Seabed Act 2004 (Warren et al., 2017). That specific hīkoi is discussed in the 'He tirohanga Māori' introduction of Chapter 5, which explores protest in Aotearoa.

To find out more about Rua Kēnana and Maungapōhatu, visit:
https://nzhistory.govt.nz/arrest-of-rua-kenana

Māori standing up for their rights has been a necessity to have Māori voices heard on issues that intimately affect Māori communities. At times, protest was the only option Māori had left to challenge injustices. This has been an historical reality, and continues to be a modern reality, for indigenous communities throughout the world.

Ngā matatini Māori: Diverse Māori realities

This brings us to the modern day, when Māori people experience a range of diverse realities influenced by access to culture, marae, whānau, housing, healthcare, education and employment, among many other determinants. This final section will focus on this diversity with reference to te reo Māori and marae.

First, it is important to acknowledge that being Māori is determined by whakapapa; somebody is Māori because of descent from a Māori person or people. Māori are not a homogenous group and live what Durie (1995) describes as 'diverse Māori realities', and 'are as diverse and complex as other sections of the population' (p. 1). Therefore, it is unnecessary to narrow the perspective of who a Māori person is in the modern time. However, some indicators will give insight into the diverse nature of living as a Māori person today with regard to participating in Māori culture.

A Māori individual may be a te reo Māori speaker, or more likely, and as a consequence of the sorts of destructive processes described above, may not be a te reo Māori speaker. Many Māori people have heard stories of our elders being physically punished at school for speaking Māori (Hoskins et al., 2020). As of 2020, there are 22,391 students in Māori medium education of Level 1 and Level 2, with 97.1 per cent of those being Māori students (Education Counts, 2021). According to Stats NZ (2020), in 2018 nearly half of the 8500 Māori who completed Te Kupenga 'had some te reo Māori speaking ability'. Those who can 'speak fairly well' ranged from 14.6 per cent to 19.7 per cent across the different age groups of 15 to 55 years, with the highest percentage of speakers being in the 15–24 years age bracket (Stats

NZ, 2020). Although these numbers give some information on the percentage of speakers of te reo Māori, they still do not clarify what it is to be a Māori person in the present time, as experiences differ from individual to individual.

With reference to marae, Māori people's experiences range from being fully involved with activities on their marae to not even knowing the name of their marae. Regardless of these circumstances, they are still Māori because of their whakapapa. Some 66 per cent of Māori adults know their marae (Stats NZ, 2020). Māori living in rural areas tend to visit their marae more often than those living in urban areas; however, many of those living in urban areas do have a longing to visit their marae (Stats NZ, 2020). Marae are still important to Māori identity, regardless of how often an individual visits.

As this illustrates, the Māori population is varied in terms of connections to cultural practices such as speaking te reo Māori, and possession of a sense of belonging to cultural institutions such as the marae. Durie (1995) states that 'the relevance of so-called traditional values is not the same for all Māori, nor can it be assumed that all Māori wish to define their ethnic identity according to classical constructs', and that people will 'reject the notion that they are "less-Māori" than their peers' (p. 15). A Māori person is Māori because of our whakapapa; whakapapa is the inseverable tie that binds descendants to the mana of our tūpuna, reaching back to time immemorial and pushing forward into the distant future.

Conclusion

This chapter has sought to give the reader an insight into the Māori world, with perspectives presented on the beginnings of the universe, the natural environment and the descent of humanity. It has discussed important concepts such as mana and tapu. The distant homeland of Hawaiki, the name of Aotearoa, and the actions of Māui Tikitiki a Taranga in relation to the landscape have been acknowledged. The expression of identity and belonging through pepeha was shown with reference to the landscape, Māori communities and Māori spaces. Descriptions of whānau, hapū and iwi have been given, followed by the bastion of Māori culture, the marae. He Whakaputanga o te Rangatiratanga o Nu Tireni and Te Tiriti o Waitangi, critical documents in the history of Aotearoa New Zealand, have also been explained in this chapter. The wars waged by the Crown on Māori, and the subsequent confiscations that left many Māori communities landless, were mentioned, and some of the negative consequences of that exposed. Subsequent acts of resistance from Māori communities to colonisation have been highlighted.

Finally, the diverse reality of a Māori person was spoken of with reference to cultural participation.

It is important to emphasise here that this chapter is merely an introduction to what may constitute Māori identity and a sense, or a feeling, of belonging to place, community and cultural institutions. A single chapter, or even publication, cannot cover the depth of this topic — but it can help stimulate thought and reflection on what being Māori is, where someone comes from, and the myriad circumstances that influence who Māori are and how Māori can be.

Chapter 2 — Tangata whenua: Māori, identity and belonging: http://turangawaewae.massey.ac.nz/ch2.html

Further reading

Mead, H. M. (2016). *Tikanga Māori: Living by Māori values* (2nd ed.). Huia.

Shaw, R. (2021). *The forgotten coast*. Massey University Press.

Te Rangi Hīroa. (1949). *The coming of the Māori*. Māori Purposes Fund Board.

References

Anderson, A., Binney, J., & Harris, A. (2014). *Tangata whenua: An illustrated history*. Bridget Williams Books.

Belich, J. (1998). *The New Zealand Wars*. Penguin. (Original work published 1986).

Best, E. (1924). *Maori religion and mythology: Part 1*. A. R. Shearer, Government Printer. (Available in the New Zealand Electronic Text Collection, http://nzetc.victoria.ac.nz/collections.html)

Bixley, D., Joseph, D., & Opai, K. (2018). *Te Hīnga ake a Māui i te Ika Whenua*. Upstart Press.

Collins, H. (2010). *Ka mate, ka ora! The spirit of Te Rauparaha*. Steele Roberts.

Durie, M. (1995, February 15). *Ngā matatini Māori: Diverse Māori realities*. [Paper presentation]. Māori Health Framework Seminar, Ngāruawāhia.

Durie, M. (2019, October). *Te āhua o te kāinga: Shaping the house*. [Paper presentation]. Māori Housing Network Seminar. Te Puni Kōkiri, New Zealand.

Education Counts. (2021). *Māori language in schooling.* https://www.educationcounts. govt.nz/statistics/6040

Fama, T. (1937, February 1). Maori fishing. *The New Zealand Railways Magazine, 11*(11), 45–46. http://nzetc.victoria.ac.nz/tm/scholarly/tei-Gov11_11Rail-t1-body-d17.html

Grace, W. (n.d.). *Kupe and the giant wheke.* https://eng.mataurangamaori.tki.org.nz/ Support-materials/Te-Reo-Maori/Maori-Myths-Legends-and-Contemporary-Stories/ Kupe-and-the-Giant-Wheke

Hongoeka Marae. (1997). *Te Whakatuwheratanga o Te Heke-Mai-Raro.* Huia.

Hoskins, T. K., Tocker, K., & Jones, A. (2020). Provocation: Discouraging children from speaking te reo in schools as a strategic Māori initiative. *Mai Journal, 9*(2), 143–151. http://www.journal.mai.ac.nz/sites/default/files/MAI_Jrnl_2020_V9_2_Hoskins_ FINAL.pdf

Kawharu, I. H. (1989). Appendix. In I. H. Kawharu (Ed.), *Waitangi: Māori and Pākehā perspectives on the Treaty of Waitangi* (p. 319). Oxford University Press.

Keenan, D. (2021). *Wars without end: Ngā pakanga whenua o Aotearoa.* Penguin Random House.

King, M. (2003). *The Penguin history of New Zealand.* Penguin Group.

Kingi, T. K. (2005, November 25). *Indigeneity and Māori mental health* [Paper presentation]. Te Pūnamawa Hauora/Te Mata o Te Tau Research Centre for Māori Health and Development. Massey University.

Marsden, M. (2003). God, man and universe: A Māori view. In T. A. Royal (Ed.), *The woven universe: Selected writings of Rev. Māori Marsden* (pp. 2–23). Estate of Rev. Māori Marsden.

Mead, H. M. (2016). *Tikanga Māori: Living by Māori values* (2nd ed.). Huia.

Moorfield, J. C. (2021). *Māori dictionary.* https://maoridictionary.co.nz/

Orange, C. (2004). *An illustrated history of the Treaty of Waitangi.* Bridget Williams Books.

Royal, T. A. (2005a). First peoples in Māori tradition — Kupe. In *Te Ara: The Encyclopedia of New Zealand.* https://teara.govt.nz/en/first-peoples-in-maori-tradition/page-6

Royal, T. A. (2005b). First peoples in Māori tradition — Tāne, Hineahuone and Hine. In *Te Ara: The Encyclopedia of New Zealand.* https://teara.govt.nz/en/first-peoples-in-maori-tradition/page-2

Stats NZ. (2020). *More than 1 in 6 Māori speak Te reo Māori.* https://www.stats.govt.nz/ news/more-than-1-in-6-maori-people-speak-te-reo-maori

Taonui, R. (2012). Te ture — Māori and legislation — The Native Land Court. In *Te Ara: The Encyclopedia of New Zealand.* https://teara.govt.nz/en/te-ture-maori-and-legislation

Te Ipukarea. (2017a, August 13). *He Pātaka Mātauranga 1:04 — Te Tangihanga* [Video interview conducted in October 2009]. YouTube. https://www.youtube.com/watch?v=aPPrQYxlPyQ

Te Ipukarea. (2017b, August 13). *He Pātaka Mātauranga 1:06 — Te Tapu, te Noa* [Video interview conducted in 2009]. YouTube. https://www.youtube.com/watch?v=b6zx5Ovv3Fo&t=1209s

Te Kotahitanga o Te Atiawa. (n.d.). *Parihaka.* https://teatiawa.iwi.nz/history/parihaka

Te Puni Kōkiri. (2001). *He tirohanga ō kawa ki te Tiriti o Waitangi: A guide to the principles of the Treaty of Waitangi as expressed by the Courts and the Waitangi Tribunal.* Te Puni Kōkiri.

Te Puni Kōkiri. (2021). *Changes to the rating of Māori land.* Te Puni Kōkiri.

Te Rangi Hīroa. (1949). *The coming of the Māori.* Māori Purposes Fund Board.

Te Tiriti o Waitangi. (1840). https://waitangitribunal.govt.nz/treaty-of-waitangi/te-reo-maori-version

Treaty of Waitangi. (1840). https://waitangitribunal.govt.nz/treaty-of-waitangi/english-version

Walker, R. (2004). *Ka whawhai tonu matou: Struggle without end* (2nd ed.). Penguin. (Original work published 1990).

Warren, T. R., Forster, M., Tawhai, V. (2017). Tangata whenua: Māori identity and belonging in Aotearoa New Zealand. In T. Cain., E. Kahu, & R. Shaw (Eds.), *Tūrangawaewae: Identity and belonging in Aotearoa New Zealand* (pp. 53–69). Massey University Press

Williams, H. W. (n.d.). *A dictionary of the Maori language* (5th ed.). Legislation Direct.

03. Aotearoa's ever-changing face

Diversity as an unfinished project

Trudie Cain and Tracey Nicholls

E koekoe te kōkō, e ketekete te kākā, e kūkū te kererū.
The parson bird chatters, the parrot gabbles, the pigeon coos.

This whakataukī is an acknowledgement that every bird has its own distinct sound (Massey University, n.d.). Even though it champions birds in the forest, it is a metaphor for humans in society — that each and every one of us is unique and has something to offer no matter where we come from, our gender, our age, or indeed any other identity thread.

He tirohanga Māori: A Māori perspective

Te Rā Moriarty

Māori communities have valued mana motuhake, independence and self-determination, since time immemorial. Although iwi have, and do, work together, iwi have always valued their independence. This is evident in the regions where individual iwi have mana whenua status, in the protection of iwi resources, in the localised customs that are practised, in the stories that are told, and in the many dialects of te reo Māori that are upheld in modern times. However, inclusivity is a fundamental moral of te ao Māori which is at the roots of Māori culture and ways of being, and which influences our shared responsibilities to each other as citizens.

This is reflected in core Māori values: manaakitanga is an integral tikanga that means to care for, look after and to treat people hospitably; whanaungatanga is a word used for the connections between people — while originally based on whakapapa this can also extend to friends; kotahitanga means to be together in unity. These values can be seen in one of the most visual and distinct Māori customs, the pōwhiri. The pōwhiri is the act of the haukāinga, or tangata whenua, welcoming manuwhiri (guests) onto their marae. Welcoming people, hosting people, and making connections to work together are tightly woven into Māori ways of being.

This was evident when early Pākehā sealers, whalers, traders and missionaries arrived in Aotearoa, and Māori were keen to learn about new beliefs, to adopt reading, writing, new tools and clothing. This was while still being Māori, speaking te reo Māori, practising tikanga Māori and living by Māori values. They were interested in and inquisitive about new technologies and incorporated these into their life as Māori.

Today, even though a person is Māori because they have Māori whakapapa, they may also have whakapapa from other parts of the world, such as the rest of the Pacific, Australia, Britain, Ireland, the continents of Europe, Asia, Africa, America and so on. This will influence the social and cultural experiences that many Māori have, which then influences their identity as a Māori individual within their collective communities. As I explained in Chapter 2, Māori live realities that are diverse. However, they are still Māori. They can still positively contribute and maintain their social and cultural worlds as Māori by participating in, and supporting, their whānau, hapū and iwi.

Introduction

In the first chapter of the book, Ella discussed the multiple threads of self that weave together to create an individual and a collective sense of identity. This chapter extends that introductory work by considering how some very specific and significant identity threads — ethnicity, sexuality and age — influence our individual and collective sense of self, including how these aspects of identity shape the encounters we have with others. Importantly, each can provide both opportunities and challenges for fully participating in society and securing a sense of belonging and inclusion. The chapter also explores how changing patterns of ethnicity and age, and changing understandings of sexual orientation and gender identity, have altered the demographic face and complexion of Aotearoa New Zealand. Population change has social, cultural, economic and political implications, each of which impacts on the lives of those who live here in Aotearoa New Zealand. What we hope will also become clear is the extent to which rapidly changing populations create new contexts in which diverse identities might emerge.

Ethnicity and identity

Ethnicity is a particularly significant identity thread for many New Zealanders. The concept 'ethnicity' may be taken for granted in some contexts, but in Aotearoa New Zealand it is strongly contested. Stats NZ (2005) defines 'ethnicity' as 'the ethnic group or groups that people identify with or feel they belong to. Ethnicity is a measure of cultural affiliation, as opposed to race, ancestry, nationality or citizenship. Ethnicity is self-perceived and people can affiliate with more than one ethnic group' (p. 1).

This definition highlights a number of important points. First, although ancestry (biological and social roots) continues to perform an important role in ethnic identification, it provides only part of the story. Indeed, official classifications of ethnicity in the five-yearly New Zealand census are regularly updated to reflect the fluidity and multiplicity of ethnic identity, moving away in recent years from an emphasis on biological criteria and descent.

More important are the subjective understandings and perceptions that individuals might have of a given ethnicity, what it means to them, and the extent to which they feel they belong or not. Ethnic identity is fluid and dynamic, and can change over the course of one's life. Perhaps related to this, many New Zealanders (especially younger New Zealanders) identify with more than one ethnic group (Boven et al., 2020). Ethnic identification is both profoundly personal and a powerful marker of shared cultural values, knowledge and beliefs, and customs and practices that are shaped in a given historical and socio-cultural context. In a local context, ethnic identification can be complex, especially in relation to ethnic categories such as Māori and Pākehā.

If you are interested in the approach Stats NZ takes to defining and classifying ethnicity, visit: https://www.stats.govt.nz/topics/ethnicity

Our ethnic affiliation and identification weave their way into many, if not all, aspects of our lives. With regard to our everyday lives, ethnicity can shape the clothes we wear, the way we wear our hair, and the food we choose to prepare and eat. The body itself can also be an important marker of ethnic identity. For example, culturally specific tattoos such as tāmoko (traditional Māori tattoo), tatau (traditional male Samoan tattoo) and malu (traditional female Samoan tattoo) provide ways of inscribing culture and ethnicity onto the body. Such tattoos are often deeply personal, and serve as a symbol of respect for cultural heritage and whakapapa (genealogy). Ethnicity is also likely to shape our religious beliefs and linguistic practices; ultimately, ethnicity helps shape how we understand and make sense of the world.

Importantly, ethnicity also intersects with other aspects of our identity, such as age and gender, each of which shapes how ethnicity is experienced and expressed. Some of you might find it fairly easy to identify your ethnicity in the first instance, and also to think about the ways you perform your ethnic identity in different settings. Others of you might find it a little trickier. As Ella noted in Chapter 1, it can be especially difficult when we identify with the dominant ethnic group — as Pākehā/New Zealand European. Arguably, when we identify with the majority ethnic group we have less reason to reflect on our own ethnic identity, because our way of seeing and being in the world becomes the norm against which others might be measured. To paraphrase the point Ella made early in her chapter, we may struggle to reflect on our own ethnic identity 'because it is so simply and obviously a fact' (Barker, 1948, p. 195). But whether you are part of the majority or not, there is nothing 'given' about ethnic identity.

We encourage you to take some time to reflect on your own ethnic identity while you continue reading this chapter. To what extent does your ethnicity as New Zealand European, Māori, Pākehā and so on, impact on how you see the world, how you behave in the world, and how you negotiate the world in everyday life?

Ethnic superdiversity and identity

We want to turn away now from an understanding of an individual ethnic identity and move towards a discussion of the demographic change that is occurring in Aotearoa New Zealand. For a long time now, this country has been described as 'ethnically diverse'. But we are increasingly being described as 'superdiverse' (Chen, 2015). The term 'superdiversity' was coined in 2007 by anthropologist Steven Vertovec to describe the 'level and kind of complexity' (p. 1024) of diversity that now exists in many migrant receiving nations, such as New Zealand. Vertovec argues that, as the world has become 'smaller', with people moving more easily between one place and another, increasingly complex social formations have developed that produce a dynamic interplay of country of origin, ethnic identification, migration pathways, languages spoken, religious affiliation and socio-cultural practices and values. So superdiversity is not simply about 'more ethnic groups' represented in a given country, although that is certainly part of it: it is about the 'diversification of diversity' (p. 1025).

Check out this report on the diversity of 'Asian Auckland' lives and culture by Ward Friesen for the Asia New Zealand Foundation: https://www.asianz.org.nz/assets/Uploads/Asian-Auckland-The-multiple-meanings-of-diversity.pdf

Viewed in this way, it is not difficult to think of New Zealand as superdiverse. As a settler colonial society, Aotearoa New Zealand has a long history of attracting migrants from the United Kingdom, to the point where, historically at least, the country was often described as 'the Britain of the South Seas' (Beilharz & Cox, 2006, p. 560). In Chapters 10 and 11 we look at some of the stories of New Zealand that were told to attract those migrants. However, in 1986/87, the country's immigration policy context changed, and the privileging of immigrants from the United Kingdom was abandoned in favour of a new immigration policy that explicitly targeted those with the skills, capital and other means of contributing to the economy (Spoonley & Bedford, 2012) that Aotearoa New Zealand required. Since then, the number of New Zealanders who were born overseas has increased dramatically in a very short space of time, climbing from just 19.5 per cent of the total population in 2001 to 27 per cent in 2018 (Stats NZ, 2018a).

These new migration flows have certainly changed the face of Aotearoa New Zealand. A report produced by the Royal Society of New Zealand Te Apārangi (2013) states that 'New Zealand is, increasingly, a country with multiple "national"

AUCKLAND TOURISM, EVENTS AND ECONOMIC DEVELOPMENT

Embracing diversity

Auckland's annual Lantern Festival, with its astounding lit-lantern artworks, marks the Chinese New Year and celebrates traditional and contemporary Chinese culture. It has drawn thousands of visitors every year since it was first staged in 2000. By 2016, attendance had grown so much that it was moved from Albert Park in the central city to the Auckland Domain. The 2018 census recorded 171,309 Chinese living in Tāmaki Makaurau Auckland, up more than 30 per cent from 118,233 in 2013. Festivals like this both represent immigrant cultures and encourage cross-cultural engagement in urban communities.

identities and values' (p. 8). These identities and values can be seen in a range of ways. For example, over 160 different languages are now spoken across the country (Royal Society of New Zealand Te Apārangi, 2013), and over 20 per cent of people are able to speak more than one language (Stats NZ, 2018a). After English, te reo Māori, Samoan, Northern Chinese (including Mandarin), and Hindi are the most common (Stats NZ, 2021).

We can expect all of these indicators of diversity to increase in the wake of the Covid-19 global pandemic, as New Zealanders return home, often from years abroad, and bring increasingly cosmopolitan lives and habits with them and perhaps also overseas-born partners or children. But we also need to appreciate that, however thoughtfully and scientifically these statistics have been collected, they are only part of the picture: the face drawn by any census is obscured by non-participation — by those who struggle with literacy, perhaps, or those whose voices are marginalised, including tangata whenua (Kukutai & Cormack, 2018; Kukutai & Taylor, 2016) — and by socio-technological challenges involved in initiatives like New Zealand's 2018 online census (Stats NZ, 2019).

As the country, and especially Auckland (our 'gateway city' for newly arrived immigrants), becomes 'diverse in new ways' (Hawke et al., 2015, p. 7), new emerging identities take shape. Auckland is the most ethnically diverse city in New Zealand, with more than 40 per cent of the city's residents having been born overseas (Stats NZ, 2018a). This stands in stark contrast to the situation in, for instance, Gisborne, where only 9.8 per cent of the resident population was born overseas (Stats NZ, 2018a).

Cultural festivals are a material consequence of population change across New Zealand, and they provide opportunities for the construction, negotiation and expression of ethnic identity. Writing about Auckland's annual Pasifika Festival, for example, Mackley-Crump (2015) argues that the event, which attracts more than 225,000 visitors each year, provides an opportunity for Pasifika peoples to deploy 'polycultural capital'; that is, to draw on an 'accumulation of distinctive cultural resources, intertextual skills, the power to negotiate between them and the ability to deploy these cross-cultural resources strategically in different contexts' (p. 8). What this means in practice is that people are able to straddle the boundaries of the Pacific and Aotearoa at this festival.

Festivals provide just one example of a context within which intercultural encounters might take place. Another example is the rise of ethnic precincts — new sites of work and consumption that are designed to meet the employment, social and consumer needs of new immigrant communities at the same time as providing both social and culinary experiences for non-migrants. Ethnic precincts

STUFF LIMITED

Pride in Ponsonby

While Aotearoa New Zealand has always housed a multitude of queer networks, our first recognised pride event, 'Gay Day', took place in 1972, just three years after New York's 1969 Stonewall riots (commonly labelled 'the first pride'). Activists gathered in Albert Park chanting 'Will Victorian morality ever die?' next to the statue of Queen Victoria (see Chapter 5 on protest for more on New Zealand's gay movement). Following the passage of the Homosexual Law Reform Act 1986, other festivals such as Hero Parade and Big Gay Out flourished, often as expressions of joy and solidarity during the darkness of the AIDS pandemic.

Currently, the largest of these events is the Auckland Pride Festival, which was first held in 2013. These days there are concerns regarding the loss of Pride's early protest roots, as well as the commercialisation of the event and shallow displays of inclusivity by corporations for financial gain ('pinkwashing'). The presence of police at the event has also become a point of contention — supported by some, but opposed by others — given the justice system's history of discrimination and violence against gay/trans communities. Nevertheless, the visibility of Pride and the rainbow community has helped garner support for tackling issues such as the mental health challenges experienced by LGBTQIA+ youth, protection from hateful violence, securing trans rights and banning gay conversion therapy.

are defined as the 'co-location of businesses that are owned by members of the same ethnic/immigrant group' (Cain et al., 2011, p. 7). For migrants, especially those who are recently arrived, ethnic precincts help foster a sense of belonging and connectedness by offering the familiar sights, sounds and tastes of home.

The sights of home might include roast ducks hanging in restaurant windows and the presence of Chinese script on the streetscape — what Cain et al. (2011) describe as the street's 'linguistic landscape' (p. 33). The sounds of home reference being able to hear and communicate in one's own language. Finally, the tastes of home are concerned with the very specific provincial flavours of migrants' hometowns; much of the Chinese food on offer in ethnic precincts is not generic, but reflects styles and flavours of cooking that are redolent of very specific places in China (Meares et al., 2015). Both food and language are important cultural identity markers, and being able to embody them in this space fosters and reinforces a sense of familiarity, belonging and connectedness both in Aotearoa New Zealand and in migrants' home countries.

Importantly, these sites of consumption also perform an important role for non-migrants. For example, the primarily Chinese ethnic precinct located in the Balmoral shops (Dominion Road, Auckland) is also frequented by many non-Chinese New Zealanders (both overseas- and local-born); one survey found that nearly two-thirds of the people who visited the precinct identified with a non-Chinese ethnicity (Meares et al., 2015). An Auckland Council study asked visitors to the precinct about their reasons for visiting. The responses often centred on the diversity of 'ethnic' foods available to them, and the 'authenticity' of the flavour profiles (Meares et al., 2015). Visitors also reported their appreciation for the vibrancy of the place and its unique characteristics, especially when compared with the ubiquitous food halls that can be found in most shopping malls.

While some might argue that ethnic precincts and ethnoburbs — defined as suburban residential areas with notable clusters of particular ethnic minority populations (Friesen, 2015; Li, 2009) — are divisive, research suggests that they have social, cultural and economic benefits for the people who live there (Skop & Li, 2010), creating a sense of connectedness, belonging and a shared social context in which migrants can feel at home (Cain et al., 2015). Where we live is important for fostering a sense of identity, community and belonging. We create a sense of place through the physical environment we inhabit, but also through the relationships we have there — relationships that are socially and culturally specific and reflect one's 'place-in-the-world' (McCreanor et al., 2006, p. 198). Part 3 of the book looks more closely at the relationship between place and identity.

A sense of identity and belonging is also mediated by the extent to which a person feels 'included and accepted within the institutional fabric of neighbourhood and community' (McCreanor et al., 2006, p. 198). There is a large body of literature that speaks to the difficulty of 'making home' in a strange land (Li et al., 2010; Phillip & Ho, 2010), and for those who are newly arrived in a country it can be difficult to attain this sense of belonging. This goes *some* way to explaining the rise of ethnoburbs (although there are other important structural and historical explanations, too). The interactions and encounters that people might have in these diverse regions across the country are undoubtedly shaped by the socio-political context in which they are situated.

Sexuality and identity

Asked to think about sexuality as an identity thread, many of us might immediately consider sexual orientation: whether our desires for physical intimacy tend to be directed towards members of our own sex (homosexual), towards members of the opposite sex (heterosexual) or towards both (bisexual). Māori social attitudes in pre-colonisation Aotearoa were more accepting of homosexuality than those imposed by British law when Te Tiriti o Waitangi came into effect in 1840 (Aspin, 2021). At that time, British law in Aotearoa New Zealand made sexual acts between men criminal acts. Sexual acts between women were never illegal, but this was not social tolerance — it was erasure of women's ability to build lives without men.

As Ella discusses in Chapter 5, in the context of protest histories, the 1986 Homosexual Law Reform Act corrected legal discrimination against gay men, and all discrimination on the basis of sexual orientation was subsequently banned in the Human Rights Act 1993 (Ministry for Culture and Heritage, 2014). These anti-discrimination protections do not, however, have the same legal force in the associated states of Niue and the Cook Islands, or in Tokelau, because each has a constitutionally or practically independent legislature (Angelo, 2008). Decriminalisation of homosexuality was considered by the Parliament of the Cook Islands in 2019, but pressure from churches resulted in a decision to maintain the criminal status for male homosexuality and extend the existing law to include criminalising female homosexuality ('Cook Islands retains ban', 2019).

Culturally, Aotearoa New Zealand has been celebrating 'gay pride' since the 1970s, and we are now widely recognised as a welcoming and progressive nation for people with diverse sexualities — members of what we have come to call our 'rainbow community'. After our 2020 election, we were hailed as having 'the queerest parliament in the world' as a result of 10 per cent of the members of the fifty-third Parliament identifying themselves as lesbian, gay, bisexual or trans (Maurice, 2020). We see this growing acceptance of diversity of sexual orientation in, for example, the fifty-third Parliament's choice to mark the thirty-fifth anniversary of the Homosexual Law Reform Act with a dawn ceremony in which the rainbow flag of the LGBTQIA+ community was raised in the forecourt of the Beehive (Chumko, 2021).

Sexuality as an identity thread becomes even more complex, and constitutive of the changing face of Aotearoa, when we consider its close relationship to gender identity, which is about who you feel yourself to be rather than who you find yourself attracted to. They are not the same thing and neither determines nor predicts the other. Worldwide, the general categories that are used to recognise different gender identity threads are 'cis' (people whose felt-identity as a girl/woman or boy/man matches their biological-genital appearance) and 'trans' (people who feel themselves to be a different gender than suggested by their body). For many in Aotearoa New Zealand the most recent public face of our trans communities is weightlifter Laurel Hubbard — the first transgender athlete ever selected for Olympic competition — even though New Zealand's Parliament swore in its first transgender Member of Parliament, Georgina Beyer, back in 1999, on 10 December, which is Human Rights Day ('Laurel Hubbard', 2021; Ministry for Culture and Heritage, 2020).

But, as Schmidt (2021) observes about umbrella terms like 'rainbow' and 'LGBTQIA+', 'cis' and 'trans' are not always as inclusive as they strive to be. People with more fluid understandings of their own gender can experience this binary concept of gender as exclusionary, and it is a way of talking about identity threads that does not line up well with more diverse conceptions in Māori and Pasifika cultures (Schmidt, 2021). The Samoan gender identity fa'afāfine ('in the manner of a woman'), for instance, describes a boy who likes household tasks classed as 'feminine' and takes on behaviours or social roles traditionally performed by women (Schmidt, 2021).

Weaving together ethnicity and gender is challenging in a world still structured by colonial attitudes and binary thinking, and we see this in the way terminology changes, as time passes or as we cross cultures. Aspin (2021) identifies the Māori Sexuality Project — a University of Auckland research project in the early 2000s into Māori attitudes and experiences — as revealing a preference among gay, lesbian, bisexual, trans and intersexual Māori for describing themselves and their culture as takatāpui, a contemporary adaptation of an identity thread long familiar in Māori culture.

And we can see the changing face of gender identity in the way the use of the pronoun 'they' has shifted. As recently as the 1990s, using 'they' to speak of an individual was considered a grammatical error; now references to individuals that use 'they' and 'their' are increasing in institutional contexts like university websites and in the media.

At present, legal protections for trans, intersex (people with ambiguous genitalia or biological-sex identity), and gender non-conforming New Zealanders are sometimes uncertain because they are grounded in the gender binary and the expectation that we all want to fit ourselves into the existing categories: men and women. Legal recognition is also a patchwork: New Zealand passport holders can apply for passports that identify them as male, female or gender diverse, but the ability to change gender on your birth certificate will only be possible with the passage of the Births, Deaths, Marriages, and Relationships Registration Bill, which the majority Labour Government is shepherding through Parliament in the current legislative session (New Zealand Parliament, 2021).

Age and identity

Age is also an important and significant thread of identity that shapes the kinds of experiences we might have on a daily basis, as well as how we might make sense of those experiences. Our age structures the kinds of encounters we have with the outside world: whether we celebrate our birthday with 21 shots or a quiet meal with friends and family; whether we curate ourselves on Facebook or TikTok; or whether we take a river cruise or backpack around India.

Of course we are not suggesting that age *determines* what one can and cannot do — there is nothing stopping a 75-year-old from backpacking around India. But the 'life course' approach to understanding human experience across the lifespan suggests that a series of socially defined events and roles shapes the way an individual's life plays out over time. These events are not predetermined; they are shaped by biological, psycho-social, cultural and structural contexts, and include starting school, (perhaps) going to university, (maybe) finding a life partner, and (potentially) starting a new career. Everyone's life is different, and the socio-cultural environment in which we live will influence whether various events become part of our individual life story and when.

Just like ethnicity and sexuality, age intersects with other threads of identity to shape how life is experienced at any given time. Income level and living situation, for example, are likely to determine the kind of lifestyle someone has. Those of us who live at home for free with our parents while studying full-time, for instance,

ALEXANDER TURNBULL LIBRARY, WA-69188-G

Baby boom sprawl

Local mothers meet on a street corner in a new housing area of Waiuku, south of Auckland, in the 1970s. Bare new housing subdivisions like this were common across New Zealand during the 1970s. Builders were busy as new shops, schools, churches and community facilities sprang up to meet the needs of young families. While these areas certainly appeared aspirational, the actual experience of those inhabiting them could be rather more varied. Women often found themselves socially isolated and physically restricted due to lack of public (and even private) transport. Public facilities, too, often lagged behind the development of the houses themselves. There were also ethnic disparities, with Māori families often in rented homes in city suburbs, separated from whānau support networks still located in rural areas.

NZEI TE RIU ROA, NEW ZEALAND EDUCATIONAL INSTITUTE COLLECTIONS

The new New Zealand

Māori and Pasifika children in their school playground. These are the faces of an increasingly diverse city, joined in recent years by children from China, India, Africa and the Middle East. The New Zealand education system has had to adapt over the decades to accommodate the language needs of such a diverse population, many of whom arrive at school not having English as their first language. As part of this effort, cultural diversity is one of the eight core principles in the New Zealand Curriculum, alongside the Treaty of Waitangi principles. Meanwhile ESOL (English for Speakers of Other Languages) support has been steadily growing within schools at all levels.

might have social lives that afford us great freedom and autonomy. In contrast, others of us who must necessarily work significant hours to contribute to the household income at the same time as studying full-time are likely to feel socially and financially constrained.

Age, too, is changing the face of this country. Populations are ageing worldwide, and New Zealand is no exception. The population aged 65 years and over is expected to almost double, from 635,200 in 2013 to 1,100,000 in 2030. As life expectancy continues to climb, the number of people who are among the 'oldest old' (i.e. aged 85 or over) will also continue to climb, increasing from around 74,000 to over 144,000 during the same time period (Dale, 2015). Another way of expressing this is to point out that the country's population aged 65 or more will increase from 13 per cent to 21 per cent by 2031 (Jackson, 2011).

But age intersects with ethnicity in different ways. Māori and Pasifika, for example, are significantly younger than those who identify with European and Asian ethnic groups: the average age of Māori and Pasifika in this country is 25.4 years and 23.4 years respectively. By comparison, the average age of European and Asian New Zealanders is 41.4 years and 31.3 years respectively (Stats NZ, 2018b).

The global and local phenomenon of ageing populations is the direct result of large numbers of soldiers returning home at the end of the Second World War and very quickly marrying and starting a family. Understanding the economic, social and cultural impact of those people who were born during this 'baby boom' period (approximately between 1946 and 1964) is important for thinking about identity and belonging in Aotearoa New Zealand. Baby boomers (as they have become known) have largely experienced economic growth and prosperity across their lifetime. In Aotearoa New Zealand, baby boomers have arguably benefited from free tertiary education, a generous 'cradle to the grave' welfare system and affordable state housing, then private home ownership and rising property prices. As the youngest of the baby boomers approach retirement age, they do so as members of a comparatively successful and affluent generation.

We use the word 'comparatively' to strike a cautionary note. For many baby boomers, access to non-income-tested government pensions and the possession of considerable equity in the form of their family home means that retirement does indeed represent the 'golden years'. However, this is by no means the case for all of them. Disquieting recent research suggests that a sizeable minority of the boomer generation do not own their own homes, and are only just getting by (if that) on government-provided superannuation (Johnson, 2015a). For these elderly, the future is likely to be uncomfortable and uncertain, especially as the property market bubble affects rental prices and availability.

The rapid ageing of Aotearoa New Zealand's overall population has serious consequences for the country, including but extending well beyond the costs of providing age-appropriate healthcare, housing and other services. Demographer Natalie Jackson points out that the 'bulge' in New Zealand's older adult population puts pressure on an already 'demographically tight labour market' (Jackson, 2016, p. 53). This means that, assuming present policies remain as they are, there are not enough of us who are of working age to fully support the growing number of retirees. A related concern is around the provision of the necessary health and social services to support an ageing population.

The national and regional problem of an ageing population is not going to disappear in a hurry. (See Spoonley, 2016, for an extended discussion of these regional concerns.) As Jackson (2016) points out, it is an issue for local and central government, organisations and the business sector that requires a better understanding of the 'local drivers of demographic change' (pp. 76–77). Challenges associated with labour market supply will be felt especially keenly at regional levels, but there are also significant infrastructure development challenges: how, for instance, can local governments create infrastructure to support an ageing population within a region with a declining total population?

Stats NZ has published the data from the 2018 census as a series of interactive maps: https://www.stats.govt.nz/tools/stats-maps

Regional differences matter because they shape the 'types of opportunities people have and the quality of life they might expect' (Johnson, 2015b, p. 5); where we live impacts on our lives in material ways. A 2015 report by the Salvation Army, *Mixed fortunes: The geography of advantage and disadvantage in New Zealand*, showed that location has a profound impact on economic opportunities (Johnson, 2015a). While areas such as Northland, Gisborne and Waikato — which, coincidentally, have significant Māori populations — have faced economic stagnation, large cities such as Auckland have benefited from a positive agglomeration effect (which is the self-reinforcing process by which large, prosperous cities attract more business and become larger and more prosperous as a result). These regional diversities not only contribute to inequitable outcomes (more on this in Chapter 10), they also contribute to the identity threads of residents.

Ultimately, different age cohorts have different life experiences that are a function of the political context into which they were born. Many millennials (those born in the 1980s and 1990s) argue that 'rolling back the state' — which occurred between 1984 and 1990 — and removing free tertiary education in 1989 have disadvantaged them and created an unfair financial advantage for older New Zealanders. The story that is often told is of the retiree who has had it all through their life course and continues to have it all in their retirement, while millennials face the impossible task of locating an affordable home in which to live. This distinction not only misrepresents the material circumstances of some older people, it also creates a false dichotomy that stigmatises older adults and constructs them as a financial burden on other members of society. As we explore in Part 4 of the book, national narratives such as that of the 'selfish boomer generation' may contain elements of truth, but they also obscure others, which results in the exclusion of the experiences of those to whom the narrative does not apply.

You don't have to look far to find articles that speak to the 'selfishness' of baby boomers and the martyrdom of millennials; however, narratives are also expanding to recognise the impact of macro-level forces on the 'generational battle':
https://www.nzherald.co.nz/nz/the-big-read-reality-of-new-zealands-generation-gap/2RUE5NUJOUGCVMM6B76KVP7ADM

Conclusion

All too often when diversity is discussed in the public arena, it is framed as a conversation about ethnicity. But the core purpose of this chapter has been to show that ethnic diversity is just one strand of diversity that impacts on the lives of New Zealanders. Age, sexuality, household income level (to name just a few variables): each shapes expressions of identity and belonging in this country. When we weave these threads together we can start to see the particularly rich context from which identity can emerge.

This chapter argues that new demographic diversities are changing the face and complexion of Aotearoa New Zealand. This necessarily places emphasis on a rapidly changing population, and this is undoubtedly important. But it is also important to remember that a population comprises many individuals. And these individuals each have a complex sense of identity that is informed by the socio-cultural, economic and political context into which they were born and raised, and currently live.

Chapter 3 — Aotearoa's ever-changing face: Diversity as an unfinished project: http://turangawaewae.massey.ac.nz/ch3.html

Further reading

Besnier, N., & Alexeyeff, K. (Eds.). (2014). *Gender on the edge: Transgender, gay, and other Pacific Islanders.* University of Hawai'i Press.

Friesen, W. (2015). *Asian Auckland: The multiple meanings of diversity.* Asia New Zealand Foundation.

Spoonley, P. (Ed.). (2016). *Rebooting the regions: Why low or zero growth needn't mean the end of prosperity.* Massey University Press.

Tse, C., & Barnes, E. (Eds.). (2021). *Out here: An anthology of takatāpui and LGBTQIA+ writers from Aotearoa.* Auckland University Press.

References

Angelo, T. (2008). In and about the Realm of New Zealand. *New Zealand Yearbook of International Law, 5,* 261. http://www.nzlii.org/nz/journals/NZYbkIntLaw/2008/10.html

Aspin, C. (2021). Hōkakatanga. In *Te Ara: The Encyclopedia of New Zealand.* http://www.TeAra.govt.nz/en/hokakatanga-maori-sexualities

Barker, E. (1948). *National character and the factors in its formation* (4th ed.). Methven & Co.

Beilharz, P., & Cox, L. (2006). Nations and nationalism in Australia and New Zealand. In G. Delanty & K. Kumar (Eds.), *The Sage handbook of nations and nationalism* (pp. 555–565). Sage.

Boven, N., Exeter, D., Sporle, A., & Shackleton, N. (2020). The implications of different ethnicity categorisation methods for understanding outcomes and developing policy in New Zealand. *Kōtuitui: New Zealand Journal of Social Sciences Online, 15*(1), 123–139. htpps://doi.org/10.1080/1177083X.2019.1657912

Cain, T., Meares, C., & Read, C. (2015). Home and beyond in Aotearoa: The affective dimensions of migration for South African migrants. *Gender, Place and Culture, 22*(8), 1141–1157.

Cain, T., Meares, C., Spoonley, P., & Peace, R. (2011). *Halfway house: The Dominion Road ethnic precinct.* Massey University; University of Waikato.

Chen, M. (2015). *Superdiversity stocktake: Implications for business, government and New Zealand*. Superdiversity Centre.

Chumko, A. (2021, July 8). Parliament marks 35 years since gay sex decriminalised. *Stuff*. https://www.stuff.co.nz/national/politics/125685981/parliament-marks-35-years-since-gay-sex-decriminalised

Cook Islands retains ban on homosexuality. (2019, November 15). *Radio New Zealand*, https://www.rnz.co.nz/international/pacific-news/402530/cook-islands-retains-ban-on-homosexuality

Dale, M. C. (2015). *Turning silver to gold: Policies for an ageing population* (Working Paper 2014-2). Retirement Policy and Research Centre; University of Auckland.

Friesen, W. (2015). *Asian Auckland: The multiple meanings of diversity*. Asia New Zealand Foundation.

Hawke, G., Bedford, R., Kukutai, T., McKinnon, M., Olssen, E., & Spoonley, P. (2015). *Our futures — Te pae tāwhiti: The 2013 census and New Zealand's changing population*. The Royal Society of New Zealand.

Jackson, N. (2011). *The demographic forces shaping New Zealand's future: What population ageing [really] means* (NIDEA Working Paper). University of Waikato; National Institute of Demographic and Economic Analysis (NIDEA).

Jackson, N. (2016). Irresistible forces: Facing up to demographic change. In P. Spoonley (Ed.), *Rebooting the regions: Why low or zero growth needn't mean the end of prosperity* (pp. 49–77). Massey University Press.

Johnson, A. (2015a). *Homeless baby boomers: Housing poorer baby boomers in their retirement*. The Salvation Army Social Policy and Parliamentary Unit.

Johnson, A. (2015b). *Mixed fortunes: The geography of advantage and disadvantage in New Zealand*. The Salvation Army Social Policy and Parliamentary Unit.

Kukutai, T., & Cormack, D. (2018). Census 2018 and implications for Māori. *New Zealand Population Review, 44*, 131–151.

Kukutai, T., & Taylor, J. (2016). *Indigenous data sovereignty: Toward an agenda*. ANU Press.

Laurel Hubbard: First transgender athlete to compete at Olympics (2021, June 21). *BBC News*. https://www.bbc.com/news/world-asia-57549653

Li, W. (2009). *Ethnoburb: The new ethnic community in urban America* [ebook]. University of Hawai'i Press.

Li, W., Hodgetts, D., & Ho, E. (2010). Gardens, transitions and identity reconstruction among older Chinese immigrants to New Zealand. *Journal of Health Psychology, 15*(5), 786–796.

Mackley-Crump, J. (2015). *The Pacific festivals of Aotearoa New Zealand: Negotiating place and identity in a new homeland* [ebook]. University of Hawai'i Press.

Massey University. (n.d.). *Whakataukī: Māori proverbs.* https://www.massey.ac.nz/student-life/māori-at-massey/te-reo-māori-and-tikanga-resources/te-reo-māori-pronunciation-and-translations/whakataukī-māori-proverbs

Maurice, E. (2020, October 19). New Zealand just elected the queerest parliament in the world with one in 10 MPs identifying as LGBT+. *PinkNews.* https://www.pinknews.co.uk/2020/10/19/new-zealand-election-lgbt-mps-gayest-queerest-parliament

McCreanor, T., Penney, L., Jensen, V., Witten, K., Kearns, R., & Moewaka Barnes, H. (2006). 'This is like my comfort zone': Sense of place and belonging within Oruāmo/Beachhaven, New Zealand. *New Zealand Geographer, 62,* 196–207.

Meares, C., Cain, T., Hitchins, H., Allpress, J., Fairgray, S., Terruhn, J., & Gilbertson, A. (2015). *Ethnic precincts in Auckland: Understanding the role and function of the Balmoral shops* (TR2015/015). Auckland Council.

Ministry for Culture and Heritage. (2014). *Reforming the law.* https://nzhistory.govt.nz/culture/homosexual-law-reform/reforming-the-law

Ministry for Culture and Heritage. (2020). *Georgina Beyer becomes first transgender woman elected to Parliament.* https://nzhistory.govt.nz/page/georgina-beyer-becomes-first-transgender-woman-elected-parliament

New Zealand Parliament. (2021). Births, Deaths, Marriages, and Relationships Registration Bill (Bill 296-2). https://www.parliament.nz/en/pb/bills-and-laws/bills-proposed-laws/document/BILL_74854/births-deaths-marriages-and-relationships-registration

Phillip, A., & Ho, E. (2010). Migration, home and belonging: South African migrant women in Hamilton, New Zealand. *New Zealand Population Review, 36,* 81–101.

Royal Society of New Zealand. (2013, March 5). *Languages in Aotearoa New Zealand.* http://www.royalsociety.org.nz/2013/03/05/new-zealand-superdiversity-presents-unprecedented-language-challenges-and-opportunities

Schmidt, J. (2021). Gender diversity. In *Te Ara: The Encyclopedia of New Zealand.* http://www.TeAra.govt.nz/en/gender-diversity

Skop, E., & Li, W. (2010). From the ghetto to the invisiburb. In J. W. Frazier & F. M. Margai (Eds.), *Multicultural geographies: The changing racial/ethnic patterns of the United States* (pp. 113–124). Global Academic Publishing.

Spoonley, P. (Ed.). (2016). *Rebooting the regions: Why low or zero growth needn't mean the end of prosperity.* Massey University Press.

Spoonley, P., & Bedford, R. (2012). *Welcome to our world? Immigration and the reshaping of New Zealand.* Dunmore Publishing.

Stats NZ. (2005). *Statistical standard for ethnicity 2005.*

Stats NZ. (2018a). *Census 2018*. https://www.stats.govt.nz/2018-census

Stats NZ. (2018b). *2018 Census population and dwelling counts*. https://www.stats.govt.nz/information-releases/2018-census-population-and-dwelling-counts

Stats NZ. (2019). *2018 Census collection response rates unacceptably low*. https://www.stats.govt.nz/methods/2018-census-collection-response-rates-unacceptably-low

Stats NZ. (2021). *Language*. https://www.stats.govt.nz/topics/language

Vertovec, S. (2007). Superdiversity and its implications. *Ethnic and Racial Studies, 30*(6), 1024–1054.

PART TWO:
VOICES OF AOTEAROA NEW ZEALAND

Voices
Introduction

Trudie Cain and Ella Kahu

The previous section of this book considered the many diverse faces of Aotearoa New Zealand. Its purpose was to explore Māori understandings of identity and belonging, as well as to consider the extent to which the individual and collective faces of New Zealand have altered, and to reflect on the implications of rapid demographic and other forms of change. This next part, 'Voices of Aotearoa New Zealand', considers how voice might be expressed in this country by different people and in different contexts. A related aim is also to consider what the impact of expressions of voice might have for individuals, communities and the nation.

About Part 2

Here, then, we explore voice in Aotearoa New Zealand. But what does voice even mean? In *Tūrangawaewae*, we define voice as the capacity to express one's view or tell one's story, and have that view taken as a valid contribution to public debate. Clearly, this statement has two very distinct parts. The first is about having a voice, and there are many different ways this can occur, depending on the context. Casting one's vote in local or national elections, marching up Lambton Quay with a banner in hand, or creating films that tell our individual and collective stories are all avenues for the expression of voice. To have a voice is one thing, but to be heard is quite another. It might make someone feel good that they have vented on a troubling issue, but if no one was listening and nothing changed, what does it matter? Which brings us to the second part of the definition: having one's voice acknowledged as a legitimate contribution to public debate. This is an important point that is worth underlining.

We can think about voice as operating at two levels: individual and collective. A single person's voice can be expressed or silenced; and, equally, collective voices — those of the elite or of the marginalised, for instance — may be heard or ignored. Clearly, not all voices are in agreement, and in a world of wide-ranging people with wide-ranging views it would be nonsense to expect that they would be. The problem emerges, however, when some voices are privileged, or, alternatively, when some voices are muted entirely.

The extent to which a voice might be amplified or silenced is influenced by a range of factors, perhaps the most important of which is identity. Individual or collective threads of identity shape how people choose to engage with public issues, their opinions on such issues, and also the extent to which their opinions and stories are heard. This links closely with the relations of power that are embedded in our encounters with others. Some groups of people in this country have to struggle for the right to participate in public affairs; in other words, they must struggle to have their voices heard and be legitimated. Gender, sexuality, ethnicity and geographical location are all threads of identity that might amplify or mute one's capacity to speak out and be heard. As Ella explained in Chapter 1, often it is the majority voice that is privileged, and it is the majority's views and stories that are taken for granted as the norm in society.

Another important influence on how and when the different faces of Aotearoa New Zealand get to speak is the norms or formal rules of a particular place (an idea we return to in Part 3). For instance, Parliament has very specific protocols about who can speak, and when, in the debating chamber. The Speaker of the House of Representatives chooses who will be invited to speak during debates, and ensures that the Standing Orders, the written rules of conduct that govern the business of the House, are observed.

To learn more on the history and role of the Speaker, visit: https://www.parliament.nz/en/visit-and-learn/how-parliament-works/office-of-the-speaker/role-history-of-the-speaker/role-election-of-the-speaker

The influence of identity threads on the right to speak can also be heard in the university setting. While lecturers take the floor as a matter of right, students are typically silent until invited to speak. And when they do speak, their words do not carry as much weight as those of their lecturer. In both of these examples, power structures are again evident.

Debates around issues of inclusion and participation are central to an appreciation of identity, belonging and citizenship in Aotearoa New Zealand. As Ella discussed in Chapter 1, there is a reciprocal link between participation and belonging. Being able to participate equally in a particular community and have one's voice heard and acknowledged increases people's sense of belonging to that community. Equally, people who already have a strong sense of belonging are more likely to use their voice and take an active role in the community. Voice, then, is important.

The conceptual template underpinning this part of the book and connecting it to the book as a whole has the following three components:

1. Giving voice to what you think and feel: We look at different ways in which people express or 'voice' their views in the public domain. We also examine what motivates people to engage in these various strategies, and probe the connections between a person or group's sense of identity and belonging and them seeking to have their voice heard.
2. From silence to voice: We explore the struggles different groups have had in gaining a legitimate voice as members of the community of citizens of Aotearoa New Zealand. We ask whether there is room in this country for dissenting voices, and look at what can happen to people who adopt unpopular or contentious positions.
3. Voice, identity and citizenship: We probe the consequences of giving voice for broader issues of citizenship. Voice contributes to the construction of identity and reveals certain assumptions about citizenship. Therefore, the central question here is: How does participation and engagement in the public domain (or being refused those things) shape understandings of identity and belonging at the individual, group and national levels?

Overview of chapters

The following chapters explore three different ways in which 'voice' is expressed: first, through political participation and representation; second, through political protest; and third, through various forms of art. Each topic provides a different means of illuminating the challenges associated with securing the right to engage in public life, and the subsequent consequences of this for identity.

In Chapter 4, 'Voices in the House: Political representation and participation', Richard Shaw discusses New Zealand's political system and how citizens of this country can exercise their voice through voting in general elections. He then briefly explores the political history of Māori and women in Aotearoa, as a reminder that, while we may take our right to vote for granted these days, not everyone has always had that privilege. Finally, Richard shines a light on an apparent turn away from political engagement, and raises concerns about rates of voter turnout for New Zealand. The implications for citizenship are great, given that the most vulnerable members of society are those least likely to exercise their right to vote.

In Chapter 5, 'Shout it out: Participation and protest in public life', Ella Kahu writes about political protest as a way of exercising one's voice and bringing about social, political or economic change in this country. Ella reflects on what motivates people to exercise their voice in this way, including the sense of unity and belonging that collective action brings for those with shared threads of identity. She draws on two historical case studies — the gay rights movement and the 1981 Springbok Tour — to illustrate the ways in which political protest can mobilise communities, create social change, and challenge and contest understandings of national identity. Finally, she looks at how technological developments and changes in the social world have given contemporary protests a different flavour.

The final chapter in this section, 'Voicing cultural rights: Arts, identity and belonging', takes a different focus, and considers the capacity of the art world to speak for those who might be marginalised, excluded or otherwise silenced. Here, Rand Hazou and Trudie Cain use diverse case studies to illustrate three key ideas: the role of the arts in shaping national and individual identities, art as a form of protest and a way for voices to be heard, and finally the links between art, belonging and wellbeing. Rand and Trudie conclude by affirming that participation in the arts is a crucial aspect of citizenship.

Conclusion

This text encourages you to think critically about issues of identity and belonging within Aotearoa New Zealand. The focus on voices in this section expands on our examination in Part 1 of the identities that make up our country, and explores the different ways in which those identities are expressed. The ability to exercise one's voice, to have one's story heard, and to have a say in how the community functions is fundamental to citizenship. New Zealand's history is saturated with examples of groups of people who have been excluded and marginalised, but who have fought to have their voices heard — through our political systems within government, through protest outside of government and through the diverse media of the arts. This section of *Tūrangawaewae* tells some of those stories to illustrate these important social processes, and in doing so widens our understanding of the links between identity and citizenship and the central importance of voice. And, most importantly, it can help us to hear those identities and voices that continue to be silenced.

04.
Voices in the House
Political representation and participation

Richard Shaw

He oranga kei waho, he oranga kei roto?
Is the health of the community outside or inside?

This whakataukī asks a question that many Māori have: Will the health and wellbeing (oranga) of the community come from within (roto) or externally (waho) through political participation? This question is not easy to answer. Māori people will have a variety of perspectives on the political system, and on whether central government will bring positive change for Māori or whether grassroots community transformation is more beneficial.

He tirohanga Māori: A Māori perspective

Te Rā Moriarty

A traditional institution for decision-making in te ao Māori is the rūnanga (Warren, 2004), which refers to the assembly of the community where views are expressed, arguments put forth and debate takes place to come to a consensus. Therefore, an important decision is not just left to an individual but has been traditionally put to the community to deliberate, with all views considered before agreement is made.

In response to colonisation, the history of Māori political movements is a long one. He Whakaputanga, outlined in Chapter 2, acknowledged Māori independence and the meeting of a rūnanga. The seeds of the Kīngitanga were planted in 1853 with Mātene Te Whiwhi and Tāmihana Te Rauparaha, of Ngāti Toa Rangatira, travelling around Aotearoa seeking a rangatira who could stand as Kīngi, a king, with Pōtatau Te Wherowhero of Waikato agreeing to the position in 1858 (Papa & Meredith, 2012). Māori then set up parliaments in the latter part of the nineteenth century as part of Kotahitanga movements. Rātana, the Māori Council and the Māori Women's Welfare League were set up in the twentieth century, dedicated to supporting and sustaining the wellbeing of Māori (Keane, 2012). Many protest movements have been established with the same aim.

Early Māori representation in the New Zealand government came from James Carroll, Āpirana Ngata, Māui Pōmare and Te Rangi Hīroa, who together came to be known as the Young Māori Party. Māori representation is still seen throughout Parliament, either as members of political parties across the political spectrum or as candidates who hold and contest seats in Māori electorates.

These are just a few of the ways that Māori have worked for the development and wellbeing of Māori communities, whether from within the whānau, hapū and iwi or with and within the government. So, to return to the whakataukī: 'He oranga kei waho, he oranga kei roto?' Perhaps the answer to that question is that both have value. There are obvious benefits from working for Māori wellbeing at a local level in the community, at the marae, in schools and in homes. And there are benefits from working with the political system to challenge and pass legislation that supports Māori people. So, what do you think? He oranga kei waho, he oranga kei roto?

Introduction

On 13 May 2021, the Federation of Aotearoa Migrants gathered on the forecourt of the New Zealand Parliament to protest against the state of an immigration system which, they informed parliamentarians in no uncertain terms, separates families and enables the exploitation of migrant workers. One way or another (as will become even clearer in the following chapter by Ella), Parliament is often the focus of protests: people come to the nation's most powerful law-making authority to voice — loudly, enthusiastically and often angrily (although sometimes joyously) — their views, opinions and concerns. Others, however, come because it is where they are employed as Members of Parliament (MPs). There is a direct link between those who protest on Parliament's steps and those who walk up them to go to work: in addition to doing so by protesting, the former can also express their political sentiments by participating in the election of the latter. And while it may appear that protesting occurs outside the political system while voting takes place within it, this false dichotomy should be avoided: in a parliamentary democracy, both are forms of political activity.

Voting is one of the main ways in which citizens give voice to their political hopes, fears and aspirations. In this chapter, then, I focus on the exercise of voice via engagement with, and participation in, politics at central government level, especially — but not exclusively — through the act of voting. I begin with some definitions of key terms and take a quick tour around Aotearoa New Zealand's voting system. Then I explore why people are motivated to vote, and look at the connection between this specific form of voice and people's sense of identity and belonging. I touch on the struggles some groups have had in gaining this citizenship right, and end by examining some of the identity consequences — for both individuals and the wider national community — of both participation and *non*-participation in politics.

A few words on democracy and politics

The language of politics can be a little daunting. But don't be put off: acquiring that knowledge will help you to understand and participate in politics (rather than leave the business of shaping democratic decisions that will affect you to others). Let's begin, therefore, by defining three terms that are central to this chapter: citizenship, politics and democracy.

Citizenship

You have already met the word 'citizenship' in this book: in Chapter 1, Ella defines it as membership of a social community. This broad, encompassing conception of social citizenship is a relatively recent development. Traditionally, the term has been associated with membership of a political community — usually, but not necessarily, a nation state — and comes with certain legal rights and duties. Two points about citizenship are especially relevant in the context of this chapter. First, the rights and obligations that are specified for a country's citizens (and typically denied non-citizens) are defined by political institutions. Parliament is particularly important, but so are the courts and the executive branch of government (Cabinet ministers and government departments). The benefits and obligations you might enjoy today are neither inevitable nor immutable (just ask women in Afghanistan): rather, they are a product of encounters and interactions between people — often with widely diverging views about what should be done — in the political process.

Parliament's website gives you access to pretty much everything going on in our legislature (including the passage of legislation): https://www.parliament.nz/en

Second, at different points in history, qualification for citizenship has rested on aspects of a person's identity. At various times possession of the vote (suffrage) in this country has depended on someone's place of birth, ethnicity, socio-economic class, gender, wealth, ability to read (in the language of the colonising nation), income, age and so on. In short, the right to participate as a full member of a political community is often determined on the basis of what we refer to in this publication as a person's 'identity threads'. There is nothing 'natural' about decisions regarding the bases on which people have the right to vote: they always reflect a normative contest between competing views about who should, and who should not, be able to do so — and, as we shall see, in Aotearoa New Zealand they are not set in stone.

Politics

Time to turn to a working definition of 'politics'. One useful approach is to see politics as the ways in which we express and try to address the things we disagree on without recourse to illegitimate violence (Stoker, 2006). This conception draws attention to the political institutions (e.g. Parliament) in which such contests are played out — and to the actors (MPs and ministers, etc.) who inhabit those formal institutions — but goes beyond these to suggest that politics is something that also occurs in other areas of our lives (in families, for instance, or in the sports, religious and community groups many of us are part of).

Even using this capacious definition (and it is worth noting that there are plenty who would take issue with Stoker's qualified acceptance of the use of violence), some people don't go near politics (more on that shortly). But lots do: by piling into an online furore, having arguments with friends, family or flatmates about the prime minister's latest pronouncement, signing online petitions, phoning or listening to talkback radio, marching in a protest, boycotting certain products or joining a political party (not so popular these days). All of these are ways in which people express their political voice and (sometimes) listen to those of others.

Democracy

The word 'democracy' describes a particular way of structuring the sorts of processes discussed above, and of apportioning political power. Most definitions of democracy describe political systems characterised by universal suffrage; governments chosen by free, regular and competitive elections; and political rights to freedom of speech and association (Stoker, 2006). Abraham Lincoln's defence of 'government of the people, by the people, for the people' in the 1863 Gettysburg Address captures the essence of this way of understanding democracy. It is an approach to politics based on the principle that people consent to being governed by others on the understanding that they get to participate in choosing those who do the governing.

Most of us would intuitively recognise this definition, but might not know that the formal term for this way of organising politics is 'representative democracy'. A representative democracy is one in which citizens delegate their political authority to elected representatives (MPs) through a formal electoral process and for a defined period of time (three years in our case). This delegation does not preclude directly participating in the business of making laws and policies: for instance, through the select committee process citizens in Aotearoa New Zealand are able to comment on virtually all legislation developed in Parliament. It does mean, however, that the day-to-day work of crafting and passing laws is done by MPs on behalf of all citizens, as their elected representatives. Elected parliaments connect those who govern with those who are governed: to use the language of this chapter, when MPs stand up in the House (or a select committee room) to speak, they are often giving voice to the views of those they represent.

Representative democracy is sometimes contrasted with 'participatory democracy', which describes systems in which citizens directly engage in the business of designing, passing and implementing policy. The classical example of this kind of model is ancient Athens, where citizens — a category which excluded women, slaves and *metics* (resident aliens) — directly participated in the business of governing. At the national level, at least, the size of most political communities these days is such that direct participatory democracy *à la* Athens is not feasible, although the spirit of direct participation remains alive in, for instance, debates about the pros and cons of making decisions through referendums.

Voting in parliamentary elections is one of the most significant forms of political engagement — in a representative democracy it is how elected representatives are chosen. Yes, voter turnout in Aotearoa is lower than it once was (although over the past three elections it has been slowly climbing again, including among young people). Yes, if it's all you do, then casting your vote (two of them, technically — more on which below) once every three years is a pretty limited means of engaging with politics. And, yes, there is a strong case for arguing that *not* voting is also a way of exercising the right to voice (we'll come to that shortly, too).

Nonetheless, voting matters because it is how we collectively decide who gets to make the rules that govern our lives. Indeed, in my view voting *really* matters. Here are three things that happen as a direct consequence of our triennial general elections. First, a Parliament is chosen. Second, a government is formed from that Parliament (by the party or parties controlling a majority of parliamentary seats). Third, that government starts doing things that have material consequences for people's lives — including yours. Governments and parliaments decide what is legal and what isn't, and what public money is (and is not) spent on. Governments' policies may validate, valorise and include, but they can also stigmatise, stereotype and exclude. One way or another, this stuff counts — and voting is where it all begins.

Some background on elections and electoral systems

Because voting is one key way in which people give voice to their political views, it is important to understand how the voting system in Aotearoa New Zealand operates and what its main functions are (see Hayward et al., 2021). Elections are staged according to various laws and procedures that collectively comprise an electoral system, a core function of which is to allow voters to influence the shape of the Parliament. When (or if, as voting is not compulsory here) you cast your votes in a general election, you are choosing the people you want to serve as MPs for the next parliamentary term; indirectly, you are also helping determine the identity of the next government. The job of the electoral system is to take your choice and that of every other voter, and allocate the correct number of parliamentary seats to the various political parties contesting the election.

Visit this Electoral Commission page for more information on voter turnout and demographic breakdowns for the 2020 general election: https://elections.nz/democracy-in-nz/historical-events/2020-general-election-and-referendums/voter-turnout-statistics-for-the-2020-general-election

Different electoral systems perform this task in contrasting ways. Under our mixed member proportional (MMP) system, each person has two votes. Voters generally give the party vote to their preferred political party, and the electorate vote to the candidate they want to represent their electorate. (Usually people give their candidate vote to the person representing the party to whom they have awarded their party vote, but they do not need to: around 30 per cent of people 'split' their votes at an election — i.e. they give their candidate vote to a person representing a different party). It is the party vote that determines the composition of Parliament, because the number of parliamentary seats a party is allocated reflects its support among voters.

The maths is pretty simple: a party that wins 50 per cent of the party vote, for example, as Labour did in 2020, will be awarded an equivalent proportion of all seats in Parliament. In 2020, Labour's share of the vote entitled it to 65 seats. (Some 7.7 per cent of party votes went to parties that did not make it over the threshold into Parliament — see below — which meant that each successful party's share of the 120 seats was slightly higher than its share of party votes.) Labour's candidates won 46 electorate seats and so the party received 19 list seats to take it to its entitlement. The sting in the tail is that parties have to cross an electoral threshold before they are entitled to list seats: they must win at least 5 per cent of all valid party votes or one constituency seat (either general or Māori).

There is one other important feature of the political system in Aotearoa New Zealand that is useful to understand. In this country we do *not* directly elect the prime minister. (Nor do we have any say in the selection of our head of state. Rather, at the apex of our constitutional arrangements sits a hereditary monarch who resides nearly 20,000 kilometres away. I will leave it to you to ponder whether or not this is consistent with our claim to be a fully sovereign and independent state.) In many other democracies, voters have a more or less direct voice in the process of choosing their head of government (whether called a president or a prime minister). Not here. Here, we directly elect the Parliament at national elections, but the formation of a government — the prime minister and the 20 or more members of their Cabinet — happens after the election.

The outcome of the process of forming a government depends on the distribution of parliamentary seats, and specifically on which party (or parties) can negotiate an arrangement with other parties allowing it (or them) to control a majority of parliamentary seats. The voters' contribution to this is an indirect one: our votes for the Parliament directly influence the number of seats each party has, and therefore how strong a voice, if any, each has in the government formation process, but we do not directly choose our governments.

Politics as voice: Identity threads, encounters and contexts

One of the aims of this part of the book is to explore what motivates people to give voice to their thoughts, feelings and views in different ways. In the context of this chapter, that requires exploring the range of reasons behind people's decisions to vote (or not to do so). For some, the motivation stems from a deeply held view that voting is a fundamental act of citizenship; an assertion of belonging to a sovereign, self-governing political community. For others, voting is a civic virtue: this view is reflected in the argument you sometimes hear that people *should* vote because others fought (and sometimes died) for that right. Most people, however, vote because they want to have a say — however small — in the political processes that directly influence their daily lives. The cost of a tertiary education and the size of a student's debt, the price of houses, the quality of our freshwater resources — these and myriad other things are influenced, if not wholly determined, by decisions made by parliamentarians and ministers. Many people have firm views on at least some of these things, and voting is one way in which they express these views and help shape decision-making.

In this respect, voting is as much an emotional and expressive act as it is a strictly rational one. When people exercise their voice through voting, they are taking a position on things they often feel strongly about. There is a relationship between a person's views, values, beliefs and so forth — their identity threads — and the positions they take on matters of public concern. For example, someone with social justice values may feel particularly strongly about income inequality in Aotearoa New Zealand; another person will have firm opinions on how we should treat the environment (you will read more about these issues in Chapters 10 and 11 respectively). These positions might motivate them to vote, and to do so for a party or politician whose policies are consistent with their values.

In addition, our political identities are to some extent shaped by the relationships and interactions we have with others. While there are no iron-clad rules, the sociological explanation of voting behaviour stresses the significant roles played by those with whom we have important social relationships — particularly family members, partners and peers — in shaping our political views and, therefore, how we vote. Another account, the party identification model (Fiorina, 2002), suggests that people develop an attachment to particular parties — based on their personal history and experiences, their families' voting preferences, past policies and so forth — which shapes their voting behaviour. According to this view, unless given compelling reasons to do otherwise, people tend to stick with 'their' party — it becomes a part of their political sense of self.

There are other connections between voting, and political engagement more generally, and people's personal sense of identity and belonging. Whether you use it or not, having the right to vote signifies that you are a member of a political community; not having that right marks you as an outsider. Furthermore, you are far more likely to feel connected to that political community, even if its decisions aren't always ones you like, if you know you can contribute by selecting those responsible for making those calls. The reverse also applies: people who cannot vote or who are disengaged from a political community are less likely to feel part of it (even though the rules the community puts in place will continue to apply to them).

Voting, therefore, is one way of expressing membership of a political community: 'I vote, therefore I belong'. But it also works the other way: that community — which is part of the context in which people's sense of identity is shaped — will do things that have consequences for individuals' sense of who they are. The language and substance of politics send messages about who matters and who does not. Tax cuts for higher-income earners send one type of message ('We will reward you because you are earning well'), while punitive sanctions against those on benefits send a very different message ('If you just tried harder, you could find work'). Look closely enough and you will see that governments' policies almost always reflect preferences for certain values and serve the interests of some groups over others.

But policies do more than that: they also shape people's material circumstances, and in doing so have consequences for one's sense of self. American political scientists Anne Schneider and Helen Ingram (1993) explain how this happens. Government policies are imbued with socially constructed images of the populations they are pointed at (high-income earners, the unemployed, sick people, business owners, students, investors, refugees, property owners, migrants or whomever). Those images may be positive or negative. Either way, the implicit

ELECTORAL COMMISSION

Exercising citizenship

In order to vote in New Zealand, you need to be 18 years or older and either a New Zealand citizen or a permanent resident (and must also have lived in New Zealand for one year or more at some point in your life). People from Australia, the Cook Islands, Niue and Tokelau who do not have permanent resident visas may vote, as long as they have lived in the country for more than 12 months and are enrolled to vote. While voting is not compulsory in New Zealand, enrolling is. Those who enrol at least a month before election day receive a voting information pack and EasyVote card to speed up the process on the day. As of 2020 it is also possible to both register and vote on election day itself (an initiative aiming to increase voter turnout). Voters of Māori descent can opt to enrol on the Māori roll rather than the general roll. Voting starts around two weeks before election day; in 2020, 68 per cent of votes were cast in advance of polling day proper.

LADY VOTERS GOING UP TO POLLING-BOOTH. ELECTION DAY, AUCKLAND.

The battle for equality

New Zealand women won the right to vote in 1893, with the passing of the Electoral Act, but the battle for equality was not quite over: they could not stand for Parliament until 1919. The push to get the vote was known as the women's suffrage movement, and Kate Sheppard was its public face: 'We are tired of having a "sphere" doled out to us, and of being told that anything outside that sphere is "unwomanly",' she once said. The movement grew out of concern at alcohol-related violence; women thought that if they could vote they would have more say in promoting laws to ban liquor and encourage higher moral standards, as well as enjoy more participation in society, rather than being largely confined to their homes.

messages — worthy/not worthy; lazy/hard-working; deserving/undeserving, etc. — communicated by such images are absorbed by members of the target populations.

Whether positive or negative, these representations of their identity can have a bearing on people's feelings of self-worth and their willingness to participate in (or withdraw from) the life of their communities. New Zealand writer Andrew Dean (2015) provides a local example of this very thing, explaining how the economic policy reforms of the 1980s and 1990s were associated with both a growing sense of alienation and rising suicide rates among young people in this country.

The consequences of these politically constructed representations can also reverberate out into the wider public domain. Public acceptance of the negative portrayal of a certain group may produce stereotypes based on a poorly informed understanding of that group's circumstances. Worse still, the process can become self-reinforcing. Negative stereotypes can influence voters' choices at the ballot booth, which in turn may lead to more punitive government policies that have further corrosive consequences for members of marginalised groups.

From silence to voice

Another core theme of this section of the book is that membership of any sort of political community is rarely inevitable. Often what we take for granted today is something that previous generations have been denied. That is certainly the case with voting: there is nothing natural about having the right to vote, or to engage in politics more generally, as a brief political history of Māori and women shows. Aspects of both stories are well known, but there is more to them than many of us realise.

The Māori seats were established in 1867 by Donald McLean's Maori Representation Act. The legislation — indeed, the whole history of Māori parliamentary representation, which remains one of the great untold (or misunderstood) political stories of our nation — was fascinating for a number of reasons. For one thing, for the purposes of the Act a 'Maori' was defined as 'a male aboriginal native inhabitant of New Zealand of the age of 21 years and upwards, and shall include half-castes'. You can see how at least three identity threads — ethnicity, gender and age — are in play here. For another, had the number of Māori seats been established on a population basis (as was the case for what were then known as the 'European seats'), there would have been 14 or 16 Māori seats rather than the four that were established. Finally, at the time, Māori weren't the only ones with dedicated parliamentary representation. Ring-fenced seats were de rigueur in the mid-1800s. Two had already been set aside for Otago goldminers by the time McLean's legislation was enacted, and there was a Pensioners Settlement electorate in Auckland. In fact, 1867 was a good year for separate representation: not only were Māori bequeathed four seats, but Westland goldminers were also tossed an electorate of their own.

For more detail on the history of the Māori seats, see Te Ara: http://www.teara.govt.nz/en/nga-mangai-maori-representation/page-1

There remains a surprisingly entrenched view that the Māori seats represent a privilege. I am not sure why, given that (a) the voting process on the Māori and general rolls is identical, (b) no voter can vote on more than one electoral roll, and (c) the Māori electorates are larger, and therefore harder to service, than general electorates. Also, we are certainly not alone in providing for the dedicated parliamentary representation of indigenous people. It also exists in Lebanon, Fiji, Zimbabwe, Singapore, India and the United States' dependencies of Guam and Puerto Rico. Admittedly, one or two of these are countries some of us might not like being compared with, but the point is that separate representation isn't uncommon.

Actually, the history of the Māori voice in Parliament is replete with instances in which being treated differently has not been to the advantage of tangata whenua. The secret ballot was established for male European voters in 1870, but Māori voted by show of hand until 1910, and then by declaration (in front of a returning officer and a Māori witness) until 1937. Between 1919 and 1951, voting in the Māori seats was held the day before voting in European seats ('European' seats became known as 'general' seats in 1975). Māori could not stand as candidates in European electorates until 1967, and between 1893 and 1975 a person deemed to be more than half Māori could not vote in a European seat. For long periods of time, without the Māori seats there would have been few, if any, Māori MPs.

As to women, while we are forever invoking the 1893 legislation granting all women the vote as part of our progressive, egalitarian nation-building story, there are less tasteful elements of that history that rarely feature in the popular narrative. For instance, while women won the right to vote in 1893, the law prevented them from *standing* for parliamentary election until 1919, and it was 40 years after the landmark suffrage legislation before the first woman — Elizabeth McCombs — took her seat in Parliament (Coleman, 2020).

The history of women and the vote in Aotearoa New Zealand is told here: http://www.nzhistory.govt.nz/politics/womens-suffrage

For many years, women comprised a clear minority of both MPs and ministers. The 2020 election, however, was a milestone: in the fifty-third Parliament women accounted for 48 per cent of all MPs (and 40 per cent of government ministers). To be sure, that figure masks differences within parties: women comprised 55 per cent of Labour's caucus, for instance, while the equivalent figure for the National Party was 31 per cent. Nonetheless, just three years earlier (in 2017) women had made up just 38 per cent of parliamentarians.

Historically, under-representation raises questions about women's voice in the House (the question also applies to other under-represented groups). It is an especial concern for those who support women's representation on the grounds that Parliament should resemble — in demographic terms — the wider population. (That view is itself based on the assumption that women have specific interests that can only be represented by those with the same interests, which is open to the challenge that this downplays other aspects of women's identity, such as class, ethnicity or age.) To some extent, too, it is also at odds with one of our national articles of faith, which is that everyone is, or should be, treated equally (which David discusses in Chapter 10).

From voice to silence?

There is one final story to talk about here, and it has to do with voter turnout. In recent decades the proportion of people exercising their right to vote has been falling in many (perhaps most) democracies, including our own. A government report on the 2014 election described the decline in voting in Aotearoa New Zealand as 'particularly steep and persistent' (Electoral Commission, 2014). In 2011, just 69.5 per cent of those eligible to vote did so (the lowest since women gained the vote in 1893) (Shaw, 2016). Things have since ticked up: at the 2020 election (which had the highest turnout since 1999) the proportion of eligible voters who cast at least one vote climbed to 77.4 per cent.

Still, this means that nearly a quarter of people who are eligible to vote are choosing not to do so. Groups among whom voting tends to be lower include young people (in 2020, just over 60 per cent of eligible voters aged 18 to 24 enrolled and voted, compared with nearly 90 per cent of 65- to 69-year-olds) and Māori (74 per cent of enrolled Māori voters voted in 2020, which was 15 per cent higher than it had been in 2017). Non-voting is also more common among those who are unemployed or on low incomes, and among members of migrant communities from nations with limited democratic traditions (Henderson, 2013).

Before delving into this issue, there are two points worth making. First, be careful not to assume that non-voters are politically disengaged. They may well be, but voting is just one way of participating in politics, and it is entirely possible that your parent/son/partner/flatmate who does not vote is happily engaging in other types of political activity. One obvious form this might take is online political activity — sometimes called 'information activism' — which is connective rather than collective in nature (Marsh et al., 2016). There is a smug tendency among more traditional types to dismiss such activity as 'mere clicktivism', but there is evidence that online activity also spills over into more concrete, embodied political arenas (Bennett & Segerberg, 2012, p. 19,) as Ella discusses in the next chapter.

Listen to this TED Talk by Yaël Eisenstat if you think the internet is innately democratising: https://www.ted.com/talks/yael_eisenstat_dear_facebook_this_is_how_you_re_breaking_democracy#t-153356

Second, while the act of voting is a statement ('I have a stake in this community and I wish to participate in it'), non-voting is not necessarily a statement of *not* belonging. By choosing not to vote, a person may well be saying 'I don't feel I belong to this community'. Equally, they might be saying 'I belong, and feel so strongly about the direction in which things are going that I will choose not to vote', or 'I don't see my particular identity reflected in the people standing for election'. This, too, is an active choice and a legitimate expression of a view. In short, resist the temptation to blame non-voting on lazy, irresponsible or apathetic individuals. Of course those can be factors, but, as Marsh et al. (2016) put it, the issue might not be 'political apathy, but alienation from politics as it is practised' (p. 1).

Why some people don't vote

Rather than blame people, then, we should ask two very serious questions: 'Why is non-voting higher than it was once upon a time?' and 'Is this a problem?' The first thing to be said is that falling (or lower) voter turnout is one expression of a trend towards political disengagement from formal politics. The reasons for this are deep and complex, but one is that some people no longer believe in the capacity of politics and politicians to address their problems and issues. If you are facing a future of insecure employment, low wages, increasingly unaffordable housing and a climate crisis — and some people in this country face all of those challenges and more — and see no way out of this vortex, you may well question the point of engaging with politics, via voting or other means.

This loss of faith is sometimes expressed in what has become known as 'anti-politics' (Hay & Stoker, 2009). Even if you have never heard it before, you will be familiar with what the term represents — anti-politics is that bleak view of politics which sees mendacity, duplicity and sleaze everywhere, and which holds that politicians are, without exception, lazy, self-serving, dishonest liars. There is some truth in elements of the anti-politics perspective; equally, it provides a partial explanation of affairs (often enthusiastically promoted by a media less interested in objectivity or balance than in sensationalism and reader-market share) which rests on negative assumptions rather than a rigorous examination of evidence.

Of most concern, perhaps, is where the anti-politics analysis leads us. If the diagnosis is that politics amounts to nothing more than the rampant pursuit of self-interest, then the solution, surely, is less politics. Unfortunately, 'less politics' really means that most of us get less and less (and eventually no) say in what gets decided. Instead, decision-making is removed from the public domain and becomes the preserve of other people: in effect, it gets 'subcontracted . . . to non-elected agencies and institutions' (Hay & Stoker, 2009, p. 228). This happens in one of two ways, the first of which is through the delegation of decision-making authority to appointed officials in institutions such as the Reserve Bank and sundry Crown entities. Those agencies can possess very significant powers: changes in interest rates decided by the governor of the Reserve Bank, for instance, have major consequences for homeowners, property investors and those who pay rent. But the public cannot hold the (appointed) Reserve Bank governor to account in the same way it can the (elected) Minister of Finance.

Second, we have come to rely heavily on the free market to organise social and economic life. But as the public sphere has shrunk, so the private domain has expanded. There are several potential issues with this. For one thing, marketisation has direct impacts on individuals, especially for those who are struggling (and who therefore, for instance, go cold during winter). Furthermore, it also has a bearing on what politics can achieve, because the government's influence in markets (for electricity, housing, food, etc.) is, by definition, limited. This means that politics is constrained in its capacity to support people who suffer from a lack of means. Finally, the more we rely on markets to resolve what were once public debates about who gets access to what, the less we are able to collectively resolve these issues through the political process. In competitive markets, unlike in politics, we are not all equal: it is in the nature of competition that some identities will miss out.

And this is a problem, why?

As to the second question posed above — is lower voter turnout an issue? — in a section about voice we should reflect on some of the possible long-term consequences of political disengagement (see Shaw, 2016). However compelling the reasons may be, there are risks associated with what amounts to a voluntary silencing of voice. Most obviously, non-voters' voices stand less chance of being heard when decisions are taken, and over time it may be that those decisions start to disproportionately reflect the views of those who *do* engage. Whether you vote or not, governments will go on governing, and will make choices — usually sooner rather than later — that will directly affect you. In other words, even if your voice has not been part of the relevant conversation, you will have to live with the consequences of the decisions that will inevitably be taken.

There is another risk of long-term political disengagement — and it was on stark display in the US Capitol on 6 January 2021 — which is that at some point anti-politics becomes so systemic it starts to threaten the very structure of our democracy. There are a couple of ways this could play out. One scenario sees a populist demagogue riding a wave of public anger to electoral victory, following which he or she drives illiberal laws through the New Zealand Parliament as the nation embraces a politics of intolerance and suspicion (see Shaw, 2017).

The second path can be glimpsed in data from a poll undertaken by international policy think-tank the Lowy Institute (2013), which revealed that just 48 per cent of 18- to 29-year-old Australians thought that 'democracy is preferable to any other kind of government'. Put differently, a majority of those polled thought some other form of political system would be preferable to Australia's parliamentary democracy.

We need to be careful about what we wish for. If we disparage, dismiss and denigrate our form of democracy to the point that it collapses, what will we replace it with? An absolute monarchy? A dictatorship? Some other form of authoritarian regime? Whatever its faults (and heaven knows they exist and need remedying), our type of democracy does permit people to voice their views and engage should they choose to. In some other political systems, the only voices to be heard are those of what American sociologist C. Wright Mills (1956) once called the 'power elite'. But if we leave the field of political play to the powerful, they may ignore the rest of us completely and simply write the rules in their favour.

Parliament, pandemic and protests

This photo was taken in February 2022, and shows some of the tents erected on Parliament's grounds during a protest that lasted 23 days. Unlike other protests in New Zealand's history — including the anti-Tour protests of 1981 and those in favour of gay law reform or Bastion Point/Takaparawhau (which eventually led to the return, in the late 1980s, of land to Ngāti Whātua ki Ōrakei) — this one seemed not to have a primary focus. Instead, it sprawled across many issues, stances and viewpoints: some were there to oppose the government's policy on vaccine mandates or to express their support for individual liberties, while others showed up to give vent to their anti-Semitism, misogyny and/or desire to publicly execute politicians and members of the media. It is too soon to tell what the long-term consequences (if any) of the 2022 protests (smaller events also occurred at other places, including New Plymouth, Christchurch, Picton and Auckland) might be, although there are concerns — given the nature of some of the social media activity that took place during those three weeks — that it will have radicalising effects that could produce further violence. One short-term consequence, however, is that shortly after the occupation ended a number of Covid-positive protesters arrived at hospitals seeking medical care, presumably missing the irony that having so vehemently opposed the government's Covid-19 policies they were now wanting its help in dealing with their own illness. Whatever the eventual consequences, days after police evicted them from Wellington's CBD the protesters' absorption with their individual rights was thrown into sharp perspective by Russia's invasion of Ukraine.

Conclusion

There is a clear link between voting, and political engagement more broadly, and the wider narrative in this book regarding citizenship. Participation in public life is a central aspect of citizenship. As Hay and Stoker (2009), two eminent British political scientists, put it, 'in politics the only way to get something is to use voice — to express your concerns in concert with others' (p. 234). That may be a little optimistic, given the conduct of some alleged democrats around the world in recent years, but you get their point. Bluntly, politics is something that we do with the others with whom we share this place. The bases on which participation in such processes is allowed (or prohibited), the groups who get to participate (and those who do not), the ways we can (or cannot) participate, including through voting — each is central to an appreciation of identity, belonging and citizenship in Aotearoa New Zealand.

Little of this is simple or straightforward. One of the central themes of this book is that the faces, places, voices and stories that characterise Aotearoa New Zealand are rich and varied. It is hardly a surprise, then, that this diversity often means people take opposing views on issues. In politics, people speak with different voices because they hold diverging views on things that are fundamental to their sense of self. In a diverse society like ours, there cannot always (or even often) be unanimity on what matters to us: unless some false uniformity is imposed from on high, there will always be different voices regarding our values and the things we believe in. That is both healthy and entirely to be expected.

Politics is the process through which all of this occurs. Done well, it can help us 'find ways for those who disagree to rub along together . . . [and to] potentially patch up the disagreements that characterise our societies without recourse to illegitimate coercion or violence' (Stoker, 2006, p. 2). But, for this to happen, two things have to occur. First, *all* of our voices need to be heard in the political conversation; second, we must do better at *listening* to what others have to say. The current drift towards political disengagement and the degree to which social media platforms are now embedded in our lives (as Stella discusses in Chapter 9) mean that some voices are falling silent and there is a whole lot less listening going on. As a political community, our challenge is to find ways for those voices to re-join the conversation about how we wish to live together, and to nourish our ability to listen to them. It won't have escaped even the most casual observer of the aftermath of the 2016 presidential election in the United States that the price of failure to rise to this challenge might be very high indeed.

Chapter 4 — Voices in the House: Political representation and participation: http://turangawaewae.massey.ac.nz/ch4.html

Further reading

Hayward, J., Greaves, L., & Timperley, C. (Eds.). (2021). *New Zealand government and politics* (7th ed.). Oxford University Press.

Shaw, R. (2016). The harvest we will reap. In N. Legat (Ed.), *The journal of urgent writing* (pp. 124–139). Massey University Press.

Stoker, G. (2006). *Why politics matters*. Palgrave Macmillan.

References

Bennett, W., & Segerberg, A. (2012). The logic of connective action: Digital media and the personalization of contentious politics. *Information, Communication and Society, 15*(5), 739–768.

Coleman, J. (2020). *From suffrage to a seat in the House: The path to parliament for New Zealand women*. Otago University Press.

Dean, A. (2015). *Ruth, Roger and me: Debts and legacies*. BWB Texts.

Electoral Commission. (2014). *Report of the Electoral Commission on the 2014 general election*. Electoral Commission.

Fiorina, M. (2002). Parties and partisanship: A 40-year retrospective. *Political Behavior, 24*(2), 93–115.

Hay, I., & Stoker, G. (2009). Revitalising politics: Have we lost the plot? *Representation, 45*(3), 226–236.

Hayward, J., Greaves, L., & Timperley, C. (Eds.). (2021). *New Zealand government and politics* (7th ed.). Oxford University Press.

Henderson, A. (2013). *Immigrants and electoral enrolment. Do the numbers add up?* (Stats NZ Working Paper 13-01). Stats NZ.

Keane, B. (2012). Kotahitanga — unity movements. In *Te Ara: The encyclopedia of New Zealand*. https://teara.govt.nz/en/kotahitanga-unity movements

Lowy Institute. (2013). *The Lowy Institute poll*. https://www.lowyinstitute.org/publications/lowy-institute-poll-2013

Marsh, I., Vines, E., & Halupka, M. (2016). Two cheers for Richards and Smith: Beyond anti-politics? *The Political Quarterly, 87*(3), 383–388. https://doi.org/10.1111/1467-923X.12247

Mills, C. Wright. (1956). *The power elite.* Oxford University Press.

Papa, R., & Meredith, P. (2012). Kīngitanga — the Māori King movement. In *Te Ara: The encyclopedia of New Zealand.* https://teara.govt.nz/en/kingitanga-the-maori-king-movement

Schneider, A., & Ingram, H. (1993). Social construction of target populations: Implications for politics and policy. *American Political Science Review, 87*(2), 334–347.

Shaw, R. (2016). The harvest we will reap. In N. Legat (Ed.), *The journal of urgent writing* (pp. 124–139). Massey University Press.

Shaw, R. (2017). We're all in this together? Democracy and politics in Aotearoa New Zealand. In A. Bell, V. Elizabeth, T. McIntosh, & M. Wynyard (Eds.), *A land of milk and honey? Making sense of Aotearoa New Zealand* (pp. 43–56). Auckland University Press.

Stoker, G. (2006). *Why politics matters.* Palgrave Macmillan.

Warren, K. T. R. F. (2004). *Rūnanga: Manuka kawe ake. Facilitating Māori aspirations* [Master's thesis, Massey University]. Semantic Scholar. https://mro.massey.ac.nz/handle/10179/955

05.
Shout it out
Participation and protest in public life

Ella Kahu

Ehara taku toa i te toa takitahi, engari he toa takitini.
My strength is not that of a single warrior but that of many.

The proverb for this section is a whakatauākī, a quote where the author who first uttered the expression is known. It is attributed to Paterangi of Ngāti Kahungunu (Grove & Mead, 2001), and reminds us that collective effort influences the success of an activity and elevates a united voice in protest and resistance.

He tirohanga Māori: A Māori perspective

Te Rā Moriarty

Māori communities have been at the forefront of many protests since the nineteenth century. These have predominantly been in opposition to the loss of rights to land because of land confiscations and dubious land sales. In 1863, the New Zealand Settlements Act and the Suppression of Rebellion Act gave the Crown the legislative means by which to confiscate land from Māori people who resisted the sale or the surveying of their land, as such resistance was deemed to be rebellion against the Crown (Durie, 1998). The loss of land left many Māori communities of the nineteenth century without resources to survive. Previously independent hapū and iwi were left with the choice of starving, being dependent on the new colonial system or standing up for their rights in protest. As Parihaka and the Land March of 1975 have already been discussed in Chapter 2, this section will focus on Māori protest activities against the Foreshore and Seabed Act 2004. It is important to note here that this Act was eventually repealed with the Marine and Coastal Area (Takutai Moana) Act 2011.

In 1997, eight iwi of the Te Tauihu o Te Waka a Māui, the northern part of Te Waipounamu, went to the Māori Land Court seeking a declaration from the court that the foreshore and seabed in the Marlborough Sounds 'be regarded as customary land, as defined in Te Ture Whenua Māori Act 1993' (Durie, 2005, p. 87). These iwi were Ngāti Apa, Rangitāne, Ngāti Kuia, Ngāti Tama, Te Ātiawa, Ngāti Koata, Ngāti Rārua and Ngāti Toa. The High Court ruled that 'once dry land had been purchased by the Crown, any Māori customary interest in the foreshore in front of it was lost' and that 'the seabed had always been owned by the Crown' (Hickford, 2015). The iwi challenged this in the Court of Appeal, which acknowledged, in 2003, that the Māori Land Court had jurisdiction under Te Ture Whenua Māori Act 1993 to decide whether the foreshore and seabed could have the status of Māori customary title.

In 2004, the government responded with proposed legislation that looked to vest full ownership of the foreshore and seabed in the Crown (Durie, 2005). This would deny Māori applicants the ability to test customary land rights in the Māori Land Court and was tantamount to an act of confiscation, albeit in a more modern guise. The reaction from Māori at the time was a hīkoi, leaving Te Taitokerau, which eventually included Māori from throughout Aotearoa, and which arrived at Parliament on 5 May (Durie, 2005). The number of protestors has been estimated at 25,000 or more.

The hīkoi brought Māori together from all over the country in opposition to the government's proposed legislation. It was significant in that it comprised a massive number of people, descended from a large number of iwi, marching as one against an injustice. Nevertheless, the government at the time went on to pass the Foreshore and Seabed Act 2004, vesting in the Crown full ownership of the public foreshore and seabed, but excluding areas that were already in private ownership (Hickford, 2015). Regardless, the protests that occurred are still carried in Māori memory and are a clear example of the passion and ability for mobilisation to stand up for rights and to uphold the mana of the tūpuna.

Introduction

In ancient Athens, political participation — activity intended to influence government — was a duty of all citizens. (As an interesting aside, as we learned in Richard's chapter, 'citizens' excluded women, slaves and *metics* [aliens] — which left just 30 per cent of the population.) The value that was placed on participation, and on the role of the active citizen, is evident in our language: the English word 'idiot' derives from the Greek *idiōtēs* meaning 'private and self-centred' — in direct contrast to *politēs*, meaning 'citizen' or 'public' (Parker, 2005).

While participation in public life is no longer seen as an obligation (even voting is not compulsory in Aotearoa New Zealand, although it is a legal requirement to enrol), the right to have a say on how things happen, to participate, remains a critical right in modern democracies (Kaase, 2011). In the previous chapter, Richard explored a particular form of political participation: voice through voting. In this chapter I step outside of the formal structures of Parliament to explore protest: groups of citizens with a common goal aiming to bring about social, political or economic change by making their voice heard through methods such as letter-/email-writing, marches, petitions, boycotts and occupations (Grey, 2015). Protest is vital to a dynamic democratic society — it is a key way for politicians to hear citizens' views on important issues. It is often through citizen activism that change occurs. The first key aim for this part of the book is to explore how people express their voice and what motivates them to do so.

So why do people protest? The phenomena of social movements and protests have been the focus of disciplines in social science and the humanities, such as social psychology, sociology, political science, history and anthropology, with each taking a different view of this complex topic (Roggeband & Klandermans,

Resisting reform, unsuccessfully

Politician Peter Tait and businessman Keith Hay, of the Coalition of Concerned Citizens, carry a petition against homosexual law reform into Parliament in 1985. Despite the strenuous efforts of a loose coalition of conservative and Christian groups, in July 1986 the Homosexual Law Reform Act was signed into the statute books by the Governor-General, thereby decriminalising consensual sexual relations between men aged 16 and over. No longer would they be liable to prosecution and a term of imprisonment. Since then, a raft of gradual reforms, including legalising same-sex marriage, has been enacted, addressing the legal status and improving the access to equal rights of LGBTQIA+ New Zealanders.

2010). For instance, a social psychologist may look at the individual identities of activists, whereas a sociologist may look at the cultural context that shapes a protest movement. Both approaches are relevant to the theoretical framework that informs this text.

At an individual level, protest is strongly linked to identity. For example, the rights granted to citizens are often determined by the threads of their identities, and it is often shared dimensions of identity, such as gender or class, that bring a group together in protest. For instance, Anthony Marx (1995) argues that exclusion from citizenship based on ethnicity solidifies ethnic identity and results in collective action against the state. Protest also links to belonging, both as a motivation and as an outcome.

The sense of belonging stemming from a shared identity can increase the likelihood of an individual protesting, and participation in collective action is often described with terms such as 'solidarity' and 'unity', with such feelings strongly associated with continued involvement in the cause (Drury et al., 2005). Of course, protest is not always founded on pre-existing collective identities. It may be an event, political decision or action that brings a group together; for example, the Springbok tour protests, as discussed shortly. In these instances, bonding over a shared belief also results in a sense of belonging, a camaraderie of protest (Friedlander, 2013).

But to fully understand why people protest, we also need to consider the context: 'collective struggles are rooted in a social and political context' (van Stekelenburg & Klandermans, 2013, p. 899). For instance, Anita Lacey at the University of Auckland (2015) highlights how the nature of protest has changed. Prior to the 1960s, protests tended to be driven by the working class, and primarily aimed at the redistribution of power and resources. Following that era, the focus shifted to wider social issues, such as rights, identity and ecology. The homosexual law reform movement, discussed shortly, is one such example. It is also an example of how, in contemporary movements, people also protest in solidarity — using their voice to strengthen the voice of minority groups. Many of those calling for the legalisation of same-sex marriage in 2013 were heterosexual.

The other two aims for this part of the book are to explore the struggles different groups face in expressing their voice, and to understand the consequences of voice in terms of identity and citizenship. New Zealand's history is replete with examples of citizens using their voice to protest — not always with success — from the peaceful Māori settlement at Parihaka in the 1880s (and the many other instances of Māori protest, some of which are discussed by Te Rā in Chapter 2), to the 151-day long waterfront strikes in 1951, to the recent School Strike 4 Climate protests. In this chapter I use two historical case studies to illustrate voice and consequences.

Both are powerful, but they are very different stories of the forging of identity at individual, group and national levels: the gay rights movement from the 1970s until the present, and the Springbok rugby tour protests in 1981. I finish by exploring some of the key ways protest is changing in current times.

The gay protest movement

Homosexuality has been a longstanding focus of protest in New Zealand. As Trudie and Tracey highlighted in Chapter 3, sexuality is an important identity thread, particularly for those who are not heterosexual, and who have therefore been excluded from aspects of life in New Zealand (and the world). Here I take a quick overview of some of the challenges and consequences of the gay protest movement. While protests centred on issues of sexuality have tended to focus explicitly on rights (protests leading up to the passing of the same-sex marriage Bill in 2013 for instance), the goals of the movement have been much deeper and wider than just legislative change. As American sociologists Polletta and Jasper (2001) remind us, a key goal of many social movements is the development of a stronger collective identity — a sense of group pride (pun intended). For the lesbian, gay, bisexual and transgender (LGBTQIA+) community, the fight has been, and continues to be, for acceptance of their identities as both valid and valued.

As with all protest movements, the socio-political context is critical to understanding events. Following the Second World War, New Zealand prided itself on being strongly equalitarian (Hansen, 1968), an ideology that is associated with conformity — pride in not just equality of income, but also equality of customs and outlook: a 'high degree of uniformity' (Dunstall, 1992, p. 452). In Chapter 10, David explores the equality element of that ideology in some depth. The conformity of the New Zealand culture was evident in rigid gender roles, with the New Zealand masculine identity of rugged rural man sharply defined.

Deviation from this strongly held norm was deeply problematic. In a book based on his doctoral thesis exploring public debate in New Zealand on homosexuality from 1960 to 1986, Laurie Guy (2002) points out that holding onto that sense of conformity requires a blindness to others: 'it was a case of ignoring Maoris [sic], ignoring women, ignoring homosexuals — male Pakeha heterosexuality ruled' (p. 25). In addition to rigid gender roles, the strong Christian beliefs of the time meant sex was acceptable only within marriage. Legally, male-on-male sex was a criminal act, and morally it was held to be a sin. This was a context when the (married) two-parent family was the only acceptable structure, and so it is unsurprising that homosexuals were seen as sick or sinful, and homosexuality was at best ignored and at worst abhorred.

 The NZ History website has an excellent summary of the history of homosexual law reform in New Zealand up until 2013: https://nzhistory.govt.nz/culture/homosexual-law-reform/homosexual-law-reform

But contexts change, and as contexts change so do identities. The late 1960s and the 1970s was a period of significant social change in Aotearoa New Zealand, with the emergence of numerous social movements, including second-wave feminism, abortion rights, anti-war protests and Māori land issues. Alongside these changes, we saw a shift in sexual morality and a decrease in the Church's influence over society. Together, these changes provided a context in which the gay liberation movement, and more specifically homosexual law reform, could become part of the New Zealand conversation (Guy, 2002).

It is not possible to pinpoint the exact start of the movement, although Guy argues that a tragic case in 1964, where a homosexual man was attacked and killed by six youths in Christchurch, acted as a catalyst for change. The offenders were subsequently acquitted, following a trial that focused, in part, on the victim's sexual preferences. This event stands both as a reflection of the societal attitudes in New Zealand of the time and as a mark of the start of the protest movement.

One of the challenges facing the early homosexual protest movement was that it did not centre on a single shared identity. For instance, Guy's (2002) examination of the gay movement in New Zealand, from the 1960s until homosexual law reform in 1986, highlights that lesbian women faced very different issues to gay men. Homosexual women faced a battle not just against heterosexism, but also against the male patriarchy. But male homosexual behaviour was seen as more abhorrent than female homosexual behaviour, which was not legally proscribed and therefore not a criminal offence.

In addition, much of the early debate and protest centred on viewing homosexuality and heterosexuality as binary identities. Despite there being an increasing acknowledgement, particularly in academia, of the fluidity and variability of sexuality in terms of both orientation and behaviour, viewing homosexual identity as clear-cut and fixed was a critical part of the reform argument — if a group has a clearly delineated identity, then the justification for acceptance and rights becomes easier.

As mentioned earlier, the gay liberation movement was about more than just legal reform. Gaining individual rights was important, but for many the acceptance and even celebration of homosexuality was also critical: 'the problem was not just the laws but societal attitudes' (Guy, 2002, p. 94). The protest was against the hegemony of heterosexuality and the 'patriarchal family', and the movement was characterised by defiance and pride. An important part of that defiance was encouraging gays to come out. Coming out was an act of protest: not just an individual act, but the joining of a community, which provided a sense of solidarity and, importantly, a visibility that would allow the community's voices to be heard. It is a potent example of how the act of protest shapes and in some cases forms a collective identity (Polletta & Jasper, 2001). As Australian academic and gay rights activist Dennis Altman (1983) explains, shifting the debate from behaviour to identity was a powerful move that forced opponents 'into a position where they can be seen as attacking the civil rights of homosexual citizens rather than attacking . . . antisocial behaviour' (p. 9).

The gay liberation movement and associated legislative reform protests spanned decades and is not yet a closed chapter. The first official meeting took place on the University of Auckland campus in 1972, followed by the first of many 'public and provocative' events (Guy, 2002, p. 96) — for example, a Gay Day in Albert Park. This event took place at the site of a statue of Queen Victoria, with 'Will Victorian morality ever die?' as one of the key catchphrases.

While legislative change was only one part of the agenda, Fran Wilde's Homosexual Law Reform Bill was a critical, and arguably the most memorable, part of the fight. The 18 months leading up to the Bill's final success were characterised by fierce debate and protest by both sides, inside and outside of Parliament. The oppositional forces were formidable. Homosexual law reform was representative of a range of other liberal issues, such as abortion, and many conservative or Christian people viewed this as a fight against the broad 'decline of moral standards' in society (Guy, 2002). The final parliamentary vote was 49 in favour and 44 against, with the age of consent (set in the Bill at 16, the same as for heterosexual sex) considered to be one of the primary reasons for the closeness of the vote.

While a defining moment in the history of gay pride, this legislative change was not the end of the political and public protests and successes. Another important achievement was the new Human Rights Act of 1993, which extended its protection against discrimination to include sexual orientation. But, in 1994, the first Hero Parade through the streets of Auckland triggered protest from conservative Christians, among other groups; clearly, the question of whether homosexuality was normal and acceptable was still not settled (Guy, 2002). The next legislative landmark was the passing of the Civil Union Act by the Labour-led Government in 2004, which enabled same-sex couples to register their unions and thus gain some of the rights of heterosexual couples.

However, marriage was still the preserve of heterosexual relationships and, for many, the Civil Union Act labelled homosexuals, once again, as second-class citizens (Baker & Elizabeth, 2012). The most recent achievement for the gay movement in New Zealand has been the passing of the Marriage (Definition of Marriage) Amendment Act 2013, which redefined marriage as the union of '2 people, regardless of their sex, sexual orientation, or gender identity' (section 4). Once again, a range of Christian groups (although by no means all Christians) vigorously protested against the legislative change, but the legislation passed with a clear majority of 77 to 44 votes.

Watch a video of the passing of the Marriage (Definition of Marriage) Amendment Act 2013, and the ensuing waiata: https://www.youtube.com/watch?v=DW4DXOAXF8U

So is there no longer a need for a gay protest movement? Have we reached a point where homosexuality is not merely tolerated but is accepted by society? Certainly this has been a successful movement. In the 55 years since the rainbow community first started raising their voice in protest, they have gained much in terms of equal legislative rights based on sexuality. Alongside those political changes, they have achieved increased acceptance of their identities by the majority of the population. For many, homosexuality is no longer something to be hidden, and pride in that identity is increasingly possible. But not for everyone. For instance, many gay Muslim men in New Zealand still live dual lives — out in mainstream areas of society, but living a life of pretence when in the context of their Muslim families and communities (Anonymous, 2015). 'Muslim' and 'gay' continue to be incompatible identity threads. And the fight for legislative change continues — at the time of writing, legislation banning conversion therapy (the practice of trying to change someone's sexual orientation, gender identity or gender expression) has just passed its first reading, and will shortly be up for public consultation.

Until relatively recently, the primary focus was sexuality rather than gender, but a growing concern is the rights of people who do not conform to strongly held binary gender norms. The evolving and expanding acronym LGBTQIA+ (lesbian, gay, bisexual, trans, queer/questioning, intersex, asexual, plus others) is testament to this widening focus. The Human Rights Act 1993 prohibits discrimination on the basis of sex, and the Human Rights Commission interprets this to include gender identity. However, the Commission's 2008 report demonstrated that transgender people experience considerable discrimination, and concluded that specific reference in the Act to gender identity would offer better protection. This is still needed, with recent research demonstrating that transgender people in Aotearoa New Zealand still experience high levels of discrimination, associated with higher levels of distress, self-harm and suicidality (Treharne et al., 2020). In 2021, gender identity is explicitly included in the Labour Government's *Proposals Against Incitement of Hatred and Discrimination,* which also proposes adding 'to the grounds of discrimination in the Human Rights Act to clarify that trans, gender diverse, and intersex people are protected from discrimination' (Ministry of Justice, 2021, p. 23).

Transgender rights are being debated with protest from both sides of the debate increasing. In 2021, the Births, Deaths, Marriages and Relationships Registration Bill, which includes provision for people to easily change their gender on their birth certificate (to male, female or non-binary), is resulting in activism and protest both for and against the Bill. Also in 2021, the inclusion of Laurel Hubbard, a transwoman weightlifter, in the New Zealand Olympic team triggered international protests against her participation. These examples highlight that sexuality and gender identity, and their associated rights, are still matters of protest. The details of the identities at stake may have shifted, but the underlying goal — to be treated as equal citizens — remains the same.

The 1981 Springbok tour

The gay liberation movement is an ongoing protest movement centred on personal identity threads and focused on achieving change for a specific community in New Zealand. In contrast, the 1981 Springbok tour protests were triggered by a sporting (and political) event and centred on our national identity, what it means to be a New Zealander. The questions of why people protested, the struggles they faced and the nature of the consequences are therefore quite different.

The fierce rivalry on the rugby field between New Zealand and South Africa — which operated a separatist political and social system known as apartheid — was long tainted by racial divides. Historically, only whites could play for South Africa's national rugby team, the Springboks, while their counterparts, the All Blacks, were multiracial. However, in the 1960s Māori and Samoan players were excluded from All Black tours of South Africa, a discrimination that triggered protest in New Zealand and resulted in the cancellation of a planned tour there in 1967.

Worldwide condemnation of South Africa's apartheid regime was also growing, and in 1968 the United Nations (UN) declared a sports boycott of South Africa. Despite this, All Black teams toured South Africa in 1970 and 1976, with the South African government deeming Māori and Samoan players to be 'honorary whites'. Following the 1976 tour, 28 African nations boycotted the Olympic Games in protest. In 1981, Prime Minister Robert Muldoon, despite having endorsed the 1977 Gleneagles Agreement, in which Commonwealth governments agreed to discourage sporting contact with South Africa, supported the New Zealand Rugby Union's decision to invite the Springboks to tour New Zealand.

The resulting protests have been described as 'a defining point in contemporary New Zealand history' (Lacey, 2015, p. 505). Continuing for 56 days, the demonstrations were widespread, involving groups such as students, women's groups, churches, sports clubs and trade unions joining anti-racism groups, such as HART (Halt All Racist Tours) and the Polynesian Panthers. The country was split roughly equally between supporters and protesters. But there were intersections with other threads of identity: protesters included more women, city dwellers and Labour Party supporters (Fougere, 1989). As photographer Marti Friedlander (2013) said, 'The tour gathered New Zealanders together as never before, but it also divided them' (p. 224). The level of protest and civic unrest, and the intensity of the police response, were unparalleled. But why? What was it about this event that polarised and galvanised such a response?

View *Patu!*, Merata Mita's feature-length documentary on the Springbok protests: https://www.nzonscreen.com/title/patu-1983

On the surface, for protesters, it was about racism: welcoming a racially selected team was supporting apartheid. For tour supporters, it was about individual freedom: there was no place for politics in sport, and sportspeople should have the right to play who they wanted. But at a deeper level this was a protest about what it meant to be a New Zealander: were we a nation of rugby players and fans, or a nation that stood up against injustice in the world? It was a protest, a dispute, about collective identity.

Two aspects of New Zealand identity were challenged: the role of sport, particularly rugby, and our race relations. According to sociologist Geoffrey Fougere (1989), to understand the response to the tour, we must understand how rugby has shaped our individual and national identity. Sport, through local, regional, franchise and national team support, enables a collective identity that can integrate and unify a diverse nation (Fougere, 1989). And, although its central role in the national identity is waning, sport — especially rugby — remains central to New Zealand life. Rugby aligned well with New Zealand's masculine, frontier culture — a place of raw but controlled physical violence. Rugby enabled masculine friendship, and its appeal to all classes and ethnicities fitted well with the narrative of Aotearoa New Zealand as an egalitarian, classless society. (This idea is also explored by David in Chapter 10.) Rugby's strong link with rural life, central to New Zealand's view of itself as a nation, was also critical (MacLean, 2003). Given these strong alignments between rugby and New Zealand identity, it is perhaps unsurprising that tour supporters saw the protests as a challenge to their way of life.

The second aspect of New Zealand identity central to the protests was what journalist Geoff Chapple (1984) has described as 'New Zealand's sublime secret' (p. 9): that despite our reputation and view of ourselves as a country with excellent race relations, this was not a nation with racial harmony and tolerance. According to the myth, it was particularly heinous for Aotearoa New Zealand, of all countries, to be supporting apartheid by welcoming the Springboks. In reality, however, the 1970s had seen a rapid increase in Māori protest, including the 1975 Hīkoi — the Māori Land March — and the occupation of Bastion Point in 1977–78. Historical breaches of Te Tiriti o Waitangi were starting to be examined alongside a growing recognition of the impacts of colonisation and the embedded racism within New Zealand's political, economic and social structures (Pollock, 2004).

For Māori, therefore, protesting against the tour was also about protesting about the problems closer to home. For Pākehā on both sides of the protest, the link the tour showed between black South Africans and Māori, coming at the end of a decade of challenges to our race relations, was a cause of anxiety (Pollock, 2004).

The tour and protests had wide-ranging consequences in terms of identity and citizenship. In an immediate sense, the protests were largely unsuccessful: except for the calling off of the Hamilton match, the tour progressed until the end. But the impacts of the protests were far-reaching. Fougere (1989) argues that it marked the end of rugby's role as the mirror of New Zealand society.

However, the protests did not occur in isolation. This was a time of considerable social change in Aotearoa New Zealand. Historian Malcolm MacLean (2003) identifies three layers of political discontent: Māori land rights, feminism and dissatisfaction with the National Government. Fougere (1989) also points out that Britain joining the European Economic Community in 1972 had weakened New Zealand's colonial ties. These social movements, all issues of identity and citizenship, were illustrated and magnified by the tour, and ultimately meant that

ALEXANDER TURNBULL LIBRARY, EP-ETHICS-DEMONSTRATIONS-1981 SPRINGBOK TOUR-03-F

The winter of discontent

The 1981 Springbok tour was one of the most sustained, ugly and divisive periods of protest ever experienced in New Zealand. Tense and violent encounters between police (and their specially trained Red and Blue Squads) and protestors were common. The scene above took place on 29 August in Wellington. That day, 7000 well-organised protestors gathered to block road and pedestrian access to Athletic Park, where the second test match of the tour was due to be played. Police intervention involved using long batons, and injured many protestors in the process, aided by some rugby fans who lashed out. Many protestors — anticipating police violence — came equipped with helmets and DIY plywood shields.

rugby and its values and practices were increasingly 'at odds with patterns newly emerging in New Zealand culture' (Fougere, 1989, p. 120).

The protests also had an impact on race relations in New Zealand and South Africa. As part of the wider social movement, the protests helped many New Zealanders recognise the myth of racial harmony in Aotearoa and begin to address structural racism. Over the next few years, important changes included extending the jurisdiction of the Waitangi Tribunal to cover historical as well as contemporary grievances, te reo Māori becoming an official language, and changes to immigration selection criteria that emphasised skills rather than country of origin.

In South Africa, the protests were a very small part of the momentous change that occurred over the following decades, including the release from prison of Nelson Mandela in 1990, and the end of apartheid in 1994 with South Africa's first full vote. Leanne Pooley's (2006) excellent documentary *Try Revolution* portrays the tour from a South African perspective and offers insight into its importance. In the words of Desmond Tutu, the black South African Anglican archbishop who was a major figure in the anti-apartheid movement: 'You can't even compute its value, it said the world has not forgotten us, we are not alone.' It is a tragedy that the tour had to go ahead, with its accompanying division of New Zealand, for that profound message to be communicated.

A short extract from Leanne Pooley's documentary *Try Revolution* is available here: https://www.nzonscreen.com/title/try-revolution-2006

The changing face of protest: Digital, global and youth-led

This final section of the chapter comes back to the first aim of the 'Voices' section of the book: understanding the different ways that people give voice. Historically, protest action such as the Springbok tour protests and the earlier stages of the gay protest movement were primarily physical — people gathering, marching and occupying places of significance. More recently, advances in technology and changes in the social world mean protests often have a different flavour, voices are increasingly expressed through digital methods and many protest movements are global. The shift to digital media and social networking tools is also enabling greater engagement by youth in political and social issues (Tawhai, 2015); young people are not just participating in protests, as they have always done, they are starting their own movements.

There is considerable debate around digital activism, with some describing digital protest in derogatory terms such as 'clicktivism' or 'slacktivism': 'feel good online activism that has zero political or social impact' (Morozov, 2009). The fiercest critics argue that it is not just an inferior form of activism, but that it is motivated by self-interest and instant gratification (Halupka, 2014). Actions such as 'liking' or 'sharing' a political post, changing a profile picture or signing a digital petition can be seen as spontaneous reactions to content, rather than sustained and premeditated civic engagement.

Nevertheless, digital technologies do enable different forms of activism. Alongside more traditional collective action, based on shared identities and membership of overarching organisations, an emerging alternative — termed 'connective action' — replaces those group ties with fluid social networks and activism that is personal and individualised (Bennett & Segerberg, 2012). Connective action has the scope to include a range of different personal reasons for protesting a situation, relying in part on quick sharing through social networking platforms such as Twitter and Facebook. The speed and breadth of this communication can effect quick change. A local small-scale example of this was the late inclusion of the Red Peak flag in the 2015 referendum on flag change following online protest.

It is of course not a matter of either physical *or* digital methods being best; street protest is also not without its critics. Rather, it is about people drawing on the strengths of both. Digital tools, used as part of a suite of tactics including traditional protest activities, can be valuable (Karpf, 2010). And the increasing use of digital tools has undoubtedly changed how people connect and raise their shared voices in protest.

One significant impact of the connectivity enabled by social media has been the growth of global protest movements such as #MeToo and #BlackLivesMatter. That both movements are identified by a hashtag slogan illustrates how grounded these campaigns are in the digital world. #BlackLivesMatter, a broad, decentralised movement protesting about racially motivated violence against black people in the United States, is an excellent example of the digital and physical working together; it started as a social media hashtag in 2013, but has grown into a widespread community of activists who enact physical protests (Hunt, 2016). The killing of George Floyd by police in 2020 reinvigorated the campaign with international protests, including thousands of New Zealanders marching in Wellington, Auckland and Dunedin (Owen & Chumko, 2020). While initially about demonstrating solidarity with black Americans, these protests have evolved into more generalised protests against racism. As Perez (2020) points out, it would be hypocritical to support #BLM while not recognising the ongoing racism and serious

JESSICA THOMPSON CARR, MĀORI MERMAID

Ihumātao: Deal or disappointment?

The land most commonly referred to as Ihumātao holds archaeological, spiritual and historical significance, and is considered wāhi tapu by local iwi. Despite a treasured history, the land was taken during the 1863 invasion of the Waikato and acquired by Crown grant in 1867. In 2016, when a subsidiary of construction company Fletcher Building proposed a housing development, community members peacefully occupied the land in protest. An eviction notice was served on 23 July 2019, and three occupiers arrested.

Headed by SOUL (Save Our Unique Landscape), mana whenua drummed up public support with digital-media savvy young leaders. This drew thousands of supporters, many setting up camp and others bringing clothes, blankets, food and money to support the occupation. The protestors at Ihumātao thus used traditional methods of in-person protest alongside digital methods of sharing information and creating virtual support.

In 2020, the government agreed to purchase the land from Fletcher Building to allow it to be handed over to tangata whenua, a process that will take time to finalise. The deal was heralded by some as setting an important precedent for countless 'other Ihumātaos' around the country. However, the deal specifically ruled out using the land for Treaty claims settlements, raising questions about how transformational the deal really is for acknowledging and rectifying Māori land alienation.

inequities here in Aotearoa New Zealand. Issues such as racism may be global, but local context matters.

A second positive impact of the increase in digital tools for protest and activism has been the strengthening of young people's voices. Digital activism led by young people can look very different to traditional protest, with young people more likely to use humour, satire and creative artefacts to make their point (Cho et al., 2020). Importantly, a recent UNICEF report found that 'digital civic engagement by young people is positively correlated to offline youth political participation' (Cho et al., 2020, p. 12), offsetting accusations of clicktivism.

Youth-led movements also move fluidly between the digital and physical world as the Fridays for Future campaign illustrates. Started by activist Greta Thunberg in Sweden when she was just 15, School Strikes 4 Climate have subsequently taken place around the world, including in Aotearoa New Zealand. The global Covid-19 pandemic has also played its part in changing the face of protest, with lockdowns limiting physical gatherings, including protests. In Germany in April 2020, Fridays for Future met that challenge with what has been described as 'the biggest digital demonstration yet' with more than 230,000 livestream viewers (Gheorghiu, 2020). Covid-19 has undoubtedly accelerated the shift to digital protest.

Make It 16 is a recent example of youth-led protest:
https://www.youtube.com/watch?v=HSWM85jFGFc&t=2s

Conclusion

Protest, be it face-to-face or digital, is a critical form of participation and an important right in a thriving democratic society. Freedom of expression and the right to peaceful assembly are enshrined in the New Zealand Bill of Rights Act 1990. Whether motivated by the rights accorded to a shared identity thread, as in the example of the gay rights movement, or by disagreement with a political event or action, as in the Springbok tour example, protest is a way for people to come together to join their voices and to effect change, often when formal political channels have failed.

The two case studies explored here serve as illustrations of the importance of protest; the diverse motivations that drive protest; and the wide-ranging consequences, particularly in terms of identity. While linked to individual identity, protest is also a function of the socio-political context in which it occurs. Both the gay rights movement and the tour protests were part of a wider period of social change during which the New Zealand identity evolved from a rural, rugby-playing masculine culture to a more liberal and inclusive society, with a wider recognition of the importance of equality of rights and recognition for different identities.

Zeynep Tufekci (2014), a sociologist working in this field, argues that we need effective social movements to deal with the world's large social and ecological issues, but the movements need to move beyond large-scale, fast expression of voice — clicktivism — and instead focus on consensus decision-making to establish policy proposals that can effect real change. Tufekci ends her TED Talk by highlighting new digital tools that can facilitate this process. One of these, Loomio, is a collaborative decision-making tool developed by social activists here in Aotearoa New Zealand. Loomio's byline offers a fitting concluding remark on this topic: 'When we hear all voices, we make better decisions.'

Watch Zeynep Tufekci's TED Talk here: https://www.ted.com/talks/zeynep_tufekci_how_the_internet_has_made_social_change_easy_to_organize_hard_to_win

Chapter 5 — Shout it out: Participation and protest in public life: http://turangawaewae.massey.ac.nz/ch5.html

Further reading/viewing

Friedlander, M. (2013). *Self-portrait*. Auckland University Press.

Guy, L. (2002). *Worlds in collision: The gay debate in New Zealand, 1960–1986*. Victoria University Press.

Pollock, J. (2004). 'We don't want your racist tour': The 1981 Springbok tour and the anxiety of settlement in Aotearoa/New Zealand. *Graduate Journal of Asia-Pacific Studies, 2*(1), 32–43.

Pooley, L. (Director). (2006). *Try revolution* [Television documentary]. Spacific Films.

Watson, G. (2017). Sport and citizenship in New Zealand. In A. Brown & J. Griffiths (Eds.), *The citizen: Past and present* (pp. 197–221). Massey University Press.

References

Altman, D. (1983). *The homosexualization of America: The Americanization of the homosexual.* Beacon Press.

Anonymous. (2015). Muslim and gay: Seeking identity coherence in New Zealand. *Culture, Health and Sexuality, 18*(3), 280–293. https://doi.org/10.1080/13691058.2015.1079927

Baker, M., & Elizabeth, V. (2012). Second-class marriage? Civil union in New Zealand. *Journal of Comparative Family Studies, 43*(5), 633–645.

Bennett, W. L., & Segerberg, A. (2012). The logic of connective action. *Information, Communication and Society, 15*(5), 739–768. https://doi.org/10.1080/1369118X.2012.670661

Bill of Rights Act 1990. http://www.legislation.govt.nz/act/public/1990/0109/latest/DLM224792.html

Chapple, G. (1984). *1981: The tour.* Reed.

Cho, A., Byrne, J., & Pelter, Z. (2020). *Digital civic engagement by young people.* UNICEF Offices of Global insight and Policy. https://participationpool.eu/wp-content/uploads/2020/07/UNICEF-Global-Insight-digital-civic-engagement-2020_4.pdf

Civil Union Act 2004. http://www.legislation.govt.nz/act/public/2004/0102/latest/DLM323385.html website

Drury, J., Cocking, C., Beale, J., Hanson, C., & Rapley, F. (2005). The phenomenology of empowerment in collective action. *British Journal of Social Psychology, 44*(3), 309–328. https://doi.org/10.1348/014466604X18523

Dunstall, G. (1992). The social pattern. In G. W. Rice (Ed.), *The Oxford history of New Zealand* (2nd ed., pp. 451–481). Oxford University Press.

Durie, M. (1998). *Te mana, te kāwanatanga: The politics of Māori self-determination.* Oxford University Press.

Durie, M. (2005). *Ngā tai matatū: Tides of Māori endurance.* Oxford University Press.

Fougere, G. (1989). Sport, culture and identity: The case of rugby football. In D. Novitz & B. Willmott (Eds.), *Culture and identity in New Zealand* (pp. 110–122). GP Books.

Friedlander, M. (2013). *Self-portrait.* Auckland University Press.

Gheorghiu, D. (2020). *How coronavirus makes us rethink youth protests.* Child Rights International Network. https://home.crin.org/latest/how-coronavirus-makes-us-rethink-youth-protests

Grey, S. (2015). Citizen engagement. In J. Hayward (Ed.), *New Zealand government and politics* (6th ed., pp. 496–498). Oxford University Press.

Grove, N., & Mead, H. M. (2001). *Ngā pēpeha a ngā tīpuna*. Victoria University Press.

Guy, L. (2002). *Worlds in collision: The gay debate in New Zealand, 1960–1986*. Victoria University Press.

Halupka, M. (2014). Clicktivism: A systematic heuristic. *Policy and Internet, 6*(2), 115–132. https://doi.org/10.1002/1944-2866.POI355

Hansen, D. A. (1968). Social institutions. In A. L. McLeod (Ed.), *The pattern of New Zealand culture* (pp. 49–67). Oxford University Press.

Hickford, M. (2015). Law of the foreshore and seabed. In *Te Ara: The encyclopedia of New Zealand*. https://teara.govt.nz/en/law-of-the-foreshore-and-seabed

Human Rights Act 1993. http://www.legislation.govt.nz/act/public/1993/0082/latest/DLM304475.html

Human Rights Commission. (2008). *To be who I am: Report of the inquiry into the discrimination experienced by transgender people*. Human Rights Commission.

Hunt, E. (2016, September 2). Alicia Garza on the beauty and burden of Black Lives Matter. *The Guardian*. https://www.theguardian.com/us-news/2016/sep/02/alicia-garza-on-the-beauty-and-the-burden-of-black-lives-matter

Kaase, M. (2011). Participation. In B. Badie, D. Berg-Schlosser, & L. Morlino (Eds.), *International encyclopedia of political science* (pp. 1778–1789). Sage.

Karpf, D. (2010). Online political mobilization from the advocacy group's perspective: Looking beyond clicktivism. *Policy and Internet, 2*(4), 7–41. https://doi.org/10.2202/1944-2866.1098

Lacey, A. (2015). Activism and social movements. In J. Hayward (Ed.), *New Zealand government and politics* (6th ed., pp. 499–510). Oxford University Press.

MacLean, M. (2003). Making strange the country and making strange the countryside: Spatialized clashes in the affective economies of Aotearoa/New Zealand during the 1981 Springbok rugby tour. In M. Cronin & J. Bale (Eds.), *Sport and postcolonialism* (pp. 57–72). Bloomsbury Publishing.

Marriage (Definition of Marriage) Amendment Act 2013. www.legislation.govt.nz/act/public/2013/0020/latest/DLM4505003.html

Marx, A. W. (1995). Contested citizenship: The dynamics of racial identity and social movements. *International Review of Social History, 40*, 159–183. https://doi.org/10.1017/S002085900011363X

Ministry of Justice. (2021). *Proposals against incitement of hatred and discrimination*. https://www.justice.govt.nz/assets/documents/publications/incitement-discussion-document.pdf

Morozov, E. (2009, May 19). The brave new world of slactivism. *Foreign Policy*. http://www.npr.org/templates/story/story.php?storyId=104302141

Owen, C., & Chumko, A. (2020, 14 June). Black Lives Matter: Thousands at Auckland and Wellington marches. *Stuff*. https://www.stuff.co.nz/national/politics/121745476/black-lives-matter-thousands-at-auckland-and-wellington-marches

Parker, W. C. (2005). Teaching against idiocy. *Phi Delta Kappan, 5*, 344–351.

Perez, C. S. (2020). Black Lives Matter in the Pacific. *Ethnic Studies Review, 43*(3), 34–38. https://doi.org/10.1525/esr.2020.43.3.34

Polletta, F., & Jasper, J. M. (2001). Collective identity and social movements. *Annual Review of Sociology, 27*, 283–305. https://doi.org/10.1146/annurev.soc.27.1.283

Pollock, J. (2004). 'We don't want your racist tour': The 1981 Springbok tour and the anxiety of settlement in Aotearoa/New Zealand. *Graduate Journal of Asia-Pacific Studies, 2*(1), 32–43.

Pooley, L. (Director). (2006). *Try revolution* [Television documentary]. Spacific Films.

Roggeband, C., & Klandermans, B. (2010). Introduction. In B. Klandermans & C. Roggeband (Eds.), *Handbook of social movements across disciplines* (pp. 1–12). Springer.

Tawhai, V. M. H. (2015). Youth engagement. In J. Hayward (Ed.), *New Zealand government and politics* (6th ed., pp. 511–522). Oxford University Press.

Treharne, G. J., Riggs, D. W., Ellis, S. J., Flett, J. A., & Bartholomaeus, C. (2020). Suicidality, self-harm, and their correlates among transgender and cisgender people living in Aotearoa/New Zealand or Australia. *International Journal of Transgender Health, 21*(4), 440–454. https://doi.org/10.1080/26895269.2020.1795959

Tufekci, Z. (2014, October). *Online social change: Easy to organise, hard to win.* [TED Talk]. https://www.ted.com/talks/zeynep_tufekci_how_the_internet_has_made_social_change_easy_to_organize_hard_to_win

van Stekelenburg, J., & Klandermans, B. (2013). The social psychology of protest. *Current Sociology, 61*(5–6), 886–905. https://doi.org/10.1177/0011392113479314

06.
Voicing cultural rights
Arts, identity and belonging

Rand Hazou and Trudie Cain

Nā rātou i whatu, mā tātou e tāniko.

The ancestors wove it, we will embellish it.

The above whakataukī takes the weaving of a garment and the subsequent decoration of it as a metaphor to encourage the continuation of a legacy of activities from ancestral times to the present moment, and into the future.

He tirohanga Māori: A Māori perspective

Te Rā Moriarty

Throughout history Māori artistic creativity has been practised in many forms, reaching back to Hawaiki. Art was a part of everyday life and was incorporated into many practices; for example, tāmoko, decorating whare and making clothing. While the tools used and appearance of the art have changed over time, modern Māori art still carries ancient narratives and references to traditional patterns. This allows it to be a means of connecting to one's culture, history and identity through creative mediums.

A very distinct form of art is tāmoko, Māori tattooing. This was traditionally worn on the face and legs. The designs used were not simply for decoration, but drew on pūrākau, such as that of Mataora and Niwareka, in which Niwareka fled back to her home in Rarohenga (Higgins, 2013), and Mataora followed her and was taught tāmoko by Niwareka's father, Uetonga. Māori would receive tāmoko when they reached adolescence. It was a physical sign of their identity as Māori, and was worn on the face of both women and men as a birth-right. Men would also receive the pūhoro design on their legs and buttocks. However, this practice may differ from iwi to iwi and region to region.

Wharenui have evolved over time to be fully carved on many marae where the poupou, the carved figures, represent ancestors of the whānau, hapū and iwi. The tukutuku panels that line the walls tell stories of history and pūrākau. The heke that descend from the tāhuhu, the ridge pole, contain patterns symbolising the environment, such as the mangōpare, the hammerhead shark.

There are many different garments within Māori culture that, while traditionally worn as everyday clothing, also contained elements that embellished the appearance of the clothing item and the wearer. This is evident in cloaks such as korowai and kaitaka made of muka, flax fibre. The korowai is distinct in having tassels hanging down on the outside and edges of the cloak. The kaitaka was made containing a border at the bottom and sides with tāniko patterns. Although today these types of cloaks are considered taonga and worn primarily on special occasions, traditionally they were part of everyday life.

Presently, traditional art forms such as tāmoko, decorating wharenui and making clothing are still practised with customary and modern tools to implement ancestral designs, but also with contemporary tools and designs. Tāmoko is not only worn on the face but also any part of the body that the wearer chooses. Wharenui will contain colours, designs and imagery that weren't seen in the past, but which make for a highly striking building.

Examples of this can be found at the new marae Te Raukaramu on the Pukeahu campus of Massey University. Cloaks now may have different colours than were seen historically, but are still identifiable as a cloak in a Māori style.

The continuation of art allows artists to maintain a strong link to their culture and its designs. Receiving and witnessing the creation of such taonga provides a visual reminder of Māori culture, which contributes to identity and belonging for oneself as a descendant of one's ancestors and a member of one's communities and culture.

Introduction

In March 2021, and as part of the Auckland Arts Festival, a huge mural started to take shape on a large wall off Karangahape Road in central Tāmaki Makaurau. The *Whakaako Kia Whakaora / Educate to Liberate* mural visually connects the relationship between the Polynesian Panther Party (Aotearoa) and the Black Panther Party (United States). The mural also pays tribute to the Polynesian Panthers' activism around the 'Dawn Raids' of the 1970s and the 1981 Springbok tour, and connects this protest history to the contemporary struggle at Ihumātao. Less than six months later, on Sunday, 1 August 2021, hundreds of people packed Auckland Town Hall to hear Prime Minister Jacinda Ardern's apology for the Dawn Raids. On behalf of the New Zealand government, the prime minister offered a formal and unreserved apology to Pasifika communities for the discriminatory implementation of the immigration laws of the 1970s that led to the Dawn Raids. The government also announced that it would incorporate the Dawn Raids into the history curriculum, and support Pasifika artists and historians to create an official record of the mistreatment (AAP, 2021).

It would be difficult to explicitly attribute the government's apology to the painting of the mural. Nevertheless, the mural, with its inclusion as part of an international arts festival, as well as the series of news articles, interviews and community events the artists engaged with during this time, helped to shine a light on an important history and galvanise attention on the need for an official apology for the Dawn Raids.

Using this example as a starting point, this chapter considers how the arts might be used to ensure that the viewpoints, experiences and realities of those who might be marginalised, disenfranchised or otherwise silenced can be recognised. The chapter considers the intersections between the arts, identity and belonging. How do the arts help create a 'place' for individuals and communities to 'stand'? And in what ways can engagement with the arts and culture be understood as forms of voice and citizenship?

In attempting to answer these questions, this chapter starts by reaffirming the importance of the arts to societies and individuals. Creative New Zealand (2016), the government's arts funding agency, states that the arts 'contribute to New Zealand's economic, cultural and social well-being', and empirical research supports this claim. The arts are shown to improve individual health and wellbeing outcomes (Staricoff, 2004), rejuvenate cities (Markusen & Gadwa, 2010), support democracy and social inclusion (Stern & Seifert, 2010), and contribute a sense of belonging, connectedness and place (Hall & Robertson, 2001). A recent study found that 72 per cent of participants agreed that engaging with arts and cultural experiences 'enriches their life', and 52 per cent agreed that it helps them 'feel connected to others' (Creative New Zealand, 2021, p. 25). The arts also contribute to the construction of individual, community and national identity (Johnson, 2005; Pound, 2009), and illuminate key issues facing contemporary society, fostering dialogue about those issues and potentially contributing to social change (Clammer, 2015).

In this chapter, we work through three key ideas, providing a case study for each. First, we consider the power of the arts to shape both national and individual identities. An example is provided of how art can perform racial identity through the work of Alice Canton, a New Zealand-born theatre-maker and performer of Chinese and Pākehā descent. Second, we discuss how art can challenge and contest dominant ideas as well as celebrate marginal histories. Here — and in this we echo points that Ella made in the previous chapter — we consider how the arts might also be used as a form of protest that ensures the dissenting or marginalised voices of this country are heard. Here we return to the *Whakaako Kia Whakaora* mural to explore in more detail how it celebrates the community activist history of the Polynesian Panthers to improve conditions for Pasifika and Māori communities in Auckland. Finally, we consider the place-making role of the arts, and the connections between art, belonging and wellbeing. We explore these issues through a case study of the performance *Shot Bro*, created by Māori actor and director Rob Mokaraka, which uses the arts as a way to facilitate community engagement with issues of mental health, suicide and depression. In conclusion, we introduce the notion of cultural rights to affirm the importance of participation in the arts as a crucial aspect of citizenship.

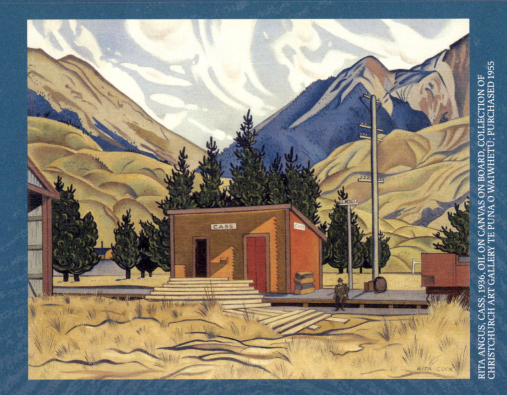

RITA ANGUS, CASS, 1936, OIL ON CANVAS ON BOARD, COLLECTION OF CHRISTCHURCH ART GALLERY TE PUNA O WAIWHETŪ; PURCHASED 1955

Cass – Rita Angus

Cass is an iconic twentieth-century New Zealand painting by Rita Angus (1908–70), depicting Cass railway station in inland Canterbury. The location was chosen for its typicality and stands for numerous small communities. The seated figure at the right in the composition is dwarfed by the surrounding landscape, accentuating feelings of isolation and remoteness. The work's direct and unpretentious style is complemented by the strong ordering of the composition. Elements typical of Angus's style, and regionalism in general, include the flattening of form by use of flat, unmodulated colour, strong outlines, and the use of simplified colour and form. When *Cass* was first exhibited in Christchurch in 1937, and later in Auckland in 1938, it received no comment in the press. At the time, Angus's work seemed to be admired only by a group of discerning friends.

Art and the shaping of national identity

There is a wealth of scholarly literature outlining the role of the arts in shaping national identity (Johnson, 2005; Pound, 2009). New Zealand artists, particularly in the mid-twentieth century, often referenced the scale and grandeur of the New Zealand landscape, but in ways that are very distinct from other influential artists around the world. Colin McCahon's *Six Days in Nelson and Canterbury*, which features the 'cumulative grandeur' of New Zealand's landscape, is a good example (McCahon, c.1950). Rita Angus's *Cass* also features the South Island landscape, but underlines the sense of isolation and seclusion arguably associated with life in the most remote parts of the South Island. Literature produced around the same time also speaks to powerful imagery of Kiwi rugged masculinity that is grounded in an equally rugged New Zealand landscape. John Mulgan's classic 1939 novel *Man Alone*, which explores a 'veteran protagonist's ability to reintegrate into civilian society and make New Zealand home', is a good example of this (Mercer, 2012, p. 77). Although these works and the worlds they depict don't speak for all of our lives, especially those of us who live in New Zealand's cities, the narrative still resonates as uniquely New Zealand.

Many artists have drawn on both Māori and European influences to tell the story of New Zealand's place in the world. Shane Cotton (Ngāpuhi) has used a combination of European painting techniques and Māori symbolism to explore cultural identity and New Zealand's colonial past. And, over half a century ago, Gordon Walters created *Painting No. 1*, which brought together two strands of his cultural identity. The stylised koru motif was revisited throughout much of his career, and has since become an important reference point for the art world and a prominent symbol of biculturalism in Aotearoa. Interestingly, Walters — who was Pākehā — has received some criticism for appropriating Māori symbolism and using it out of context. Others, however, have applauded his use, suggesting instead that his work is an 'act of homage from the outside, so acknowledging the truth of his historical, ethnic and cultural circumstance' (Pound, 2009, p. 317).

These examples demonstrate the power of the arts to tell stories of national identity. They generate a collective voice of this place, and provide ways of thinking and talking about what it means to be a New Zealander. But we need to take care that this isn't overstated. These examples demonstrate that both art and artist raise important questions about culture, ethnic identity, power and voice. If art has the capacity to 'unify the nation, to construct it as one place' (Bell, 2011, p. 91), questions must always be asked about whose version of unified place is being represented.

Performing racial identities: *OTHER [chinese]* — a case study

Alice Canton is a New Zealand-born theatre-maker and performer of Chinese and Pākehā descent. In 2017, Canton devised and directed *OTHER [chinese]*, which premiered at the Q Theatre in Auckland and encouraged other Chinese New Zealanders to share their stories directly with an audience. The production involved a core cast of 14 storytellers and a rotating ensemble cast of up to 100 participants. All of the participants were 'non-actors', in the sense that they were not professionally trained but rather recruited as members of the 'Chinese Kiwi' community.

The production was created to challenge racial stereotypes and what it means to be 'Chinese'. Auckland is being rapidly transformed by Asian immigration; just over 28 per cent of Tāmaki Makaurau's usually resident population identifies with an Asian ethnicity (Knowledge Auckland, 2020). But a study conducted in the 1990s suggested that the terms 'Asian' and 'Kiwi' were seen to be 'mutually exclusive' and unable to co-exist together (Bartley, 2004, p.163). *OTHER [chinese]* addressed what it means to be a Chinese New Zealander in Aotearoa today. The performance invited the audience to hear various snippets of real stories relating to being a Chinese or mixed-Chinese person living in New Zealand.

The production also utilised impromptu segments that involved Canton asking the non-actors questions such as: 'What do you think of this statement: "The Chinese are buying up all the houses in Auckland"? Agree, disagree, or neutral?' In reply, the actors were asked to congregate on stage left for 'agree', stage right for 'disagree' or to remain centre stage if they were neutral. Throughout the run, the participants overwhelmingly congregated on stage right to disagree with this statement, while responses to other questions changed from night to night, depending on the cast taking part. The segments worked as a kind of live "vox pop" and a representation in real time of the opinions of a diverse group of Chinese individuals.

Importantly, the production doesn't simply report these stories. The production involved movement, gesture and even dancing. In *OTHER [chinese]*, by presenting a diverse range of bodies and Chinese subjectivities on stage, the audience was immediately 'confronted' by the question of 'Chinese-ness' in a very physical and visual sense (Lam & Hazou, 2020). This important work demonstrates how the arts can challenge national stereotypes as well as broaden the definition of what constitutes being a New Zealander.

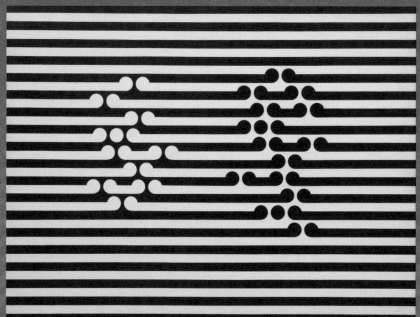

GORDON WALTERS, PAINTING NO. 1, 1965, PVA ON BOARD, AUCKLAND ART GALLERY TOI O TĀMAKI, 66/13

Art with multicultural roots

Gordon Walters was born in Wellington in 1919. Between 1935 and 1939 he trained and worked as a commercial artist and studied part-time at the art department of Wellington Technical College. In 1941 he met Theo Schoon, an Indonesian-born Dutch artist and photographer who encouraged Walters' growing interest in the abstraction of painters Paul Klee, Joan Miró, Jean Arp and Piet Mondrian. In 1946 Walters paid a visit to Schoon, who was in South Canterbury recording Māori rock art near the Ōpihi River. This encouraged Walters to introduce ideas and motifs from indigenous art into his own work.

By 1956 Walters was experimenting with the koru motif, a curving bulb-like form on a stem found in moko (tattoo) and kōwhaiwhai (rafter painting). He looked at the paintings of Giuseppe Capogrossi and Victor Vasarely to provide guidelines for making a series of compositions limited to a few formal elements. By 1958–59 he had evolved his own version of the koru as a geometric motif in which positive and negative elements mirror one another in a taut, dynamic relationship.

By using Māori titles, Walters acknowledged the inspiration he received from the koru and related motifs such as rauponga. He created a new kind of painting in which Māori motifs and European abstract painting were drawn together. He was criticised in the 1980s for appropriating these motifs, but Walters himself saw it as a positive response to being an artist with bicultural influences.

Contestation and the arts

A recurring theme throughout this book (and this section in particular) is that having a voice is rarely natural or inevitable; many people resident in New Zealand do not feel that they have a legitimate place from which to speak and be heard. People or groups are socially, culturally and politically excluded on the basis of a range of identity threads, including ethnicity, sexuality, body size and ability, gender and class. When you are different from the 'norm', it can be difficult to ensure that your experience and viewpoint are accounted for.

In the preceding chapter, Ella considered political protest as a form of voice. Here, we consider how the arts might also be used as a form of protest that ensures the dissenting voices of this country are heard. Aotearoa New Zealand has a history of using the arts to challenge ideas, and speak up and speak out against social and political injustices. For example, the unapologetically feminist photography of New Zealand-born artist Alexis Hunter speaks for the broader community of women. Her subversive collection of photographs, titled *The Model's Revenge*, examines and critiques the politics of gender and sexuality. Other examples of art activism include the poetry of Brian Turner, who has written of the degradation of New Zealand's environment in poems such as 'River Wind', and a piece of art provocatively titled *Tuhoe Never Signed the Fucking Treaty*, which was created by a collective of artists called 'Concerned Citizens'.

Perhaps one of the most well-known protest art works is Ralph Hotere's painting *Vive Aramoana*, which was created in the early 1980s as part of the protest movement to stop an aluminium smelter being built at the entrance to Otago Harbour. The work sold in 2012 for $183,000, arguably demonstrating its 'lasting voice and presence' (Booth, 2013). Undoubtedly, the arts have been used to raise political consciousness, foster dialogue about contemporary issues and promote social change, especially in support of those who are disenfranchised (Beasley & Hager, 2014; Clammer, 2015).

 Although the exhibition is no longer running, you can still see some of Alexis Hunter's works from *The Model's Revenge* here: https://www.tepapa.govt.nz/about/past-exhibitions/2016-past-exhibitions/alexis-hunter-models-revenge

Some art revisits history and ensures we do not forget. During the Anzac 100-year commemorations in 2016, a series of sculptures appeared across Wellington's

CHARLOTTE KELLY, PEACE ACTION WELLINGTON

A cruel punishment

On Anzac Day in 2016, Wellingtonians awoke to the sight of three sculptures erected outside Te Papa museum, in Frank Kitts Park and in the Civic Square. Later found to be the work of Peace Action Wellington, the statues depicted conscientious objectors who resisted conscription following its introduction in October 1916, in the field punishment No. 1 position. In the First World War around 300 conscientious objectors were imprisoned and 14 were forcibly sent overseas for service. Some of those men, including Archibald Baxter, were subjected to extreme physical and mental abuse including the depicted field punishment No. 1 — bound to a post, with ropes cutting off blood flow, for up to four hours in all weathers, often near the site of combat. This torturous experience did not break Baxter's determination to resist supporting the war. He described his experiences in a classic account, *We Will Not Cease*, which has subsequently been made into a film.

The sculpture located outside of Te Papa was quickly taken down by museum security. Nevertheless, the temporary sculptures elicited strong emotional reactions and inspired a petition for a permanent sculpture of Baxter. While this has not (yet) happened, the Archibald Baxter Peace Garden: The National Memorial for Conscientious Objectors opened in Dunedin on 29 October 2021.

central city. The sculptures were installed by 'guerrilla artists' associated with Peace Action Wellington. They depicted New Zealand's conscientious objectors, who during the First World War refused to fight and were consequently punished by being tied for long periods in the 'field punishment No. 1' position, including on the Western Front. The sculptures were designed to challenge what the artists viewed as the 'romanticisation of war and the militarisation of Anzac Day', and they certainly attracted great interest and media attention during the time of their installation. Interestingly, Wellington City Council was not in a hurry to remove the sculptures. A council spokesperson at the time stated: 'Wellington is a political and creative city and we are not in the business of stifling political expression. We'll make sure the sculptures are secure and we'll seek discussions with Peace Action Wellington about their future' (Hunt, 2016). Despite this assurance, Te Papa security staff quickly removed the statue that had been placed outside the museum.

People who were interviewed by media during this time reported finding the installations a powerful reminder of the atrocities and complexities of war. The installations certainly started a conversation about New Zealand's war history. But they also bridged the past with the present, encouraging people to reflect on New Zealand's current contributions to war.

The arts are clearly important for contesting how New Zealand is and how it ought to be. It can be a very powerful and urgent way to bring attention to issues or events often overlooked by official government accounts. The following case study provides a further example of the arts being used to tell and celebrate a marginalised history, and work as a form of protest to apply pressure on government to acknowledge past wrongs.

Performing protest: The Polynesian Panthers — a case study

The *Whakaako Kia Whakaora/Educate to Liberate* mural is a 26m x 5m artwork painted on a huge wall of a parking lot on the corner of Karangahape Road and Gundry Street in Central Auckland. The colourful mural, painted on a striking background of yellow and blue fanning stripes, serves as a reminder of the role played by the Polynesian Panthers in advocating for the social issues — including health, housing, land rights, environment and education — impacting on Pasifika and Māori communities in Tāmaki Makaurau between 1971 and the present.

The mural visually connects the relationship between the Polynesian Panther Party (Aotearoa) and the Black Panther Party (United States). This is represented by a blue 'manawa' or heart line, designed by Toa Sieke Taihia, running the length of the mural. The project was born from the ongoing engagement between Emory Douglas, the former Minister of Culture of the Black Panther Party, Tigilau Ness,

WHAKAAAO KIA WHAKAORA (2021). IMAGE COURTESY CHRIS MCBRIDE

Whakaako Kia Whakaora/Educate to Liberate

This mural was painted on a large wall off Karangahape Road in central Tāmaki Makaurau Auckland. The mural visually connects the relationship between the Polynesian Panther Party (Aotearoa) and the Black Panther Party (USA), represented by a blue 'manawa' or heart line designed by Toa Taihia running the length of the mural. The mural also pays tribute to the Polynesian Panthers' activism around the Dawn Raids of the 1970s and the 1981 Springbok Tour, and connects this protest history to the contemporary struggle at Ihumātao.

The Panther Mural Project includes artists Huriana Kopeke-Te Aho, Numa McKenzie, Toa Sieke Taihia in collaboration with Emory Douglas, the former Minister of Culture of the Black Panther Party, Tigilau Ness, the former Minister of Culture and Fine Arts of the Polynesian Panther Party and arts curator Chris McBride. The mural is an example of an artwork that celebrates an important history of community activism.

the former Minister of Culture and Fine Arts of the Polynesian Panther Party, and arts curator Chris McBride. Designed by Emory Douglas, Toa Sieke Taihia, Numa MacKenzie and Huriana Kopeke-Te Aho with contributions by Tigilau Ness and Chris McBride, the mural was painted to coincide with the fiftieth anniversary of the formation of the Polynesian Panthers.

Follow the link to learn more about the history, art and activism of the Black Panthers and the Polynesian Panthers: https://panthers.liberationlibrary.nz/

The artwork speaks directly to the history of the Polynesian Panthers, which was formed in Auckland in June 1971. Inspired by the Black Panthers party in the United States, the Polynesian Panthers shared a similar social justice agenda and formed in response to the marginalisation and discrimination experienced by the Pasifika community. Their local community activism for the Pasifika community included organising homework centres, tenancy support groups, prison visits and food programmes. The Dawn Raids between 1974 and 1976, which targeted tangata Pasifika families, helped to galvanise the group.

As early as the 1950s, immigration from the Pacific Islands had been welcomed as an answer to New Zealand's need for cheap labour. However, an economic downturn in the 1970s resulted in government rhetoric denigrating Pasifika migrants as 'overstayers' — this, despite the fact that the vast majority of people here with expired visas at the time were from Europe. This political dog-whistling led to the racial profiling of Pasifika individuals and increased surveillance about their immigration status, with police stopping individuals in the street and demanding to see their immigration papers. This culminated in the targeting of Pasifika families with a sustained series of early-morning raids on their homes by the police. People deemed to be overstayers were taken into police custody on the spot, and invariably deported. As well as splitting up families, this persecution led to deep-based trauma for all those who experienced the raids, or even just lived in fear of them.

While at the time Pasifika peoples comprised only one-third of overstayers, they constituted 86 per cent of all prosecutions for overstaying. In contrast, citizens from the United States and the United Kingdom, who also made up almost a third each of those overstaying, represented only 5 per cent of prosecutions (New Zealand Human Rights Commission, 2020).

The last official activity of the Polynesian Panthers was to participate in the Springbok protests in 1981 (which Ella discussed in the previous chapter). The Springbok tour of 1981 inspired many New Zealanders to engage in a series of protests aimed at stopping the rugby tour with an apartheid South Africa. Tiglau Ness, Polynesian Panther and one of the mural designers, hoped that *Whakaako Kia Whakaora* would help spark conversation and keep this history alive. In an interview for One News, Ness explained: 'Humans, we forget so easily . . . people come and go, but artworks, they remain. They're a reminder of who we are' (Lee, 2021).

The mural is an example of an artwork that celebrates an important history of community activism. This is something that has become increasingly important given the impact of gentrification on inner suburbs such as Ponsonby, which was previously a centre for Pasifika migrants to Auckland. With the changing demographics of the city, the history of the Polynesian Panthers, their connection to place and the issues they fought for are at risk of being overlooked. The mural forms a striking reminder that is difficult to dismiss, stretching the length of a large wall with a commanding view of K Road. It also helped to galvanise public interest and potentially shift the political will in favour of the government making an official apology for the Dawn Raids.

Place-making, belonging and wellbeing

'Place-making' is a term used in the social sciences to describe the ways in which people consciously engage in activities to make places meaningful to them (Akbar & Edelenbos, 2021). The term is also used to describe the range of activities undertaken by planners, designers and managers of public spaces in order to produce places that meet the cultural, economic, social and ecological needs and preferences of specific groups of people.

The arts are a vital feature of healthy and connected communities; art contributes to a sense of belonging, connectedness and place (Hall & Robertson, 2001; Pollock & Paddison, 2014). The next part of this book considers place explicitly, but we want to briefly introduce place here, because the arts play such an important role in supporting place-making in both formal and informal ways. (Equally, as you read through Chapters 7–9 look out for the appearance of art in its many and varied forms.) Formalised art includes commissioned public art, such as Max Patté's *Solace in the Wind* in Wellington (also known informally as 'The leaning [naked] man'), and Michael Parekowhai's *Lighthouse/Tū Whenua-a-Kura* on

Queens Wharf in Auckland (also known as 'The state house'). These nicknames are indicative of the familiarity and connection residents develop with the works, and, irrespective of whether we like or approve of the art, both of these pieces are uniquely New Zealand. While Patté's work speaks to Wellington's reputation as the 'windy city', Parekowhai's work references the heritage of state housing in New Zealand.

Cultural festivals such as Matariki, Diwali, Pasifika and the Chinese Lantern Festival perform an important role in promoting and celebrating ethnic diversity, and in negotiating identity and belonging in Aotearoa. Writing about the origins of the Pasifika Festival, Jared Mackley-Crump (2016b) argues that 'Pasifika festivals are highly public community events, in which diverse displays of material culture are offered up for consumption by both cultural tourists and Pacific communities alike' (pp. 33–34). This is an important point. Cultural festivals create opportunities to perform identity to multicultural audiences (Mackley-Crump, 2016a), but they also help to create strong, inclusive and cohesive communities (Laing & Mair, 2015). These kinds of events are important features of Aotearoa New Zealand's place-making and provide a platform for telling our richly diverse ethnic and cultural stories.

Alongside formal arts-based events, such as art installations and cultural festivals, there are many informal initiatives. Informal arts include street performers who might busk, dance or throw fire in some of New Zealand's larger cities; guerrilla knitters, also referred to as 'yarn bombers', who personalise, beautify or reclaim public places (Farinosi & Fortunati, 2013); or graffiti artists who respond to the existing built environment, creating more interesting, political and dynamic public spaces. Such forms of artistic expression are important contributors to the vitality, sociality and conviviality of street life (Simpson, 2011).

Of course, informal and formal expressions of art are not created equally; they are embedded within relations of power that legitimate their presence in public places. Informal expressions of art are constrained, for example, by by-laws that govern what can and cannot be done in a public space, and formal expressions of art are often the result of arts committees and local government determining what art and which artists will represent a given community. Some of the creative works discussed here might suggest that the arts readily provide a voice for those who are marginalised or excluded from society. While this can certainly be the case, it is a suggestion that should not be overstated. As noted throughout this book, having a voice, either as an individual or as a community, is important, but not everyone's voice is heard equally, and those in positions of authority do not always have the capacity or inclination to listen and act.

Rob Mokaraka: Performing wellbeing — a case study

Shot Bro — Confessions of a Depressed Bullet (2016) was written and performed by Rob Mokaraka (Ngāpuhi, Ngāi Tuhoe) and directed by Erina Daniels (Ngāpuhi, Ngāti Wai). It is a semi-autobiographical work that chronicles Mokaraka's undiagnosed depression, which resulted in him being shot by police in an attempted suicide in 2009. *Shot Bro* is the product of the actor's eight-year journey of healing and self-discovery, and is a production that aims to provide audiences with a safe means to discuss mental health, depression and suicide.

Since premiering in 2016, the production has toured extensively to theatres, community halls, marae and other venues, including a tour to Te Whare Manaakitanga (the Special Treatment Unit for violent offenders) at Remutaka Prison in July 2016 (Richards, 2018). The staging of *Shot Bro* at Remutaka was so impactful that Mokaraka incorporated the experience of performing the show to the 'tough' prison audience into the play, with subsequent iterations including a restaging of the prison performance in a scene that emphasised how even the most hardened of criminals need opportunities to express their emotions and fears. Given the high suicide rates in New Zealand, and given that Māori men are disproportionately represented (Flahive, 2018), *Shot Bro* provided a theatrical space to encourage healing.

An outstanding feature of the production is how it opens up a space and allows people to talk about issues of mental health and depression that might otherwise go unvoiced. The production has a powerful effect on audiences. A recurring feature of the production is how it provokes particularly stoic men who might normally find it hard to share emotions to stand up after the production and talk. The production empowers audiences to overcome the stigma of mental illness and share their experiences. While we have lots of programmes and initiatives attempting to tackle mental health issues in our communities, the embodied and experiential nature of the arts, and especially theatre, makes this a particularly potent and effective mode of communication to engage people in tackling the issues head-on.

Watch a documentary about Rob Mokaraka's *Shot Bro*. In this documentary, produced by *The Spinoff* and Māori Television, actor Rob Mokaraka shares his story of attempted suicide and his motivation for creating his one-man play *Shot Bro*. The documentary follows Rob as he tours the production around the country, and captures some of the responses from audiences to his show. Viewer discretion is advised: https://www.youtube.com/watch?v=_3G6boYCxXg

Pasifika celebrates

The first Pasifika Festival was held in Auckland in 1992, and it is now one of the largest annual events in the Auckland area. Activities include fashion shows, food and craft stalls (over 200, no less!), theatre performances, sports competitions and even pop opera concerts. Pasifika attracts over 60,000 visitors over its two days and contains 11 'villages' representing Sāmoa, the Cook Islands, Fiji, Hawai'i, Niue, Tahiti, Tuvalu, Tonga, Tokelau, the Solomon Islands and Aotearoa. This concept allows the nations to showcase the unique aspects of their individual food, visual and performance cultures, while also promoting a collective Pasifika identity.

Conclusion: Cultural rights

The arts provide a powerful voice for the nation, for communities and for individuals. Art serves as a nation-building project, telling a unique story of this land and the people who live here. Art serves as a community-building project, with artists using creative expression and action to generate communities and neighbourhoods that are designed for the people who want to live, work and play there. And art serves as a self-building project, offering possibilities for the expression, representation and construction of individual identity.

The arts are used in countless ways to tell the many diverse stories of this country. In doing so, creative practice potentially provides a voice for those who are silenced. Whether they are socially silenced through discriminatory practices or politically silenced through inadequate representation in the political sphere, art can tell their stories in powerful and authoritative ways. The arts are well positioned to contest and challenge dominant ideas about this land, or revisit limited and reductionist histories that offer only a partial historical truth. But this is not to suggest that the arts should be valued only for their capacity to represent a diversity of perspectives. We conclude by suggesting that both access to, and participation in, the arts are a vital aspect of citizenship.

One way to think about the intersections between the arts and citizenship is through the notion of 'cultural rights'. Cultural rights are a fundamental expression of human rights, and have become increasingly important in rights discourse given the associations between culture, identity and social equity. Cultural rights include the notion that 'all citizens should have access to and be able to participate in the artistic and cultural practices of their choosing' (Caust, 2020, p. 1). Those who participate in cultural life may have a stronger sense of fulfilment as a human being, a stronger sense of social cohesion, and a stronger sense of responsibility and commitment towards the wider community. As Annamari Laaksonen (2010) explains in a report commissioned by the Council of Europe on the provision of cultural rights:

> Without the right to participate in cultural life, individuals fail to develop the social and cultural connections that are important to maintaining satisfactory conditions of equality. When people are excluded from cultural life, this can have consequences for the well-being and even sustainability of the social order. Participation in cultural life is closely linked to citizens' ability to build a sense of responsibility in areas such as respect for others, non-discrimination, equality, social justice, the preservation of diversity and heritage, and curiosity for other cultures. (Laaksonen, 2010, p. 16)

Filling the gap

Gap Filler was initially formed in response to the September 2010 earthquake in Christchurch, then expanded after the February 2011 quake. It is supported by the Gap Filler Trust and is a registered charity. Its first project ran from late November until early December 2010, transforming an empty site on Colombo Street into a temporary garden café, with pétanque, live music, poetry readings, outdoor cinema and more. The project was incredibly well received and utilised, leading to further projects, including art installations, concerts, workshop spaces and eventually semi-permanent structures such as the Pallet Pavilion, RAD Bikes and the Dance-O-Mat (shown above).

Gap Filler continues to operate, describing itself as: 'a creative urban regeneration initiative that facilitates a wide range of temporary projects, events, installations and amenities in the city. These short-term and comparatively small-scale projects are far less risky than new permanent developments — and consequently open up opportunities for experimentation: trying new ideas, pushing social boundaries, adopting participatory processes to get everyday people involved in creating their city. Working with local community groups, artists, architects, landowners, librarians, designers, students, engineers, dancers — anyone with an idea and initiative — they activate city spaces for temporary, creative, people-centred purposes.

'By recycling materials, teaming up with suppliers, harnessing volunteer power and being creative, Gap Filler proves that the regeneration of the city does not rely solely on large-scale developments by the private or public sectors. Great things can be achieved with community power and resourcefulness; we can be flexible and swift in adapting to our changing city, meaning our projects will always provide contemporary reflection on the state of society' (Gap Filler, 2015).

The notion of cultural rights helps to shift considerations about the importance of participation in the arts from notions of representation and voice to their centrality as basic requirements for citizenship, as an important right that deserves to be promoted and protected.

Chapter 6 — Voicing cultural rights: Arts, identity and belonging: http://turangawaewae.massey.ac.nz/ch6.html

Further reading

Hall, T., & Robertson, I. (2001). Public art and urban regeneration: Advocacy, claims and critical debates. *Landscape Research, 26*(1), 5–26. https//doi.org/10.1080/01426390120024457

Hyland, N., Syron, L. M., & Casey, M. (2018). Tūrangawaewae: A place to stand in contemporary indigenous performance in Australasia and beyond. *Australasian Drama Studies, 73*, 1–16.

Mackley-Crump, J. (2016b). *The Pacific festivals of Aotearoa New Zealand: Negotiating place and identity in a new homeland* [e-book]. University of Hawai'i Press.

Pound, F. (2009). *The invention of New Zealand: Art and national identity, 1930–1970.* Auckland University Press.

References

AAP. (2021, August 2). Jacinda Ardern apologises for New Zealand 'dawn raids' on Pasifika people in 1970s. *The Guardian.* https://www.theguardian.com/world/2021/aug/02/jacinda-ardern-apologises-for-new-zealand-dawn-raids-on-pasifika-people-in-1970s

Akbar, P. N. G., & Edelenbos, J. (2021). Positioning place-making as a social process: A systematic literature review. *Cogent Social Sciences, 7*(1). https://doi.org/10.1080/23311886.2021.1905920

Bartley, A. (2004). Contemporary Asian migration to New Zealand: Challenging the 'settler' paradigm. In P. Spoonley & D. G. Pearson (Eds.), *Tangata tangata: The changing ethnic contours of New Zealand* (pp. 157–174). Dunmore Press.

Beasley, M. M., & Hager, P. M. (2014). Intervention, instigation, interruption: Art, activism, and social policy. *Journal of Poverty, 18*, 1–4.

Bell, A. (2011). That strange fissure opened by discovery/invention: The invention of New Zealand in art. *New Zealand Sociology, 26*(2), 88–102.

Booth, C. (2013, January 23). *Art speaks action.* https://artspeaksaction.wordpress.com/page/2

Canton, A. (Director). (2017, September 6). *OTHER [chinese]* [dramatic work]. Live performance at Q Theatre, Auckland.

Caust, J. (2020). Cultural rights as human rights and the impact on the expression of arts practices. *Journal of Citizenship and Globalisation Studies, 31*(1), 1–14.

Clammer, J. (2015). *Art, culture and international development: Humanizing social transformation.* Routledge.

Creative New Zealand. (2016). *The evidence to support your advocacy.* http://www.creativenz.govt.nz

Creative New Zealand. (2021). *Audience Atlas Aotearoa 2020.* Wellington. https://www.creativenz.govt.nz/assets/ckeditor/attachments/2407/audience_atlas_final_20210901.pdf

Daniels, E. (Director). (2016, May 11). *Shot Bro — Confessions of a Depressed Bullet* [dramatic work]. Live performance at OneOneSix, Whangārei.

Farinosi, M., & Fortunati, L. (2013). A new fashion: Dressing up the cities. *Textile: The Journal of Cloth and Culture, 11*(3), 282–299.

Flahive, B. (2018, August 24). New Zealand suicide rate highest since records began. *Stuff.* https://www.stuff.co.nz/national/health/106532292/new-zealand-suicide-rate-highest-since-records-began

Gap Filler. (2015). https://chchcentral.co.nz/business-listings/gap-filler

Hall, T., & Robertson, I. (2001). Public art and urban regeneration: Advocacy, claims and critical debates. *Landscape Research, 26*(1), 5–26. doi: 10.1080/01426390120024457

Higgins, R. (2013). Tā moko — Māori tattooing. In *Te Ara: The encyclopedia of New Zealand.* https://teara.govt.nz/en/ta-moko-maori-tattooing

Hunt, T. (2016, April 26). Conscientious objector Archie Baxter remembered in guerrilla sculpture. *Stuff.* http://www.stuff.co.nz/national/last-post-first-light/79299545/Conscientious-objector-Archie-Baxter-remembered-in-guerrilla-sculpture

Johnson, H. (2005). Dancing with lions: (Per)forming Chinese cultural identity at a New Zealand secondary school. *New Zealand Journal of Asian Studies, 7*(2), 171–186.

Knowledge Auckland. (2020). *Asian people in Auckland: 2018 census results.* https://knowledgeauckland.org.nz/media/1443/asian-people-2018-census-info-sheet.pdf

Laaksonen, A. (2010). *Making culture accessible. Access, participation in cultural life and cultural provision in the context of cultural rights in Europe.* Council of Europe.

Laing, J., & Mair, J. (2015). Music festivals and social inclusion: The festival organizers' perspective. *Leisure Sciences, 37*(3), 252–268.

Lam, C. H. Y., & Hazou, R. T. (2020). Decoloniality and contemporary Asian theatre in New Zealand. *Theatre Journal, 72*(3), 325–343.

Lee, I. (2021, 15 June). 'We forget so easily'— art keeps Polynesian Panthers' legacy alive 50 years on. *One News.* https://www.1news.co.nz/2021/06/15/we-forget-so-easily-art-keeps-polynesian-panthers-legacy-alive-50-years-on

Mackley-Crump, J. (2016a). From private performance to the public stage: Reconsidering 'staged authenticity' and 'traditional' performances at the Pasifika Festival. *Anthropological Forum, 26*(2), 155–176.

Mackley-Crump, J. (2016b). *The Pacific festivals of Aotearoa New Zealand: Negotiating place and identity in a new homeland* [e-book]. University of Hawai'i Press.

Markusen, A., & Gadwa, A. (2010). *Creative place-making* (White Paper). National Endowment for the Arts.

McCahon, C. (c.1950). *Six days in Nelson and Canterbury* [painting]. In the collection of Auckland Art Gallery Toi o Tāmaki. Discussed at https://www.aucklandartgallery.com/explore-art-and-ideas/artwork/4888/six-days-in-nelson-and-canterbury

Mercer, E. (2012). War, homecoming and genre: John Mulgan's 'Man alone' and Jack Kerouac's 'On the road.' *Journal of New Zealand Studies, 13,* 77–88.

Mulgan, J. (2021). *Man alone.* Victoria University Press. (Original work published 1939).

New Zealand Human Rights Commission. (2020). *Talanoa: Human rights issues for Pacific peoples in Aotearoa New Zealand.* Human Rights Commission.

Pollock, V. L., & Paddison, R. (2014). On place-making, participation and public art: The Gorbals, Glasgow. *Journal of Urbanism, 7*(1), 85–105.

Pound, F. (2009). *The invention of New Zealand: Art and national identity, 1930–1970.* Auckland University Press.

Richards, S. (2018). *Shot Bro:* A theatrical kōrero about depression and suicide in Aotearoa/ New Zealand. *Australasian Drama Studies, 73*(October), 42–68.

Simpson, P. (2011). Street performance and the city: Public space, sociality, and intervening in the everyday. *Space and Culture, 14,* 415–430.

Staricoff, R. L. (2004). *Arts in health: A review of the medical literature* (Research Report 36). Arts Council England.

Stern, M. J., & Seifert, S. C. (2010). *Arts-based social inclusion: An investigation of existing assets and innovative strategies to engage immigrant communities in Philadelphia.* William Penn Foundation.

Turner, B. (2012). *Elemental: Central Otago Poems.* Random House New Zealand.

PART THREE:
PLACES IN AOTEAROA
NEW ZEALAND

Places
Introduction

Trudie Cain and
Juliana Mansvelt

The title of this book is *Tūrangawaewae: Identity and belonging in Aotearoa New Zealand.* 'Tūrangawaewae' means 'one's sacred or special place of belonging', and as such we ask those who read this book to reflect on the place on which they stand, whether it is here in Aotearoa New Zealand or elsewhere. The first two parts of this book support such an endeavour: Part 1 considered the identities of the people who live here, and Part 2 explored how voice might be expressed in different ways and in different contexts. A key theme running through these sections was that identity threads shape experience in multiple and powerful ways. This third part of the book, titled 'Places in Aotearoa New Zealand', considers more explicitly how identity might be shaped by the places we inhabit and the people we might encounter, and, conversely, how places might be informed by the people who inhabit them.

About Part 3

Human geographers define 'place' as a space which is given social meaning by human activity and/or imagination. With this fairly all-encompassing definition as a starting point, it is easy to see how places provide the contexts through which the sociality and materiality of life manifest. Places are a key source of belonging and identity as sites of inclusion, security, comfort, freedom, and material and social wellbeing. But they are also sites of exclusion, marginalisation, alienation, fear and anxiety. In a related way, places are where the communities to which we belong (or to which we aspire) come together to address matters of mutual concern; and equally, they can provide a refuge (or a place of disengagement) from such collective interactions. Undoubtedly, place matters.

One of the most powerful ways of creating a sense of place is through shared understandings of the conventions and norms enacted *in situ*. Conventions can be thought of as typical or common ways of interacting in a given place. For example, it is fairly accepted and conventional that in a dining room we might eat, read at the table, drink coffee or chat with friends. But sometimes conventions become norms which comprise the traditions, customs and practices that govern behaviour. Norms might include queuing to be served at the supermarket rather than pushing in, and not talking on your phone at the movies — although it is important to note that norms and rules may vary across cultures, time and place. While some norms are explicit, they are often based on tacit knowledge which is learned through experience. This means that those who are unfamiliar with a place may find themselves experiencing discomfort, unease or even censure or punishment if they behave in a way that is beyond the norm. Norms tend to be associated with moral values, and are powerful because they become indicative of how people *ought* to behave in a given place.

The idea that norms dictate behaviour is important, because it underlines the ways in which power is embedded in place. There is a tendency to think of places as neutral, but they rarely are, because how they are structured, organised and understood influences the social relationships and encounters that might occur. Some places — private gyms and golf clubs, for example — are quite literally exclusive, and have restrictions about access and participation. Importantly, inclusion and exclusion often reflect specific identity threads, such as being of a certain age or gender, or having the disposable income to pay membership fees. The extent to which an individual is included and able to fully participate has significant consequences for identity, citizenship and a sense of belonging.

The three chapters comprising this section consider the extent to which place matters for the construction of identity in different place-based contexts. Each considers a different kind of place, and argues that place matters very much indeed. Like the preceding sections of this book, this one has a conceptual template which binds the contributing chapters together and links the section to the overall themes of the book. The conceptual template underpinning Part 3 has four key elements:

1. Interactions with others: We consider the ways in which our presence and engagement with others in different places help shape identity. Importantly, we think about this as a reciprocal process, so we also consider the extent to which such interactions shape the very places in which they occur.
2. Structuring relations: We recognise that places are shaped by formal and

informal norms, conventions or regulations that shape the interactions between people that occur in different contexts.

3. Place and power: Power is the capacity to bring about consequences for others, whether negative or positive. We examine how power is exercised in different places and to different effects.

4. The consequences of place for citizenship: Finally, we look at the extent to which the places we inhabit — whether they are physical or digital places — hinder or facilitate our membership of different social and political communities.

Overview of chapters

It is not easy to choose just three places to include in a book about identity and belonging when all of social life happens 'in place'. Our final decision reflected a desire to consider a balance between private and public, digital and non-digital, and regulated and non-regulated places. In providing a range of places, we hope to illuminate how each operates and, more specifically, the ways in which interactions between people in these different places shape individual and collective identities.

In Chapter 7, 'Physical places: Home as place', Trudie Cain and Juliana Mansvelt address the importance of house and home in creating a sense of place, identity and belonging. They first consider the many diverse meanings of home, depending on factors such as geography, culture and age. Second, they illustrate that home is where our identities are constructed, and in particular where we are socialised into gendered norms around the home and family. Finally, Trudie and Juliana make the important point that home is not a place of stability for everyone — that the current housing crisis, increasing homelessness and the prevalence of gender-based violence in the home all contribute to a lack of home security for some. Underpinning this chapter is an understanding that this most private of places provides profound opportunities for developing a sense of identity, belonging and citizenship.

Chapter 8, 'Institutional places: The university', focuses on the university as an institutional place that provides a very specific and regulated context in which identity is shaped. Written by Richard Shaw and Matt Russell, this chapter comments on the social norms, conventions and regulatory practices that exist in universities and the impact they have on notions of identity, belonging and citizenship. They explore some of the social encounters through which students' identity is formed, and consider how power is exercised in order to illustrate the links between universities and wider citizenship considerations. In doing so, Richard and Matt interrogate the role and function of the university, and how it is located within normative political debates that stress the need for a work-ready graduate. This chapter creates a space for considering the significant consequences of universities for an individual's sense of self, as well as the wellbeing of the wider community.

The final chapter in this section, Chapter 9, is called 'Digital places: Identity, participation and power'. In it, Stella Pennell considers how our identities are shaped in often unseen ways by the digital places within which we increasingly interact. She highlights how data provided by us and collected from our activities forms an algorithmic identity which then shapes our participation in society. We are also curating and presenting a digital self, representing our multiple identities whether through an avatar in an online game or a CV on LinkedIn. The chapter reminds us that the digital world is not equally open to everyone, and that the accessibility of information it provides can be both positive and negative. Finally, Stella makes the important point that digital places are sites of power; digital companies shape our personal, social and political lives, which has serious implications for citizenship.

Conclusion

The key message of this section of the book is that our sense of self, and our understanding of what it means to be a citizen of this country, is intimately connected to different places and the relationships that we have in them. Each of the following chapters considers the role of place in shaping identity, and, in some cases, the impact that identity might have on the places themselves. In other words, they emphasise the importance of different sorts of places, and, more specifically, the importance of the interactions between people in those places in shaping individual and collective identities.

These chapters are closely connected with citizenship. The power structures that underpin specific places can provide an economic, political and socio-cultural context in which inclusion or exclusion can be determined. Such power structures can manifest in different ways that are both formal (e.g. policy documents that outline eligibility for membership to a given place) and informal (e.g. the tacitly understood knowledge about appropriate interactions in a given place). Undoubtedly, these structures, which occur in both digital and physical places, have implications for notions of identity, belonging and citizenship.

07.
Physical places
Home as place

Trudie Cain and Juliana Mansvelt

Tangata ākona i te kāinga, tū ana ki te marae, tau ana.
S/he who is taught at home will stand on the marae with confidence.

This whakataukī, and its variations, refers to the benefit of being brought up in the community by the elders and the competence that comes with that experience when conducting oneself in public (Grove & Mead, 2001). It acknowledges the importance of home, the kāinga, in the growth of an individual as a member of their community.

He tirohanga Māori: A Māori perspective

Te Rā Moriarty

What is a kāinga? A kāinga can be a village, a fortified area, the place of the community, a whare, a place of residence and, therefore, a home. In the broadest sense, the kāinga is the region where someone's marae is, or are, located. But it is also where their elders grew up, where their ancestors lived and are buried, and where their whanaunga reside. An individual may have been raised on their kāinga and still dwell there, or they may have never been to their kāinga. However, their kāinga is still their kāinga: it is from here that their rights to stand on their tūrangawaewae are passed down through whakapapa.

For many Māori today, a district, town or city outside of their marae will be the place in which they predominantly live — and will still feel like a home. By digging deeper into the ancestral realities of people and place, a kāinga is a main pillar that supports identity and allows one to feel a strong connection to the areas to which one belongs — a feeling that is shared by the multitude of whānau, hapū and iwi members who descend from the same ancestors and places.

Perhaps a personal story may help to exemplify the intricacies of a kāinga for Māori. I have spent most of my life living between the Rangitīkei and the Manawatū rivers, where I was born, raised, schooled and still live today. However, my marae of Takapūwāhia is in Parirua (often spelt Porirua) in the Kāpiti region of Te Upoko o Te Ika. Although my connections to Rangitīkei and Manawatū are ones of experience and very valuable to me, once I return to the kāinga, see Kāpiti Island, read the place names and arrive at my marae, I am reminded of my tūpuna, their feats, their lives, their knowledge and their stories — and that makes me feel that I belong, which is where my whānau, hapū and iwi belong.

Therefore, for Māori the notion of a kāinga is inseparable from the mountains ascended, the waterways swum, the forests walked, the gardens dug, the places named and the homes occupied by our tūpuna.

Introduction

I (Trudie) started working on this chapter in my office at home. I say 'my office', but it's not really my office. It's a shared space, variously occupied by me, my daughter or my partner. Before the days of Covid-19, negotiation of the use of this space was straightforward. The rhythm of home life meant that when my daughter or partner wanted to use the home office, I was usually at my office at the university. And when I wanted to use the home office, they were typically happy to oblige by retreating to the lounge or dining room to work. But Covid changed everything. Now, we all work from home almost all of the time, and the office has become serious real estate that supports the professional working lives of three people.

We have unwritten rules about whose work takes priority. Zoom meetings and teaching always takes precedence. It's the one space in the house we can go where the backdrop is semi-professional — a bookcase rather than a headboard or kitchen paraphernalia. The professionalism of teaching via Zoom, however, is tenuous. My private world continually intrudes upon my professional identity as a lecturer. As I deliver a class (or write this chapter), Frankie the schnauzer scratches at the door, asking to come in. In meetings, one or other of the cats slink across the screen. Frankie scratches at the door, asking to go out. The courier arrives, reminding me that there is a world beyond my front gate. And Frankie scratches at the door yet again, asking to come back in. But why am I telling you all this? Well, because it speaks to the changing and multifaceted nature of home.

We often think of the home as a private space, one distinct from the public world. The home is a haven, a place of refuge from the outside world, where we can enjoy the company of those we live with, where we can be ourselves away from public scrutiny. To paraphrase sociologist Erving Goffman (1990), home is the place where, on walking through the front door, it is possible to relax, drop our front, forgo speaking our lines and step out of character. With these words, Goffman creates a clear distinction between the 'front stage' of our public worlds and the 'backstage' of our private worlds.

This is a powerful idea, and one that has some traction — home *feels* private; it is readily distinguishable from obviously public places, such as the park, the local library or the beach, and from quasi-public places such as the shopping mall, the local café or the workplace. But home is set within a changing context which can disrupt things. As I write this, Covid-19 is making the distinction between private and public spheres far more fluid than ever before. New technologies mean we communicate across the borders of the home every day, inviting people into our personal places, sometimes without ever meeting them in person. We hold meetings, deliver and attend lectures, get interviewed for new jobs, and some of us even have date nights online. This is not entirely new; the boundaries between home and the outside world have always been somewhat tenuous. But Covid has amplified this, resulting in the dissolution of the boundaries of home as we navigate the social, familial and professional threads of our identity within the private space of the home.

Home is one of the most important places in many of our lives, and one to which we attribute great meaning. In this chapter, we consider the multifaceted, fluid meanings of home, reflecting on the ways in which our threads of identity are both represented and constructed in and through the home. We critically examine the practices that are performed there, adopting a feminist lens to consider the way those practices often reflect gendered norms and values that align women with the private sphere. We conclude by considering the idea that home has the potential to afford people stability and security in an unstable world. Throughout the chapter, we scrutinise common and sometimes taken-for-granted meanings of home, and consider how having a place we call home might be important to our sense of self, belonging and tūrangawaewae.

The meaning and place of 'home'

While 'home' is a word we all use easily, defining it is challenging. Within the humanities and social sciences disciplines, its meaning is undoubtedly contested (Easthope, 2004). Formal definitions include functionalist accounts of the home as a physical structure located in a specific location (Blunt & Dowling, 2006). The home, however, is more than bricks and mortar. It is the place where we learn about the world and our place in it. The home is described by Rose (1993) as a social, cultural and familial gendered unit. Here, Rose underlines the gendered nature of home life — the way that many of us are socialised into normative feminine and masculine roles, often through the enactment of everyday routines (Highmore, 2010). Rose (1993) also underscores the fact that, for many of us, our home is a relational place and the centre of family life, even though our familial relationships might, at times, be somewhat fractured or dislocated. The meaning of home, however, is also somewhat amorphous, representing a sense or feeling (Mallett, 2004), a deep affective attachment to place that 'grows around you like a skin and can never be put off' (Barrowman, 2015, pp. 14–15, quoting Maurice Gee, one of New Zealand's most celebrated writers of fiction). The home is a multidimensional concept encompassing both objectively and subjectively constructed meanings.

But what does home mean to you? If you are asked where your home is, your answer, we're sure, will depend on the context in which you find yourself — who is asking the question and where you are at the time of being asked. For example, if you are travelling overseas, you will likely reply 'New Zealand'. But if you are holidaying in Queenstown and are asked the same question, your response will be more geographically specific. Depending on who is asking the question, you might respond with the place where you were born or grew up. In other contexts, your answer might be a specific house that you associate with home — perhaps the house you lived in as a child, or the house where you currently live. Those of us who have migrated between one country and another might feel we have two homes — our country of birth and our adopted country — or perhaps even no home at all. And let's not muddy the waters even further by thinking about those places we might visit and just *feel* as though we are home . . . As we said, 'home' is complicated!

Geographical and cultural constructions of home

The meaning of home is geographically and culturally specific. For many of us, denoting the place from which we come is an important part of speaking to our sense of home. This can be important for those of us who live somewhere other than our country of birth, circumstances that can result in a renewed sense of what home is, and an appreciation of how our current dwelling place differs from what and where we consider home to be (Wiles, 2008).

Speaking to the place from which we come, however, is especially important in Aotearoa New Zealand. The traditional Māori way of formally introducing oneself is through a mihimihi, a greeting which introduces the speaker, their connections to others via waka, iwi and hapū, their whakapapa, and their place of origin. This is a powerful way of anchoring oneself in place and sharing understandings of place and home with others. A pepeha is part of a mihimihi, and helps frame the ways in which the person's identity is connected to whenua and the significant features of place where one comes from, typically incorporating geographical features such as maunga, awa and moana.

This description makes it sound little more than a list of geographical and familial associations, but mihimihi and pepeha are so much more than this. They represent the ways in which one's spiritual, emotional and physical sense of self is deeply and intimately connected to place and people, present and past. These provide those listening with a sense of the standing place or tūrangawaewae of the speaker, as well as giving them an opportunity to recognise and acknowledge connections through shared whakapapa.

PHOTOGRAPHED AND DESIGNED BY CHLOE ALDERTON, 2022

Refuge in the quarter-acre dream

'Take Refuge' was the theme of the 2021 Simon Devitt Prize for Photography, awarded to Chloe Alderton, a Masters of Urban Planning (Professional) and Urban Design student. The photo, *The Quarter Acre Dream*, depicts her bedroom at the very beginning of lockdown. 'I wanted to capture a small fragment of what a space of refuge looks like in these strange times. The idea of refuge seemed funny in relation to this idea of a "perfect but very imperfect community" of Frank Lloyd Wright's *Broadacre City* and the "Quarter Acre Dream" — when we are living in tiny spaces through lockdowns in the best way we can,' says Chloe. In her case and space, that refuge included the collection of pot-plants that have travelled with her from flat to flat over the years, and capturing 'the peace that comes from surrounding ourselves with nature inside — what seeking refuge in the best way we can looks like'. The image will no doubt also elicit feelings of claustrophobia in many, given the reminder of how our worlds have been shrunk by the pandemic (it is precisely this ambiguity of emotion that won Chloe the prize). *The Quarter Acre Dream* prompts us all to consider how lockdown has forced a renegotiation of our relationships with spaces we previously inhabited without much conscious thought.

We can also see such attachments to place and home reflected in numerous spheres of social and cultural life. For example, Dave Dobbyn's 2006 song 'Welcome Home' contains profoundly New Zealand imagery that speaks to *this* place: 'there's a woman with her hands trembling, and she sings with a mountain's memory'. This line is a clear reference to wiri — the shaking or trembling of hands during waiata that is performed by Māori to demonstrate a deep affinity to nature. The song and the accompanying video, which features a number of migrants — including then asylum-seeker Ahmed Zaoui — were inspired by anti-racism protests in Christchurch, and have become synonymous with powerful discourses of unity and inclusion that shape what it means to call New Zealand home.

Watch the video for Dave Dobbyn's song 'Welcome Home' here:
https://www.youtube.com/watch?v=Wlz2uEuxyyk

Changing meaning of 'home'

For many of us, the meaning of 'home' shifts over time in accordance with our stage of life. During childhood, home might be understood as the place of caregivers and the 'feelings and activities associated with them' (Campo et al., 2020, p. 299), social imperatives might drive our decision to go flatting in our young adult years (see Clark et al., 2017), and the prospect of 'settling down' might inform our ideas of home when preparing for having children of our own. The meaning of home can change yet again in our older years.

The first author of this chapter, Trudie, worked on a research project exploring the changing meaning of home for older adult residents (aged 65 and older) of a multiply diverse neighbourhood in Tāmaki Makaurau Auckland (CaDDANZ, 2021). Many of the participants had moved to the neighbourhood (Northcote on Auckland's North Shore) in the mid-1960s when the suburb was first developed and they were starting a family. They expressed pride in the home they had built, and recalled many stories of raising a family there. Indeed, their homes were repositories of those special memories (Mallett, 2004) — the birth of children, first days at kindergarten and school, celebrations over the years, as well as the passing of loved ones, for example.

But often, their stories of home centred on a sense of community generated between neighbours: children playing in each other's backyards; chatting over the fence with the neighbour; and helping neighbours do odd jobs around the house.

These relationships contributed to their sense of home and were important to their identities as parents. But these neighbourly encounters have largely disappeared over the years as the context of their lives and the local community have changed (Irvine et al., 2020). Participants lamented the loss of the connection they had felt when their children were younger and 'everyone knew and supported each other'. Interestingly, they attributed the loss of connection primarily to changes in labour market participation, including more dual-income families, housing affordability and gender roles, rather than a change in their individual circumstance of no longer being responsible for dependent children:

> '[As a woman] you were at home while your husband was working. We have neighbours on one side . . . they're both working flat out and I am lucky if I say two words to them in a year . . . they're gone first thing in the morning, they're home late at night, they don't want to see anybody, they don't want to talk to anybody . . . I know very few people in my street now'. (Irvine et al., 2020, p. 7)

Participants' earlier experiences of the community they called home were underpinned by their role as parents; most residents in the neighbourhood were raising young families, with children forming the common bond. But the neighbourhood is not as homogenous as it once was. Patterns of migration and processes of gentrification have resulted in greater diversity in ethnicity, age and income level, which has also altered these older residents' sense of connection to their home and the community (Cain et al., 2020; Terruhn et al., 2020). The meaning of home has changed considerably for them, not only as their stage of life altered, but also as the community around them changed. Where once they felt their home and neighbourhood afforded them a sense of belonging and inclusion, several now feel somewhat disconnected. Home and community remain important to them, but their changing needs and expectations of home have led several of them to consider downsizing to something that better accounts for their reduced mobility, smaller world and continued desire for social connection. This case study serves as a useful exemplar of the changing meaning of home over time, not only in accordance with people's life stage, but also in accordance with the changing context of their lives.

Practices of home: A site of familial and gendered routines

Home is a key site where identities are constructed — where we become who we are (Young, 2020). It is the site in which we are first socialised into various threads of our identity — our culture and ethnicity, our class or socio-economic status, and our gender, for example. This most private of places provides the setting in which the very 'socialness' and the material 'stuff' of life is made. One of the ways this occurs is through the routinised habits and practices we perform in the home that come to shape who we are and how we perform our identity to others. Home is also the place we learn how to 'do' family life.

Take a moment to reflect on the kinds of routines you have in your own home. It might be difficult to think of any at first, because our norms become so embedded in our everyday lives that we largely take them for granted. But do you do any of the following: take off your shoes at the door when you arrive home; say grace/karakia before eating a meal together; or have a roster around cleaning responsibilities? All of these things are indicative of the everyday routines we establish that shape our domestic lives. Although not practised every day (and certainly not practised by everyone), annual events such as birthdays, Matariki, Christmas and Easter are also occasions for the display of family practices that signify how your family celebrates and what they value.

It is easy to think that these quotidian and celebratory practices are deeply personal and unique to our own familial setting. But whether we realise it or not, many of our practices in the home reflect our identity threads: removing our shoes on arriving home might reflect our national identity; our religious beliefs might inform whether we say grace/karakia before a meal; and the assigning of chores might be informed by gendered norms.

Gendered social norms

The home is a key site in which we are socialised into *gendered* norms and practices that often reflect narrow ideas of masculinity and femininity (Gorman-Murray, 2007). For much of the twentieth century, homes were sites for the establishment of conventions and norms around forms of gendered domesticity (Mitchell, 1972). For men, this included a culture of do-it-yourself (DIY) enshrined in notions of frontier masculinity (Cox, 2016). For women, gendered domesticity centred on home provisioning through baking, bottling and cooking. The 'ladies, a plate' culture — which is quintessentially Kiwi in origin — as well as the scientific management of families and households, further strengthened understandings of gendered norms in the home (Park, 1991).

These observations are not benign; they speak to relations of power in domestic life that have material effects. Historian Jock Phillips (1996) noted:

> But what if he spent the weekend at home, then what? Was not the home the woman's world? The man's response was to cordon off from the domestic environment certain exclusive male territories. Fences of sexual segregation were erected at home. The man would not cook unless it was over a campfire; he would not clean unless it was the car; he was prepared to garden so long as it was always vegetables and not the herbaceous border; he was prepared to mend things so long as it was a washer and not socks, and he was ready to cut wood. The jobs that were acceptable were those that generally involved heavy physical work or mechanical skills — outside tasks which allowed him to relive the fantasy of the pioneering life. (p. 243)

We can see from Phillips's quote how homes are riven with gendered meaning. From this perspective, for much of the twentieth-century 'home-making' might be viewed as a largely feminine act of caring, involving the use of domestic appliances, decoration, consumption and filling one's house with material objects. These acts can be considered as distinct from 'making home', a practice which relied primarily on masculine ingenuity, an emphasis on DIY improvement and repairs using tools, and productive outdoor pursuits such as vegetable gardening.

Despite the rise in dual-income households and men's increased involvement in childcare, the greatest share of domestic and caregiving labour in the twenty-first century is still performed by women (Charmes, 2019). In Aotearoa New Zealand and elsewhere around the world, among partnered heterosexual couples, mothers undertake the majority of parental childcare, even when both parents work full-time (Stats NZ, 2013). Non-care-related domestic work is also still primarily carried out by women (Ministry for Women, 2019).

The gendered division of unpaid care work in the home is not benign either; it 'partially explains the slow and uneven progress toward gender equality and women's economic empowerment' (Ministry for Women, 2019, p. 3), and normalises the 'undervaluation of caring occupations . . . because of the pervasive cultural association between care work and the traditional roles of women' (Meagher, 2016, p. iii). These gendered practices within the home have always had social and economic implications, but these implications are amplified in the context of a global pandemic, which disproportionately impacts on women, especially women of colour (Bahn et al., 2020).

Housed by the state

In 1937, Prime Minister Michael Savage lifted a dining table through the door of the first state house in New Zealand, in Wellington. Although there had been various previous attempts at social housing, it wasn't until the Great Depression of the 1930s that the Labour Government began a concerted building effort to provide people with homes of their own with state backing.

This image is of neighbourhood children in a state housing street in Mount Albert, Auckland. In 2020, state housing waiting list numbers soared to a record high of 14,869, despite 10 new houses being built by the government daily.

Home: A place of security and stability?

In the previous sections, we explored the meaning of home and examined the gendered norms and practices performed there that shape gendered expectations. In this final section we turn our attention to the potential security and stability that is offered by having a home — a place of residence. Housing scholars Ann Dupuis and David Thorns (1998) argue that home, especially home ownership, affords inhabitants 'ontological security', which they define as follows:

> [Home as] the site of constancy in the social and material environment; home as a spatial context in which the day to day routines of human existence are performed; home as a site free from the surveillance that is part of the contemporary world which allows for a sense of control that is missing in other locales; and home as a secure base around which identities are constructed. (p. 24)

This idea certainly has traction, but it also calls into question the extent to which it remains applicable, given it is widely agreed that Aotearoa New Zealand is in the midst of a 'housing crisis' (Paul et al., 2020). In the following section, we examine the norm of home ownership, the shift towards a generation of renters, and the experiences of those who face extreme housing instability, to better understand people's relationship to house and home.

For a graphical representation of the decline in housing ownership and future projections, see: http://www.tradingeconomics.com/new-zealand/home-ownership-rate

House, home and the norm of home ownership

For much of the twentieth century, meanings of home in this country have been connected to the phenomenon of home ownership (Mitchell, 1972). Historically, Aotearoa New Zealand had some of the highest home-ownership rates in the world. As early as 1911, over half of New Zealand's households were owner-occupied, compared with only 10 per cent of households in the United Kingdom at the same time. Although these rates experienced a temporary decline during the Depression of the 1930s, rates steadily increased to reach a high of 73.8 per cent in 1991. Since then, we have seen a downward trend in home ownership, as income levels have failed to keep pace with property prices (Eaqub & Eaqub, 2015). Most recently, the 2018 census showed that home ownership had fallen to 64.5 per cent of households (with or without a mortgage), with disproportionately low home-ownership rates for Māori and Pasifika peoples (Stats NZ, 2020).

For a more detailed history of state housing in New Zealand and its relationship with homeownership, see this *New Zealand Geographic* deep-dive: https://www.nzgeo.com/stories/state-housing/

Both the high rates of home ownership experienced in the twentieth century, and the more recent decline in this century, have much to do with context: the policies and practices in place. State support for home ownership began in the nineteenth century. However, mass ownership was established with three major initiatives in the 1950s and 1960s: 3 per cent loans; the capitalisation of the family benefit, which allowed for future family support payments to be taken as a lump sum and used as a deposit on a home; and the Group Building scheme, which stimulated housing supply by supporting private builders. These factors provided a perfect policy context in which to encourage home ownership.

Social and economic investment in home has historically been an important element of identity and belonging for generations of New Zealanders (Ferguson, 1994). One journalist went as far as to suggest that 'becoming a home owner is a rite of passage; anybody who reaches 40 without buying a house is decidedly suspect, not fully adult' (McLeod, 1989, p. 11). This would be an absurd proposition today. Home ownership is now beyond the reach of many New Zealanders, and those who do own their own homes often have excessively large mortgages (Eaqub & Eaqub, 2015), which can foster financial stress and ontological *in*security. In a contemporary context, declining home-ownership rates, and the related issues of affordability (Eaqub & Eaqub, 2015) as well as urban intensification and gentrification (Terruhn, 2019), are now challenging the home-ownership model, leading to a new generation of renters.

New patterns of home life — Generation Rent

Long-term renting is not part of this country's national narrative, even though more than one-third of New Zealand households rent (Stats NZ, 2019). Indeed, renting has historically been constructed as a somewhat inferior 'second-class option' (Eaqub & Eaqub, 2015) when compared with a 'housing as investment' model that prioritises private ownership and wealth accumulation through capital gain. But the number (and proportion) of people renting has increased considerably in recent years, especially in the larger cities. For example, in Tāmaki Makaurau Auckland, the percentage of households who rent their home increased by 18.5 per cent between 2006 and 2013. Children are likely to live in rented accommodation; in 2013, 46.5 per cent of children under the age of four lived in rented accommodation (Goodyear & Fabian, 2014).

Renting is not inherently problematic, but it does bring specific vulnerabilities for tenants. First, the shortage of rental stock means that rents are high. Indeed, those who are least able to afford it are spending the greatest percentage of their income on housing: in 2014, 41 per cent of those in the lowest household-income quintile spent more than 30 per cent of their income on housing costs, compared with just 10 per cent of those in the top income quintile (Ministry of Social Development, 2016). Second, although new laws designed to protect tenants have recently been introduced, evidence suggests that the quality of rental housing stock remains variable, potentially impacting on the health of tenants (Camaira & Mafile'o, 2018). Third, despite legal protections, tenants often report feeling a perpetual fear of eviction, especially given limited housing stock should they need to move (Chisholm et al., 2020). This fear is not unfounded, as renting is also correlated with greater transience. In 2013, 35 per cent of people in households who rented had lived in their current home for less than one year (compared with 14.4 per cent of those in households who owned their home) (Goodyear & Fabian, 2014). This transience has negative impacts on health (Timmins, 2018) and education outcomes (Ministry of Education, 2021) for New Zealand's young people, and hinders the development of friendships and a sense of community connectedness and belonging (Dale et al., 2014).

These health, education and social implications are not the responsibility of those who rent. Rather, they are the consequence of a housing policy context that enables higher-income groups to leverage economic capital, including intergenerational wealth. This policy context has shaped narratives of housing as investment, with obtaining a home an important first step on the 'property ladder', and then buying a better property and/or buying investment properties seen as a viable means of asset accumulation. This can provide choice and ontological security in later life: with 'downsizing' or reverse mortgages as a means of 'realising' wealth accrued through housing, or with an intergenerational transfer of wealth through inheritance. By comparison, lower-income groups, including state housing tenants and sole-parent families, face increased housing instability and insecurity (Stats NZ, 2016).

Some scholars argue that access to a home is a fundamental human right, and reject the model of 'housing as an investment' accordingly. Vanessa Cole

(2020), a critical housing scholar, has argued that creative and critical thinking is required to respond to a housing crisis that most negatively impacts the most vulnerable members of society. She presents a case for a universal state-housing policy that would democratise access to affordable, safe, secure housing; combat gentrification, displacement and stigma; and ensure the development of housing that is environmentally sustainable. Ultimately, she puts forward a model of house and home that would afford everyone ontological security.

Homelessness and sleeping rough

The high turnover of rental properties, short tenancies and an inability to afford adequate rental housing all increase the vulnerability of many New Zealanders. It is estimated that one in 100 New Zealanders is now in severe housing deprivation (defined as those living in housing without adequate security of tenure, privacy and/or control, or in structurally inadequate properties) (Amore, 2016). Of those who are housing-deprived, 70 per cent are staying with extended family or friends in severely crowded houses; 20 per cent are staying in a motel, a boarding house or a camping ground; and 10 per cent are living on the street, in cars, or in other improvised dwellings (Amore, 2016). The continued housing crisis and Covid-19 have both exacerbated these statistics, leading to increased numbers of homeless people and rough sleepers. This raises the question: What is the meaning of home for those whose lives are characterised by extreme housing and social instability?

Like other home dwellers, the meaning of home for those who are homeless or sleeping rough is complicated. For the most part, despite not having a physical place to call home, they nonetheless generate a sense of home. A study of people sleeping rough in central Auckland, which Trudie was involved in, found home was relationally oriented (Beaton et al., 2015). This means that the meanings of home had less to do with the physical materiality of a dwelling, and more to do with the encounters people shared with others on the street, people they described as street family or whānau. Indeed, they shared numerous stories about the close, complex and contradictory relationships they had with their street whānau — stories of care, support and encouragement, alongside stories of frustration, mistrust and betrayal. Despite not having a physical dwelling to call home, they didn't necessarily *feel* homeless because they generated their sense of home through these familial relationships.

An Australian study similarly found that people who sleep rough readily articulated their idea of home as the emotional security they shared with others on the street (Parsell, 2012). Many of them contrasted this affective meaning with the physical insecurity of the house they grew up in, declaring it could not be considered a home because it had failed to provide them safety and stability. But a social imagining of home beyond the realm of their own experience also emerged for participants: an imagined home as a physical dwelling was 'constructed as a signifier of normality, and as a commitment to participation in Australian society' (Parsell, 2012, p. 159), something that was beyond their reach, given their sense of disconnection from society.

These ambivalent articulations speak to the complexity of home, and to our capacity to hold competing ideas, understandings and experiences of home. Certainly, it is a misnomer to describe someone sleeping rough as 'homeless', despite them not having the ontological security and stability of a single dwelling to return to each day.

Gender-based violence in the home

The idea that home offers stability and security is appealing, but research shows that for many of us — women especially, although not exclusively — the home is not stable, secure or safe. Domestic violence has reached epidemic proportions in Aotearoa New Zealand, and police records make for a sobering read. Around half of all homicides in New Zealand are committed by family members, 76 per cent of intimate-partner violence-related deaths were perpetrated by men between 2009 and 2012 (Family Violence Death Review Committee, 2014), and every five and a half minutes a family violence investigation is recorded in this country (Stats NZ, 2015). Over three-quarters of recorded assaults against women are committed by an offender who is identified as family (New Zealand Family Violence Clearinghouse, 2017), and one in three women in New Zealand will experience physical and/or sexual violence from a partner in their lifetime (Fanslow & Robinson, 2011). Children, too, do not always experience the home as a safe place; 14 per cent of young people report having been hit or physically harmed by an adult at home (Adolescent Health Research Group, 2013).

 Sadly, home does not represent safety for all. Visit the New Zealand Family Violence Clearinghouse directory for more detailed statistics and resources for understanding family violence: https://nzfvc.org.nz/family-violence-statistics

At the time of writing, due to the Covid-19 pandemic, much of the country has been exhorted to 'stay home and save lives'. Local and international research, however, has pointed to the sharp increase in incidents of gender-based and intimate-partner violence during periods of lockdown as economic and social pressures have been magnified (Bradbury-Jones & Isham, 2020). In this context, the privacy of home and associated freedom from surveillance has exacerbated risks of violence. For those who experience domestic violence of any kind, the home offers little in the way of protection or safety, given it is the primary site where such abuse occurs. Indeed, in this context, the home can become a 'place where dynamics of power can be distorted and subverted by those who abuse, often without scrutiny' (Bradbury-Jones & Isham, 2020, p. 2047).

Conclusion

In this chapter we have explored the centrality of the home in the shaping of identity and belonging. Exploring notions of places as homes, and homes as places, has enabled us to reflect on the ways in which places are intimately connected with our sense of self and our relations to others. Importantly, we have shown that our identity threads — gender and ethnicity, for example — play an important role in shaping how domestic life will be enacted through a range of conventions and norms. Everyday practices that are informed by identity demonstrate the extent to which home and 'place as home' are not neutral spaces but are sites in which power is expressed and produced.

Meanings of 'home' are currently being shaped in the context of a housing crisis that makes it challenging to maintain a secure sense of home, place and belonging. Housing and income insecurity, rising prices, and shortages of suitable dwellings in parts of Aotearoa, mean that for many New Zealanders the normative rite of home ownership is well beyond reach, and renting in the current competitive rental housing market produces a different set of challenges. Irrespective of housing tenure, the meaning of home is fluid and multifaceted. But the housing policy context has resulted in economic and social inequalities between owners and non-owners, and such changes not only challenge constructions of home, but also provoke questions about the extent to which all citizens can access a home that provides security, stability, and a sense of place, identity and belonging.

Chapter 7 — Physical places: Home as place:
http://turangawaewae.massey.ac.nz/ch7.html

Further reading

Chisholm, E., Howden-Chapman, P., & Fougere, G. (2020). Tenants' responses to substandard housing: Hidden and invisible power and the failure of rental housing regulation. *Housing, Theory & Society, 37*(2), 139–161. https://doi.org/10.1080/14036096.2018.1538019

Eaqub, S., & Eaqub, S. (2015). *Generation rent: Rethinking New Zealand's priorities.* Bridget Williams Books.

Paul, J., McArthur, J., King, J., Harris, M., & Figenshow, S. (2020). *Transformative housing policy for Aotearoa New Zealand: A briefing note on addressing the housing crisis* (Policy Briefing: 7/2020). Public Policy Institute, University of Auckland. https://cdn.auckland.ac.nz/assets/auckland/arts/our-research/research-institutes-centres-groups/ppi/policy-briefings/ppi-housing-full2.pdf

Young, I. M. (2020). House and home: Feminist variations on a theme. In I. M. Young (Ed.), *Intersecting voices: Dilemmas of gender, political philosophy, and policy* (pp. 134–164). Princeton University Press.

References

Adolescent Health Research Group. (2013). *Youth '12 overview: The health and wellbeing of New Zealand secondary school students in 2012.* The University of Auckland. https://www.fmhs.auckland.ac.nz/assets/fmhs/faculty/ahrg/docs/2012prevalence-tables-report.pdf

Amore, K. (2016, June 3). *Homelessness accelerates between censuses.* University of Otago. http://www.otago.ac.nz/news/news/otago613529.html

Bahn, K., Cohen, J., & van der Meulen Rodgers, Y. (2020). A feminist perspective on COVID 19 and the value of care work globally. *Gender, Work and Organization, 27*(5), 695–699. https://doi.org/10.1111/gwao.12459

Barrowman, R. (2015). *Maurice Gee: Life and work.* Victoria University Press.

Beaton, S., Cain, T., Robinson, H., Hearn, V., & ThinkPlace. (2015). *An insight into the experience of rough sleeping in central Auckland.* Lifewise, Auckland Council, Auckland City Mission & ThinkPlace.

Blunt, A., & Dowling, R. M. (2006). *Home.* Routledge.

Bradbury-Jones, C., & Isham, L. (2020). The pandemic paradox: The consequences of COVID-19 on domestic violence. *Journal of Clinical Nursing, 29*(13–14), 2047–2049. https://doi.org/10.1111/jocn.15296

CaDDANZ. (2021). *Capturing the diversity dividend of Aotearoa New Zealand.* University of Waikato & Massey University. http://www.caddanz.org.nz

Cain, T., Terruhn, J., Ran, G. J., & Irvine, J. (2020). *Living with diversity: Negotiating difference in Northcote* (CaDDANZ Brief 10). The University of Waikato.

Camaira, J., & Mafile'o, T. (2018). Noqu Vale: Community organisation professionals' views on what works and what needs to change for Pasifika housing. *Aotearoa New Zealand Social Work, 30*(4), 70–83.

Campo, M., Fehlberg, B., Natalier, K., & Smyth, B. (2020). The meaning of home for children and young people after separation. *Journal of Social Welfare and Family Law, 42*(3), 299–318. https://doi.org/10.1080/09649069.2020.1796218

Charmes, J. (2019). *The unpaid care work and the labour market: An analysis of time use data based on the latest world compilation of time-use surveys.* International Labour Office.

Chisholm, E., Howden-Chapman, P., & Fougere, G. (2020). Tenants' responses to substandard housing: Hidden and invisible power and the failure of rental housing regulation. *Housing, Theory & Society, 37*(2), 139–161. https://doi.org/10.1080/1403609 6.2018.1538019

Clark, V., Tuffin, K., Frewin, K., & Bowker, N. (2017). Shared housing among young adults: Avoiding complications in domestic relationships. *Journal of Youth Studies, 20*(9), 1191–1207. https://doi.org/10.1080/13676261.2017.1316834

Cole, V. (2020). A case for universal state housing in Aotearoa New Zealand. *Counter Futures: Left Thought and Practice Aotearoa, 9*, 19–45. https://doi.org/10.26686/cf.v9.6773

Cox, R. (2016). Materials, skills and gender identities: Men, women and home improvement practices in New Zealand. *Gender, Place and Culture, 23*(4), 572–588. https://doi.org/10.1080/0966369X.2015.1034248

Dale, M. C., O'Brien, M., & St John, S. (Eds.). (2014). *Our children, our choice: Priorities for policy.* Child Poverty Action Group Incorporated.

Dupuis, A., & Thorns, D. C. (1998). Home, home ownership and the search for ontological security. *The Sociological Review, 46*(1), 24–47. https://doi.org/10.1111/1467-954X.00088

Eaqub, S., & Eaqub, S. (2015). *Generation rent: Rethinking New Zealand's priorities.* Bridget Williams Books.

Easthope. H. (2004). A place called home. *Housing, Theory and Society, 21*(3), 128–138. https://doi.org/10.1080/14036090410021360

Family Violence Death Review Committee. (2014, June 26). *Fourth annual report: January 2013 to December 2013.* Health Quality and Safety Commission. http://www.hqsc.govt.nz/our-programmes/mrc/fvdrc/publications-and-resources/publication/1600

Fanslow, J. L., & Robinson, E. (2011). Sticks, stones, or words? Counting the prevalence of different types of intimate partner violence reported by New Zealand women. *Journal of Aggression, Maltreatment and Trauma, 20*(7), 741–759. https://doi.org/10.1080/1092 6771.2011.608221

Ferguson, G. (1994). *Building the New Zealand dream.* Dunmore Press.

Goffman, E. (1990). *The presentation of self in everyday life.* Doubleday.

Goodyear, R., & Fabian, A. (2014). *Housing in Auckland: Trends in housing from the census of population and dwellings 1991 to 2013.* Stats NZ.

Gorman-Murray, A. (2007). Contesting domestic ideals: Queering the Australian home. *Australian Geographer, 38*(2), 195–213.

Grove, N., & Mead, H. M. (2001). *Ngā pēpeha a ngā tīpuna.* Victoria University Press.

Highmore, B. (2010). Homework: Routine, social aesthetics and the ambiguity of everyday life. *Cultural Studies, 18*(2–3), 306–327. https://doi.org/10.1080/0950238042000201536

Irvine, J., Ran, G. J., Terruhn, J., & Cain, T. (2020). *Ageing and wellbeing in Northcote* (CaDDANZ Brief 10). The University of Waikato.

Mallett S. (2004). Understanding home: A critical review of the literature. *The Sociological Review, 52*(1), 62–89. https://doi.org/10.1111/j.1467-954X.2004.00442.x

McLeod, M. (1989, December 18). A home of your own. *New Zealand Listener.*

Meagher, G. (2016). *Valuing care work and care workers: Workforce and equal pay issues in NZ aged residential care* (Research report). E tū.

Ministry for Women. (2019). *Gender inequality and unpaid work: A review of recent literature.* Ministry for Women.

Ministry of Education. (2021). *Education indicator: Student engagement/participation.* Ministry of Education. https://www.educationcounts.govt.nz/statistics/transient-students

Ministry of Social Development. (2016). *The social report 2015: Te purongo oranga tangata.* Ministry of Social Development.

Mitchell, A. (1972). *The half-gallon quarter-acre pavlova paradise.* Whitcombe and Tombs.

New Zealand Family Violence Clearinghouse. (2017). *Data summary: Violence against women.* University of Auckland. https://nzfvc.org.nz/our-work/data-summaries/violence-against-women

Park, J. (Ed.). (1991). *Ladies a plate: Change and continuity in the lives of New Zealand women.* Auckland University Press.

Parsell, C. (2012). Home is where the house is: The meaning of home for people sleeping rough. *Housing Studies, 27*(2), 159–173. https://doi.org/10.1080/02673037.2012.632621

Paul, J., McArthur, J., King, J., Harris, M., & Figenshow, S. (2020). *Transformative housing policy for Aotearoa New Zealand: A briefing note on addressing the housing crisis* (Policy Briefing: 7/2020). Public Policy Institute, University of Auckland. https://cdn.auckland.ac.nz/assets/auckland/arts/our-research/research-institutes-centres-groups/ppi/policy-briefings/ppi-housing-full2.pdf

Phillips, J. (1996). *A man's country? The image of the Pakeha male, a history.* Penguin.

Rose, G. (1993). *Feminism and geography: The limits of geographical knowledge.* Blackwell Publishers.

Stats NZ. (2013). *Caring for children: Findings from the 2009/10 Time Use Survey.* https://www.stats.govt.nz/reports/caring-for-children-findings-from-the-200910-time-use-survey

Stats NZ. (2015). *New Zealand Police recorded crime and apprehension tables.* http://nzdotstat.stats.govt.nz/wbos/Index.aspx?DataSetCode=TABLECODE740

Stats NZ. (2016). *Changes in home-ownership patterns 1986–2013: Focus on Māori and Pacific people.* https://static1.squarespace.com/static/57176f9f20c6478937696378/t/5a21e3fc419202083af7f0a9/1512170501777/home-ownership-maori-pacific.pdf

Stats NZ. (2019). *Renting vs owning in NZ.* https://www.stats.govt.nz/infographics/renting-vs-owning-in-nz

Stats NZ. (2020). *Housing in Aotearoa: 2020.* https://www.stats.govt.nz/reports/housing-in-aotearoa-2020

Terruhn, J. (2019). Whose dividend? Diversity as a selling point in urban development projects in Auckland. *New Zealand Population Review, 45,* 160–184. https://population.org.nz/app/uploads/2019/12/NZPR-45_whole-doc-final.pdf#page=162

Terruhn, J., Irvine, J., Cain, T., & Ran, G. J. (2020). *Urban regeneration and community building in Northcote* (CaDDANZ Brief 11). The University of Waikato.

Timmins, J. (2018). *What is the scale of vulnerable transience in New Zealand?* Oranga Tamariki. https://www.orangatamariki.govt.nz/assets/Uploads/About-us/Research/Research-seminars/May-2018/The-scale-of-vulnerable-transience-in-New-Zealand.pdf

Wiles, J. (2008). Sense of home in a transnational social space: New Zealanders in London. *Global Networks, 8*(1), 116–137. https://doi.org/10.1111/j.1471-0374.2008.00188

Young, I. M. (Ed.) (2020). *Intersecting voices: Dilemmas of gender, political philosophy, and policy.* Princeton University Press.

08.
Institutional places
The university

Richard Shaw and Matt Russell

Whāia te arapiki a Tāne-te-wānanga.
Follow the pathway of Tāne-te-wānanga.

The above expression encourages students to pursue a greater understanding of their studies and the world in which they live. The statement references the pūrākau of Tāne and the ascent into higher realms of knowledge to obtain three baskets, called Ngā Kete o Te Wānanga. Within these kete is all knowledge relevant to the world.

He tirohanga Māori: A Māori perspective

Te Rā Moriarty

In te reo Māori, the name for a university is a whare wānanga. This refers to ancient houses of learning that taught higher forms of knowledge such as karakia, whakapapa, history, and celestial and terrestrial knowledge. The word 'whare' refers to the buildings and the vicinity where the teaching and learning takes place; the word 'wānanga' is the action of discussing, debating, teaching and learning.

For many Māori students, a university can be a place where they struggle to belong and to positively identify as a student, partly because much of the knowledge taught within such institutions tends not to be drawn from or reflect te ao Māori. This has led to many initiatives on campuses to create spaces and environments that are comfortable and confirm Māori identity. The offering of courses and programmes focusing on te reo Māori, tikanga Māori and Māori history work to inform Māori communities of their culture, which connects Māori to their identity as descendants of their ancestors.

Many universities have a marae located on campus. The first, Te Kupenga o Te Mātauranga, built in 1979, was a part of the previous Teachers College of Massey University in Hokowhitu, Palmerston North. The Massey campus in Wellington, Pukeahu, opened a new marae in 2021 called Te Raukaramu. Situated on Victoria University of Wellington is the marae Te Tumu Herenga Waka. On Waikato University is the marae Te Ao Hurihuri. Ngā Wai o Horotiu is a marae located at Auckland University of Technology. Waipapa is the marae located at the University of Auckland. This is not an exhaustive list of all spaces dedicated to Māori students on all tertiary education campuses, but is an example of the creation of culturally comfortable spaces.

All of these marae provide a location for Māori students to be in a Māori environment on a university campus that may otherwise lack a familiar visual Māori presence in the form of buildings, structures and cultures. Through engaging with spaces such as these marae, students are able to have their identity as Māori promoted, supported and cared for. These places also create a Māori space for students who don't descend from Māori ancestors to experience Māori culture and to acquire Māori knowledge.

Introduction

Universities matter. In a powerful defence of the critical importance of the social sciences and humanities in the twenty-first century, American journalist and author Fareed Zakaria (2015) cites biologist E. O. Wilson's concern that we are drowning in information while starving for wisdom. Zakaria's point — which is that what the world needs now are people who can think critically and act wisely — seems as good a place as any to start this chapter, given that one of the historic *raisons d'être* of universities is to transform information into knowledge in the hope that this will lead to wisdom. It is one thing, for example, to know that at the 2020 general election in Aotearoa New Zealand just over 60 per cent of eligible voters aged 18 to 24 enrolled and voted (compared with nearly 90 per cent of 65- to 69-year-olds), but quite another to parse that data into knowledge of the complex causes of political disengagement as discussed in Chapter 4 (and thus to avoid making the mistake of blaming low voter turnout on lazy, apathetic individuals).

In tertiary institutions such as whare wānanga, universities and polytechnics, the processes of shifting from information (or data) to knowledge and wisdom can have significant consequences for both individuals' sense of self and the wellbeing of the wider community. In short, universities provide useful examples of the ways in which institutions shape people's sense of identity (and vice versa). In this chapter, therefore, we explore some of the identity encounters through which students' identity is formed, examine the rules that structure interactions in a university, look at the ways in which power is exercised, and interrogate the role of tertiary institutions within a pluralist, liberal democratic society.

Being at university: Identity threads and encounters

A core theme of this book is that places comprise the contexts in which we interact with others and, in so doing, shape our sense of identity. In turn, the ebb and flow of such exchanges have consequences for the rules, whether formal or informal, which structure the ways in which people interact in those places. Let's begin by reflecting, then, on the sorts of identity encounters people have in the different communities that make up their lives as students.

The word 'student' has many different hues. Any student's experience will reflect not only the specifics of their university, choice of programme and mode of study, but also their own history and circumstances. The choice of a particular degree and specific courses, decisions made regarding which other students to associate with

MASSEY UNIVERSITY ARCHIVES

Mortar board and gown

A graduation day procession at Massey University in 2015. It's far too happy a day to be worrying about the size of their student loans, but no doubt some of these students are. Since the introduction of fees, the meaning of a university education in New Zealand, and the value we place on such an education as a society, have shifted: the private dimension of taking a degree has become more prominent, and the case for a public education has correspondingly diminished (although it is far from dead).

(and what conversations to have — or avoid having — with them), and the sense that is made of the books, chapters and articles encountered along the way: these and countless other elements of a student's life will be influenced by the threads — age, socio-economic class, sexuality, ethnicity and so forth — that 'produce the fabric of a person's identity' (Burr, 2015, pp. 123–124). Those things do not rigidly determine the trajectory of our lives (indeed, part of the point of being a student is to reflect on the ways in which we can exercise agency over future outcomes), but our choices are not wholly independent of them. In short, 'student' is not a unitary category.

Nor is being a student a homogeneous experience. Rather, it plays out in contrasting ways for different people, as is illustrated by considering how a person's identity as a student intersects with their living arrangements. Some students live on campus; some in flats; some in homes that are far from the university at which they are studying. The rituals, routines and behaviours that occur in these different contexts vary. For example, the lives of students living in hostels are to a degree regulated by institutional rules: when and where they eat, the times of the year during which they must vacate 'their' rooms, the standards of behaviour expected in the hostel, and so on — all of these reflect the regulatory regime in place at any given time. Some of these rules are formal and the consequences of breaking them are made blindingly obvious, but others are tacit and the sanctions that apply may only become clear after the event.

As to life in student flats, there is typically an expectation that flatmates will engage in the communal life of the flat. Indeed, the very term 'flatmate' tells you something about the relationships you are expected to have with the others you share a flat with. It carries a normative expectation of amiability that is missing, for instance, from the equivalent French term *colocataire*, which simply suggests an arrangement in which people share a living space. The advent of digital technologies is shifting the practices associated with this normative rule; for instance, it is much more common now than it used to be for flatmates to spend time alone streaming content. However, the expectation that as a member of a flat you will contribute to the shopping and cook for your flatmates continues to exert a significant influence over student life in this country. It operates with the force of a rule, yet it isn't codified anywhere.

Check out this episode from one of New Zealand's early reality TV shows, *Flatmates*: https://www.nzonscreen.com/title/flatmates-episode-one-1997

For distance students, that part of their identity labelled 'student' typically demands juggling multiple family, work, community, study and other responsibilities. To put this differently, navigating the interplay — if not outright contradiction — between one's different identity threads can be highly challenging for students who, having already split the day between childcare and work obligations, can hit the books only once dinner has been prepared and served, the dishes and folding done, and the kids put to bed.

The rules of the university game

Students have other encounters, particularly in the context of the formal environment of the university, which are also structured by certain 'rules of the game' (Bourdieu, 1977). The rules in question might be explicit: for instance, a student cannot hand in an assignment that has been plagiarised (at least, not without running the risk of being detected and punished). Others are tacit. The following claim from Arran Stibbe (2010), who teaches English and Creative Writing at the University of Gloucester, provides a clear sense of the breadth of the scope of these formal and informal rules of the game:

> All the rules — explicit and implicit — which guide students in how they should talk and act in the classroom, how they should write their essays, how they should give presentations, all the assessment briefs, assessment criteria, regulations for assessment, referencing guides [and] feedback on written work, are guiding them into particular disciplinary identities. (p. 91)

Stibbe's suggestion is that a university is a 'totalising' institution — one which shapes all (or at least an awful lot) of the conduct of those who inhabit it. His references to talking and acting are particularly relevant. The general point is that such interactivity is structured by expectations of appropriate behaviour. That expectation is most marked in the relationship between academics and students, in which talking and acting tends to reflect clearly defined roles and accepted ways of doing things. Thus, it is generally considered poor form (by academics, at least) for students to routinely check their digital devices in lectures or to talk audibly in a lecture about something that is not relevant to the topic under discussion. There are also conventions around engaging with people whose views you do not agree with: for instance, launching personal attacks on other students in online discussion forums or tutorials is well and truly out of bounds.

Designing rules into the furniture

These rules and roles are even designed into the architecture of universities' learning environments. Think of a traditional lecture theatre comprising banked rows of seats facing a lectern. This particular built environment — which is nothing if not a secular interpretation of a sacred space — encourages certain kinds of interactions between staff and students but makes others a little tricky. Students do not sit facing each other — they face the front of the room. That arrangement does not encourage discussion among students; rather, it is expressly intended to focus their attention on the person delivering the lecture. The divide — or, to put it differently, the 'symbolic order' (Lacan, 1991) — of the lecture theatre is emphasised by the physical distance that exists between students' seats and the space the lecturer inhabits.

Such arrangements also embody clear messages about the possession of knowledge and the respective roles of students and staff. The fundamental assumption built (literally) into a lecture hall is that this is a place where intellectual novices come to learn from acknowledged experts. The layout of the theatre — and lecturing does have a performative or theatrical dimension to it — privileges certain types of knowledge (those acquired through rigorous, disciplined study) and specific ways of learning (by listening and asking questions).

To a degree, the traditional symbolic order within universities is changing, as our understanding of learning and education shifts to a more constructivist approach. The use of digital learning technologies, recourse to more interactive teaching methods, and the gradual replacement of the traditional banked lecture theatre with flat-floored teaching spaces — these and other changes alter the dynamic between academics and students. Established ways of doing things are remarkably resilient, however, and it is far from clear that these new developments will ever wholly disrupt what is a fundamentally unequal relationship. Even in the Zoom (or Blackboard, Bluejeans or Google Meets) 'classrooms' in which students increasingly find themselves in a world proscribed by the Covid-19 pandemic, the ancient hierarchy of learned and learnee plays out: the former doing most of the talking while the latter dutifully listen (often with video feed turned off).

Disciplining students

There is one other defining feature of studying at a university that is central to a student's identity, and that is the part that is defined by their academic discipline. This person is a Politics student; that one is majoring in Sociology; and those three over there are English, French and Media Studies students respectively. Each is a student, but the preceding qualifiers clearly distinguish one from the other. And that qualifier matters a great deal, because disciplines explain the world in particular ways that are shared by members of those disciplinary communities. In quite a literal sense, a discipline uses theories, concepts and research methods to teach someone to see and understand the world in a particular way: the phenomena studied, the theories used to explain relationships or interactions between those phenomena, the methods used to collect and analyse empirical data, and so on, combine to socialise (i.e. discipline) students into the ways and conventions of a very specific intellectual community.

Disciplines play a central role in crafting students' intellectual worldviews. They also shape the professional identities people take into their lives after graduating. When students leave university, they carry with them these disciplined, structured ways of making sense of things, and use them to interpret the world beyond university. Making sense of literature, language, society, art, politics, events in the wider world and so on is, after all, one of the reasons many of us seek a university education.

We're all equal here. Aren't we?

Well, no, we're not. Universities are innately hierarchical institutions in which power — that is, the capacity to bring about consequences for others — is unequally distributed. Those imbalances take different forms, not all of which will be visible to students. Gender, for instance, is one of the identity threads discussed throughout this book, and is one of the bases on which power is unequally distributed across the university. Gender and formal authority tend to be interwoven in universities. Women comprise a little over 50 per cent of all academic staff in New Zealand's eight universities, but account for just under 30 per cent of all professors (Lynn, 2016). Moreover, recent research has found that, across New Zealand universities, women can earn up to $400,000 less than men across a career — only half of which can be explained by age or research performance, and even though women apply for promotions just as regularly as do their male colleagues (Brower & James, 2020).

There are also relations of power based on research performance (measured in publications and research grants): star researchers usually enjoy higher status and greater influence than star teachers. A division between academic and professional staff also exists, with the activities of the former often accorded greater status (and money) than those of the latter.

See this Ministry for Women page for more on the gender pay gap: https://women.govt.nz/work-skills/income/gender-pay-gap

Inequalities also apply in what is arguably the most fundamental relationship within a university: that between academic staff and students. What goes on in a lecture is fundamentally a relationship of power in which academics radiate knowledge which students passively absorb. This imbalance is perhaps most obvious in the gatekeeping role academics play. Bluntly, academics decide whether students pass or fail their courses. There are, of course, procedural means for seeking redress, but in the final instance the determination of whether or not a student has learned what an academic has asked them to learn is for the latter to determine (and this may be entirely appropriate, given that academics are, or should be, specialists in their fields).

The fact that students contribute to the cost of that learning does not render the staff–student relationship one of equals. There is a view that the advent of student fees has reinvented the student as a consumer. In other words, some argue that a student who pays fees for a course of academic study is purchasing a commodity, and as such is entitled to the same levels of responsive service that (should) attach to the consumption of other goods and services. The issue of exactly *what*, if anything, is being purchased is not moot. A student may believe they are buying a certificate, diploma or degree, but an academic is likely to counter that what is being purchased is the opportunity to learn, not an outcome on an essay or exam.

The latter view is buttressed by the fact that, in this country, a tertiary education remains substantially publicly funded. The precise balance of public funding versus private contribution (in the form of fees) varies from year to year and course to course, but in the humanities and social sciences students generally meet around 20 per cent of the total cost of their degree. Put differently, the rights and obligations of students are not equivalent to those who consume commodities that are not publicly subsidised to the tune of 80 per cent or so.

That is not to gainsay the impact of fees, or of the challenges students face meeting the costs of living and course-related expenses (both of which are discussed shortly). Nor is it to ignore that, in the quasi-market that is New Zealand's tertiary education sector, students choose where they take their academic custom (albeit increasingly within economic constraints). The point, however, is that debates about how the burden of paying for tertiary students' education is allocated do not substantially detract from the fundamental basis of the relationship between academics and students. That has to do with the authority academics possess that is grounded in their membership of both an institution and a discipline.

The university and citizenship

Finally, let's address the citizenship dimensions to all this. To that end, in this section we shift gears and reflect on the place of universities in — and the contributions they make to — the wider national community.

A central aspect of this discussion concerns the policy context that shapes the experience of being a student. One of the key features of that environment concerns the funding of tertiary study and, in particular, the balance between the level of public subsidy and the amount students themselves pay to study. A little historical context is necessary here. Back in the distant past of the 1990s, levels of government funding covered a greater proportion of the total cost of a student's tertiary education than is now the case. Furthermore, students tended to fund their study through a combination of parental support and government bursaries (which were awarded to senior secondary-school students on completion of a University Entrance [UE] exam). Most students could, if they chose, avoid having to work while studying, and universities were nominally free and open to all New Zealand citizens who had attained UE (Crawford, 2016).

Of course, the system was neither 'free' nor entirely 'open'. Student fees were largely covered by the taxpayer, and nationwide scaling of UE results was used to restrict access to bursaries and scholarships, limiting overall enrolments (Crawford, 2016). (All of which meant that inequalities in the secondary-school sector were amplified within the tertiary sector.) When they were introduced by the Fourth Labour Government in 1989, the average annual student fee was a princely $129. In 1990, however, they were bumped up to $1250 — an increase of 969 per cent (O'Mannin, 2018) — and these days the average sits at just under $9000 for a full-time student.

In short, these days students incur a greater proportion of the costs of studying than they once did. Some of these are opportunity costs (e.g. forgone income), which are difficult to quantify. Others are far easier to capture. For instance, in 2018, the average amount borrowed by university students for course fees per year was $7233, plus an additional $966 for course-related costs such as books or equipment (Ministry of Education, 2019). An analysis of 50 nations with top-ranking universities ranked New Zealand fourteenth most expensive, averaging $8595 per student per annum (Keogh, 2019). Moreover, government statistics on student debt are almost certainly an understatement, given they do not include the private debt accrued by students through a combination of bank overdrafts, credit cards and other lending services that strategically target students along with other low-income groups (New Zealand Union of Students' Associations [NZUSA], 2017).

Some of the risks associated with these figures — such as the cost of providing students with interest-free loans totalling $28.8 billion since 1992 (some $17 billion of which has been repaid) — are publicly borne. However, debt also influences the later choices graduates make about their futures, including where they can afford to live (and whether or not they can take on a mortgage), plans for having families and so on. As importantly, cost deters some people from taking on tertiary education in the first instance. In what feels like another country now, Clarence Beeby (1983), the visionary educationalist and one-time director of the Department of Education, argued that 'every New Zealander, whatever his or her level of academic ability, whether she be rich or poor, whether she live in the town or country, will, at least, have a free education, absolutely free, of the kind for which she is best fitted and to the fullest extent of her powers' (p. 110). Beeby was talking about the primary and secondary sectors, but today many of those who argue against charging fees for tertiary study invoke his compelling case that a free education is a fundamental right of citizenship.

How context shapes student identities

The consequences of these policies extend beyond the financial burden borne by individuals. Indeed, the wider political and policy context sketched above has fundamentally reshaped what it means to be a student and transformed (not always for the better) what is understood as 'student culture'.

Michael Sandel (2012), a professor of government theory at Harvard, argues that when a price is attached to something, the nature of that thing changes. That is precisely what has occurred in Aotearoa New Zealand. The commodification of tertiary study has had major consequences for student identity. Most obviously, debt-anxiety clearly looms large in many students' day-to-day decision-making: it is all too common to hear students say they feel 'sick' or 'anxious' when thinking about the impact of their student loan repayments on their future (Keogh, 2019).

Given the expense involved, many students adopt an instrumental approach to their choice of degree. Rather than pursuing a course of study on the basis of passion for a subject or more abstract concepts such as civic duty, students are more likely to take an economically rational approach, deciding what to study based on notions of future employability (Grey & Sedgewick, 2014). But this instrumentalism is likely to be frustrated by structural changes in the employment market (such as the 'greening' of primary sectors), which are transforming the world of work in unknown ways. Moreover, this unpredictability contributes to a kind of ontological anxiety regarding what the future may or may not hold — which is entangled with other significant concerns, including the unknown ways in which the ecological and social impacts of climate change will transform societies and economies.

Student agency and engagement

While these anxieties have contributed to renewed waves of student activism in societies like Sweden, Russia, France, the United Kingdom and the United States in recent years, students in Aotearoa New Zealand have been conspicuously quiet. It might be useful here to briefly return to the relationship between identity and context. Contexts establish rules that enable and constrain the ways in which identity is expressed; they also enable and constrain particular types of agency (Barnes, 2000). To some degree the commercial model has enhanced student agency: it has removed some barriers to participation and arguably made tertiary institutions (and at least some academics) less élitist and more responsive to students. But while the university *itself* has perhaps become more democratic, the institutional bases of student activism and student politics *within* the university have been eroded.

Much of this is connected to changes inside universities that are beyond the historical memory of anybody born this side of the millennium. For example, the semesterisation of the academic year in 1992 had significant (but rarely acknowledged) consequences for student culture. Previously, courses ran over a full year and students' progression often depended on their performance in end-of-year exams rather than multiple assessments during a course. This, combined with relative freedom from the need to work during the academic year, meant that until the early 1990s many students experienced what theorists of democracy would call a 'surplus of leisure' (Russell, 1991, p. 76) and, therefore, more time to engage in activism (and other equally worthy pastimes).

Most contemporary students, however, face more or less relentless internal assessment; in addition, the need to minimise debt compels roughly 70 per cent of them to find part-time employment while studying (NZUSA, 2017), and the pressure on people to complete their degrees as quickly as possible means many students also take courses across the (so-called) summer recess. Few students these days have much time to engage meaningfully in anything outside of their study and employment obligations. The ancient Athenians understood that the absence of financial constraint and a surplus of free time were the two basic foundations of active democratic citizenship (Dewey, 1963). The modern student has neither.

Another decisive factor in the historic decline of student political action arrived in 2011 in the form of the Voluntary Student Membership (VSM) Act. Up to 2011, the democratic agency of students was institutionally supported by the student association, the purpose of which was to independently represent the collective interests of the student body, both in relation to university management and the government. Membership was compulsory for all students, in return for which

Louder together

Approximately 300 Massey University staff and students used their collective voice to protest the university's 'repositioning' proposals in August 2000, marching down Tennant Drive in Palmerston North towards Massey's old teaching campus in Hokowhitu. Due to both increasing costs and a drop in government funding, Massey management had proposed significant academic staff redundancies. Student associations — worried that these job losses would have negative consequences for students by increasing staff/student ratios — worked together with the Association of University Staff (now called the Tertiary Education Union) to oppose both student fee increases and redundancies for academics. Instead they called on the government to increase funding for the tertiary sector. While Massey's repositioning did eventually go ahead, only 44 academic jobs were lost, rather than the 166 originally proposed.

the associations provided services (such as university shops, student spaces, academic advocacy, political lobbying and events) and managed an independent student radio and student magazine. Every university or polytechnic housed a student association, and associations were fiercely defensive of their independence.

In 2011, the Voluntary Student Membership Act (VSM), introduced by the ACT Party, largely removed that independence. Post-VSM, student associations could no longer charge membership fees directly to students in the form of a student services levy (which was set at around $150 per student). Instead, universities now include this charge in student fee payments (in other words, it hasn't gone away) and distribute the funds to associations in the form of contract and service agreements (Meads & Smith, 2018; Nissen, 2019).

VSM has transformed student associations into something more closely resembling a business. And while it has not reduced costs for students directly, it has significantly reduced the financial independence of student associations, rendering them beholden to university management. Institutions can now exert influence over the activities of associations in both subtle and overt ways, principally via the negotiation of short-term service agreements. The continual threat of the non-renewal of agreements or of funding reductions swings the balance of power towards the university's management, and makes it much less likely that associations will engage in activity that may compromise their relationship with their funders (Nissen, 2019).

In this environment many student officers reject the relevance of 'politics' to an association's work, instead defining their role as providing services to the student body (Nissen, 2019, p. 42). If an association does adopt a political position, it tends to be about practical issues deemed to be 'uncontentious and non-divisive', such as 'improving student housing, local alcohol laws, or better public transportation' (Nissen, 2019, pp. 43–44). While some student officers speak positively of the constructive relationship they have with management, others question whether VSM has really enhanced students' collective voice — or simply turned associations into another service delivery arm of university managers.

It's about the economy, stupid

The material effects of the wider policy context are not restricted to what goes on within the university, and in this section we reflect on the extent to which a university education facilitates membership of, and participation in, various communities post-study. In Aotearoa New Zealand, the issue, as we noted above, is almost always framed as the impact a university degree has on someone's employment and earnings prospects. Bluntly, the instrumental question that is usually asked is: What's the likely return on your (and the public's) investment in your degree? By most measures, a person's income and employment prospects are enhanced by the completion of a degree. Universities New Zealand (2016) suggest that a typical university graduate will earn $1.6 million more over their working life than someone who has not graduated with a degree, while the Ministry of Education (2015) found that five years after graduating the median earnings of Bachelor's degree graduates are 46 per cent higher than those of people earning the national median income.

Universities New Zealand/Te Pōkai Tara reports on the benefits of gaining a degree: https://www.universitiesnz.ac.nz/latest-news-and-publications/degree-smart-investment-0

It is perfectly reasonable to focus on employment outcomes, not least because of the costs borne by graduates. However, to *only* do this is to assume that there is just one answer to the question: What is the purpose of a university degree? We think that is a mistake. Instead, different possible answers to that question should be considered.

Some of these lie in the reasons individuals give for having enrolled at a university. Hong Kong education researchers David Kember, Amber Ho and Celina Hong (2010) found that people's motives for attending university can be organised into a series of categories, including compliance with the expectations of family and teachers, the perceived attractions of a university lifestyle (including the sense of belonging to a community), a wish to enhance career prospects, and an interest in pursuing learning in particular subjects. Public debate in this country about the value of universities is substantially shaped by the last two of these categories. The dominant story is the employability narrative alluded to above, in which context the function of a degree — and of universities in general — is to produce a suitably credentialled supply of labour in response to employers' demands (Grey & Sedgwick, 2014).

This narrative reflects a particular view of the nature of university degrees (that they are primarily about helping graduates find work), and therefore the sorts of things that should be taught in them (technical skills rather than broader intellectual and cognitive competencies). There are three clear problems with this story. First, individuals' employment outcomes are influenced by things universities have little or no control over, including how hard students work while

MASSEY UNIVERSITY ARCHIVES

Continuity and change

A school bus parked outside of Massey University's Sir Geoffrey Peren Building, Palmerston North, in the 1960s. This was the original heart of the campus, then known as Massey Agricultural College, and consequently enjoys Historic Place Category I status ('special or outstanding significance') on the New Zealand Heritage List. The government financed its construction in 1931, alongside the Refectory (which itself holds Category II status) and dormitories to a total of £92,000. At the time the building was opened, the college had 200 students. By the time the building was earthquake-strengthened and restored to its former glory in 2016, there were over 31,000 students enrolled at Massey University.

studying, how diligently they apply themselves to searching for work, and the level of demand for labour in the wider economy.

Second, it is not immediately clear why the interests of employers should be privileged in this particular way. There may well be other sections of society for whom a university education is about something other than (or additional to) finding work, but those views are not strongly reflected in present government policy.

Third, the 'universities-should-respond-to-the-requirements-of-employers' lobby assumes that the skills employers need both now and in the future can be predicted and subsequently designed into university courses. It is notoriously difficult, however, to forecast these sorts of things. Moreover, it is clear that globalisation, automation and the global pandemic have already changed, and will continue to change, the world of work.

One particularly influential report (Frey & Osborne, 2013) anticipates that 46 per cent of the jobs presently carried out in the United States are at risk of automation within the next two decades. The authors also make the point that specific technical skills will not be enough in this new world of work. Instead, people will need transferable skills — such as critical thinking, problem-solving and social intelligence (i.e. the sorts of things found in degrees like the BA) — that will help them navigate a working life likely to contain many jobs (some of which do not yet exist) rather than a single career. Reflecting on policy in this country, we can't help but wonder if our own decision-makers are aware of this.

Except that it's not just about the economy, stupid

Frey and Osborne's (2013) conclusion is precisely why it is important to consider a second answer to the question: What is the purpose of a degree? Section 162 of the Education Act 1989 states that the principal aim of universities is 'to develop intellectual independence'; further, it requires universities to 'accept a role as critic and conscience of society'. In other words, the students and staff who make up our universities have the right (if not a legal obligation) to ask awkward questions, question received wisdoms, poke at sacred cows, and voice controversial or unpopular opinions. That doesn't mean they get to rant — these statutory rights and requirements have to be exercised ethically, transparently and within the law. All the same, that law makes it clear that universities are required to do more than prepare people for work.

These contests over the meaning and purpose of universities are not just academic (pun intended). For one thing, they have direct consequences for what is deemed to count as knowledge. The employability narrative emphasises skills and attributes with direct application to the job market. This can marginalise knowledge that is important even though it may not have direct vocational application, and can produce a university experience that more closely resembles training than education. It can also have a chilling effect on the capacity of academics to teach and students to learn about perspectives on the world that challenge the status quo. In the end, this disposition simply serves the interests of those in positions of political and economic power.

Debates about the purpose of universities also have material consequences for what is held to be acceptable (or, indeed, required) behaviour within those institutions. In Chapter 5, you read that students at our universities were among those who took to the streets to protest against climate change, apartheid in South Africa and inequality in Aotearoa New Zealand. Earlier in this chapter we made the point that the student voice — expressed through protest and student radio and newspapers — was once a vibrant element of public life both on campuses and well beyond, and was frequently directed at issues of broad social, economic and political importance. Indeed, the student voice was considered an important part of the foundations of a 'vibrant, informed and participatory democracy' (Bridgman, 2007, p. 128). Not so much these days, perhaps.

Writing for the online *Bloomberg View*, columnist Megan McArdle (2015) captures the spirit of our times:

> Cultural and economic shifts have pushed students towards behaving more like consumers in a straight commercial transaction and less like people who were being inducted into a non-market institution. The rise of [universities] as labour market gate-keepers has transformed [them] from a place to be imbued with the intangible qualities of character and education . . . into a place where you go to buy a ticket to a good job.
> A university education is supposed to accomplish two things: expose you to a wide variety of ideas and help you navigate your way through them; and turn you into an adult, which is to say, someone who can cope with people, and ideas, you don't like.

In effect, what is happening is that students' future identity as workers is squeezing out their present identity as students (Daniels & Brooker, 2014). One of the great things about a university education is that it requires you to learn things you did not previously know. That experience can be challenging, stimulating and sometimes uncomfortable, and it requires that you identify and question the limits of your own existing knowledge. But if all we want from our universities these days are job-ready students, we risk producing people who may be fine at working but poorly equipped to live in a world full of people who do not look, think or behave as they do. Not what is required, you might think, at a time when the faces, voices and stories of this country — much less the wider world — are as rich, diverse and connected as they have ever been.

Covid-19: A new type of university?

Although our focus in this chapter has been on the political economy of the tertiary sector, over the past two years it has become impossible to avoid the impact of the global Covid-19 pandemic on universities. It is too soon to reach definitive conclusions on how deep and lasting this impact will be, but several observations are worth hazarding.

Perhaps the most obvious concerns the ways in which the physical and virtual dimensions of universities are merging as an institutional space; in other words, the university is becoming more hybrid. During the lockdowns of 2020 and 2021, for instance, we were all distance students for a time — although the familial, economic and health contexts in which many students lived often made this a less than fulfilling experience.

The increasing recourse to digital technologies (for both teaching and meetings among staff) — which was trending well before the pandemic arrived, but which has since been super-charged — has consequences for our encounters with others. (Zoom classes, we have all realised, have their own norms and conventions.) There is an argument that these technologies democratise access to education. But they also exacerbate pre-existing inequalities both within and beyond the university. For one thing, the digital evangelists sometimes overlook the reality of the digital divide in this country: not everyone enjoys unfettered access to endless data and good study conditions, and the uncritical embrace of online learning by university administrators risks leaving some people behind.

For more on how the digital divide impacts different groups in Aotearoa, see the 2021 *Digital Inclusion and Wellbeing* report: https://www.digital.govt.nz/dmsdocument/161~digital-inclusion-and-wellbeing-in-new-zealand/html

There are other, broader consequences of the pandemic which are also reshaping the university sector. Following at least two years of closed borders, for example, it is not at all clear that New Zealand universities will ever again be able to rely upon full-fee-paying international students to cross-subsidise costs. Enrolments of domestic students have increased markedly since the advent of Covid-19 (they always do in times of uncertainty), but not to the extent that they offset the sizeable loss of revenue from international students. Universities are at a critical juncture: as was the case apropos the early 1990s, we might look back on the early 2020s as one of those times at which universities began charting a new course.

Conclusion

It could be argued that the modern university is in danger of becoming like the modern airport, where education is reduced to something we use to get someplace else. A university can be a strange, almost 'non-place' (Augé, 2008); a nether-zone between one life stage and another. People arrive in order to be transported from teenage-hood to adulthood; from parenthood to life after the kids have left home; from one job to another. Students briefly touch down for as long as it takes them to attain a degree (on average about four years), and then lift off into the future. There is little opportunity or reason for students to examine the political economy of the university: like airports, they are defined by their utility.

And, much like airports, at times universities can be uncomfortable, expensive and isolating places. Students collectively confront shared problems such as debt management, negotiating work and study, and maintaining mental and physical wellbeing, but often they do so as individuals. Most people eventually get to the departure gate on time, but student identity has been decisively shaped by neoliberal-inspired reforms that have socialised students to see themselves as autonomous actors; as consumers of a 'student experience' in the tertiary marketplace, rather than as active citizens engaged in co-creating and contributing to a university community.

There is another way of looking at this. A few airports still manage to be vibrant, colourful places, humming with energy precisely *because* people are leaving here to go there. So, too, the university can and does play a critical part to play in fostering and promoting public (as well as private) values. And this role — which is jointly played by students and staff — matters. And perhaps the most seductive aspect of both travel and higher-education is not the promise of new and exotic destinations, but rather the promise of reinvention, the possibility that we can escape what we were before and become somebody new — that we can 'light out for the territory', as Huckleberry Finn would say.

As Australian geographer Iain Hay (2016) has persuasively argued, the world needs more thinking people; it needs those who can distinguish information from knowledge, interpret and learn from the lives of others, and ask sharp questions of those in positions of economic and political power. It needs people who know how to disagree with others (and to do that well), and how to live alongside those with different values and other ways of living. These things are central to a society that is inclusive (rather than one which excludes) and accepting of different identities (rather than one which routinely rejects those who are somehow marked as different). And they are at the core of what it is to be a university student. So, linger awhile at this particular type of airport and see what you can learn.

Chapter 8 — Institutional places: The university:
http://turangawaewae.massey.ac.nz/ch8.html

Further reading

Grey, S., & Sedgwick, C. (2014). Go study for the economy. In D. Cooke, C. Hill, P. Baskett, & R. Irwin (Eds.), *Beyond the free market: Rebuilding a just society in New Zealand* (pp. 113–120). Dunmore Press.

Hay, I. (2016). Defending letters: A pragmatic response to assaults on the humanities. *Journal of Higher Education Policy and Management, 38*(6), 610–624. https://doi.org/10.1080/1360080X.2016.1196933

Nissen, S. & Hayward, B. (2016). Students' associations: The New Zealand experience. In R. Brookes (Ed.), *Student Politics and Protest* (pp. 147–160). Routledge.

Sandel, M. (2012). *What money can't buy: The moral limits of markets.* Farrar, Straus and Giroux.

References

Augé, M. (2008). *Non-places: Introduction to an anthropology of supermodernity.* Verso.

Barnes, B. (2000). *Understanding agency: Social theory and responsible action.* Sage.

Beeby, C. (1983). Centennial address. *National Education, 65*(3), 106–110.

Bourdieu, P. (1977). *Outline of a theory of practice.* Cambridge University Press.

Bridgman, T. (2007). Assassins in academia? New Zealand academics as 'critic and conscience of society'. *New Zealand Sociology, 22*(1), 126–144.

Brower A., & James, A. (2020). Research performance and age explain less than half of the gender pay gap in New Zealand universities. *PLoS ONE, 15*(1): e0226392. https://doi.org/10.1371/journal.pone.0226392

Burr, V. (2015). *Social constructionism* (3rd ed.). Routledge.

Crawford, R. (2016). *History of tertiary education reforms in New Zealand* (New Zealand Productivity Commission Research Note 2016/1). New Zealand Productivity Commission.

Daniels, J., & Brooker, J. (2014). Student identity development in higher education: Implications for graduate attributes and work-readiness. *Educational Research, 56*(1), 65–76.

Dewey, J. (1963). *Democracy and education: An introduction to the philosophy of education.* Macmillan.

Frey, C., & Osborne, M. (2013, September). *The future of employment: How susceptible are jobs to computerisation?* [Paper presentation]. Machines and Employment Workshop/Oxford Martin Programme on the Impacts of Future Technology, Oxford University, England.

Grey, S., & Sedgwick, C. (2014). Go study for the economy. In D. Cooke, C. Hill, P. Baskett, & R. Irwin (Eds.), *Beyond the free market: Rebuilding a just society in New Zealand* (pp. 113–120). Dunmore Press.

Hay, I. (2016). Defending letters: A pragmatic response to assaults on the humanities. *Journal of Higher Education Policy and Management, 38*(6),610–624. https://doi.org/10.1080/1360080X.2016.1196963

Kember, D., Ho, A., & Hong, C. (2010). Initial motivation orientation of students enrolling in undergraduate degrees. *Studies in Higher Education, 35*(3), 263–276.

Keogh, B. (2019, May 23). 'Eye-watering' loans leave students feeling sick and anxious about future. *Stuff.* https://www.stuff.co.nz/national/education/112905295/eyewatering-loans-leave-students-feeling-sick-and-anxious-about-future

Lacan, J. (1991). Freud's papers on technique 1953–1954. In J.-A. Miller (Ed.) & J. Forrester (Trans. & Notes.) *The Seminar of Jacques Lacan, Book 1.* Norton.

Lynn, A. (2016, July 11). Gender gap remains stagnant at universities. *Stuff.* https://www.stuff.co.nz/national/education/81851545/gender-gap-remains-stagnant-at-universities

McCardle, M. (2015, August 13). Sheltered students go to college, avoid education. *Bloomberg.* https://www.bloomberg.com/opinion/articles/2015-08-13/sheltered-students-go-to-college-avoid-education

Meads, C., & Smith, S. (2018). *The hand that feeds us: How voluntary student membership has impacted the freedom of associations and the voice of students.* New Zealand Union of Students' Associations. https://static1.squarespace.com/static/5f0515b1b1a21014b5d22dd6/t/5fa22e60d4098173eb4be0d7/1604464257589/The+Hand+that+Feeds+Us+.pdf

Ministry of Education. (2015). *Student loan scheme* (annual report).

Ministry of Education. (2019). *Student loan scheme* (annual report).

New Zealand Union of Students' Associations. (2017). *Income and expenditure report: The cost of being a student in NZ.* https://static1.squarespace.com/static/5f0515b1b1a21014b5d22dd6/t/5fa215269b07783ceda7a845/1604457815314/Income___Expenditure_Report_2017__for_online_publish_.pdf

Nissen, S. (2019). *Student political action in New Zealand.* BWB Texts.

O'Mannin, C. (2018, July 5). Campaign to repeal voluntary student membership starts. *Critic Te Arohi*, 14. https://www.critic.co.nz/news/article/7614/campaign-to-repeal-voluntary-student-membership-st

Russell, B. (1991). *History of Western philosophy.* Routledge.

Sandel, M. (2012). *What money can't buy: The moral limits of markets.* Farrar, Straus and Giroux.

Stibbe, A. (2010). Identity reflection: Students and societies in transition. *Learning and Teaching in Higher Education, 5,* 86–95.

Universities New Zealand. (2016). *A degree is a smart investment.* https://www.universitiesnz.ac.nz/latest-news-and-publications/degree-smart-investment

Zakaria, F. (2015). *In defense of a liberal education.* W. W. Norton.

09.
Digital places
Identity, participation and power

Stella Pennell

He rā ki tua.

A day to come.

The whakataukī used here is a word of encouragement that there is another sun and another day on the horizon (Williams, in Mead & Grove, 2003). It has been drawn on for this topic to show that, regardless of the pressures that are faced by communities due to the impacts of land and cultural loss, these communities are resilient in striving to find new ways to promote and maintain the wellbeing of their people and knowledge.

He tirohanga Māori: A Māori perspective

Te Rā Moriarty

Māori have always been adaptable to new ways of doing things, such as reading and writing, and to new technologies and the use of new tools such as steel chisels and nails. Through recent years there has been an increase in online activities, such as learning, discussing and sharing mātauranga Māori relevant to specific whānau, hapū, iwi and also wider Māori society. For example, a Taranaki-based broadcasting and media company called Te Korimako o Taranaki frequently broadcasts to its members regular radio shows and in-depth discussions with many knowledgeable and influential people. The broadcasts are held daily, with the discussions taking place every Monday evening on a segment named *Pupuke Te Wānanga*. These have elements of an interview, but are also wānanga-based, where listeners and watchers are informed of iwi histories and customs, with a frequent focus on contemporary initiatives and projects. Te Korimako o Taranaki is an example of how Māori communities can connect with each other through listening to, and sharing, mātauranga on an online platform.

Living by the Stars is a kaupapa that teaches knowledge of astronomy from an ancestral understanding with regular videos by Rangi Matamua. This powerful kaupapa reconnects Māori communities to specific knowledge of their tūpuna, which has been negatively impacted through the colonial process of dislocating people from their land, their culture and their mātauranga. The focus on astronomical patterns and movements also highlights the intimate relationship that the celestial and terrestrial realms have with each other. This relationship governs the natural environment that we inhabit, and, once again, connects descendants today with the mātauranga and customs of their ancestors, further strengthening their connections to themselves as Māori people.

In a final example, the podcast *Taringa*, from Te Wānanga o Aotearoa, is a weekly internet broadcast that discusses all manner of kaupapa within te ao Māori, including iwi profiles, te reo Māori, tikanga Māori and mātauranga Māori. Members from different iwi are interviewed and given the chance to share their own histories with wider Māori communities. Aspects of the Māori language and customs are chosen and discussed regularly, informing Māori descendants, and all listeners, about indigenous knowledge distinct to Aotearoa. This leads to a greater understanding of one's culture through ancestral knowledge.

The examples mentioned here are just a small collection of the ways that Māori people are using modern technology to reach Māori communities nationally and internationally. The outcome is that knowledge relevant to te ao Māori, whānau, hapū, iwi and the natural environment of Aotearoa is shared and explained. This leads to strengthening people's identity and a sense of belonging with their own culture by understanding themselves, their customs and the ancestral ways of being.

Introduction

In the Introduction to Part 3, 'Places in Aotearoa New Zealand', Trudie and Juliana define 'place' as 'a space which is given social meaning by human activity and/ or imagination'. This chapter addresses the *social meaning* of digital places, with particular attention to notions of identity, inclusion/exclusion, participation, belonging and power. More specifically it addresses how digital places explicitly shape our personal and collective identities in often unseen ways, as well as shaping opportunities for digital and offline citizenship.

The chapter opens with a consideration of the proliferation of digital places, which has normalised our interactions to such an extent that the influence of digital places on our identity construction is often overlooked. Digital places extend far beyond social media sites, and include virtually any device capable of transmitting information about your patterns of behaviour, including 'smart' devices (TVs, wearables, fridges) and even more banal devices such as garage-door openers. Collation of data from your digital interactions contributes to your algorithmic identity, which in turn has implications for issues of inclusion and exclusion. Using gaming as an example, I then examine the role of gender in both identity-making and inclusion. The discussion next shifts to consideration of belonging and participation in digital places, and the ways in which identity is shaped by individuals as well as by digital platforms. Finally, I consider issues of power in digital places, with consequences for individuals and for society writ large.

'Place' and 'space' have similar meanings and are ideas that are often used interchangeably. Both are sites that are understood through social meaning, but 'place' can be understood as being specifically bounded, whereas 'space' has less delineation in the way of rules, norms and conventions. Terminology such as 'virtual' spaces or 'online worlds' suggests that digital places are somehow separated out from reality and physical spaces, and therefore are not 'real' in the common-sense understanding (Taffel, 2017). Even the concept of a specifically 'digital' identity infers that it is fundamentally different from your 'real' identity. These types of discourses run contrary to the ideas presented in this book, which view identity as multifaceted, consisting of many threads that weave together (Burr, 2015). To address this disjunct between arbitrary divisions, such as the 'real' or offline worlds and digital environments, I begin by examining how the construction of identity in digital places incorporates both online and offline experiences.

Digital places and algorithmic identity construction

Let's imagine a scenario. On an average weekday morning over breakfast, you check your calorie intake on your Samsung smart fridge, then log onto Facebook and Instagram on your phone to check any likes or status updates. While sipping your morning coffee, you watch TV on Demand on your smart TV, while also skim-reading the local news on stuff.co.nz on your iPad, moving on to the international news through Al Jazeera or CNN. A glance at the weather outside necessitates a check of the forecast on metservice.co.nz, and you decide you'll take the train to work. On the way out you use your remote-control to open your garage door so that you can put the rubbish bin out for collection. At the train station you swipe your loyalty card at the kiosk and buy your lunch with Apple Pay. Once on the train you complain about the weather and the state of public transport on Twitter, then check out the cost of a textbook on amazon.com.

In the scenario above what has just happened (apart from being informed and entertained) is that you have unknowingly contributed to a burgeoning digital construction of your identity. Data about your movements, behaviours, preferences, political ideologies and social location is collected from your digital devices, including your fridge, TV and garage-door opener, your loyalty card, your train card, and every website you have visited. All of these separate portals to the digital 'you' are drawn from what is increasingly called the Internet of Things; referring to virtually any device that has radio-transmitting capabilities (Parker et al., 2016; Slee, 2015).

Your personal data then becomes separated out from the self and reconfigured into what Cheney-Lippold (2011) calls 'a new algorithmic identity' (p.165). In myriad unseen but interconnected databases your algorithmic identity has been updated, your identifying markers — such as age, gender, class, income bracket and ethnicity — have been logged, and parts of that algorithmically based identity have been sold to web-analytic organisations who categorise and parse your information into saleable categories. This convergence of data points enables a previously unseen level of hyper-connectivity, which means that your digital presence is almost continuously available for data mining.

The process of categorisation of personal and individual characteristics has the effect of separating these characteristics from the individual — the 'you-ness' of you — into a dissipated set of indices that are reconfigured into a group or population (Rouvroy & Stiegler, 2016). This process produces a paradox: individuals become dissociated from their individualising characteristics. As Deleuze (1992) describes, 'individuals have become "*dividuals*", and masses, samples, data, markets or "*banks*"' (p. 5). For digital commercial purposes it is not necessary to see you as a whole person. Different pieces of information about you are used for different purposes. You, under such algorithmic coding, have become a new identity: a saleable, commodifiable, repackaged, dissociated bundle of discrete data-points. 'You' are now a 'user'.

Inclusion and exclusion

All of this may sound somewhat contradictory to my opening comments that digital and offline identities weave together to make the whole 'you'. If the 'you' in digital places is just a bunch of separate, floating bits of data in cyberspace, how does that impact on identity and belonging? Your personal data has put you into a category. Cookies and software add-ons, such as application programming interfaces (APIs) that allow data sharing between webpages, aggregate this categorised information to provide users — you — with a variety of consumer choices.

You might ask, why does this even matter? After all, we all know that our online interactions are tracked, and don't the resulting 'tailored' ads just save us time by giving us choices we'll like? This point of view is reiterated through the rhetoric of digital platforms whose underlying logic is capital accumulation. Put another way, these digital corporations are just businesses whose focus is on making money, but they present themselves as cultural actors, emphasising the democratic, inclusive and benign characteristics of the internet (Langley & Leyshon, 2016). But, in this section, I hope to demonstrate that this process is not always about democratic choices, nor about free will, but rather about a more nuanced experience of inclusion and exclusion based on your identity markers.

This short YouTube video explains the use of application programming interfaces (APIs), and some privacy problems associated with their use: https://www.youtube.com/watch?v=OVvTv9Hy91Q

The Internet of Things

The Internet of Things (IoT) refers to the billions of devices and machines that can transmit information and connect over the internet or other communication systems. This includes obvious devices such as smartphones and smart TVs, as well as less obvious objects such as wearables, remote controls and home security systems. The advent of fibre broadband, and the availability of wearables and smart devices, have enabled the proliferation of the IoT.

On a wider scale, the IoT has enormous potential for connecting people and sharing and analysing data, resulting in improvements in manufacturing, healthcare, environmental issues, inventory control and transportation. On a personal level, the IoT facilitates everything from home security to garden watering to health and fitness regimes. A smart fridge can even assess your grocery purchases and alert you when particular items are running low.

However, the IoT relies on data sharing, and many IoT devices have weak security without encryption, leading to concerns about privacy; hackers are now targeting seemingly benign objects such as TVs and wearables. Other issues are also emerging. For instance, in 2018 a major security flaw came to light — US Army troops' movements at military bases in war zones were able to be tracked via the Fitbits worn by soldiers.

Let's go back to our hypothetical scenario. Imagine that you are planning a holiday to Queenstown. When you get home from work, you search flights on Air New Zealand, and over the next few days pop-up ads for bungy-jumping off the Kawarau Bridge, white-water rafting, cheap rental car options and a range of accommodation options populate your social media. Which options are presented to you, the user, are pre-configured choices based on your algorithmic identity.

This raises the question: What if algorithmic analysis not only pre-configures your choices, but it also *limits* them? Let me share a personal vignette to highlight this. My sister and I were arranging a holiday in Rarotonga. We video-called each other and used three accommodation search platforms in real time. Her search results returned luxury, resort-style accommodation, while mine were invariably cheap, dorm-style options (the outrage!). My sister's luxury choices didn't even appear on my searches, or, if they did, were buried 10 or 15 pages in. They had been effectively erased from my realm of possibilities. Even though my sister had not previously used two of the websites, her searches on those were consistently similar with the other platform's results. The platforms were clearly collating data from numerous other sites that inform our algorithmic identities.

This demonstrates that the impacts of algorithmically defined identity extend *beyond* the realm of the digital into the material existence of physical lives. They enable or restrict what options are available to you. It is through such processes that digital mediation has become the de facto method by which human experience, identity and understanding is increasingly defined (Martinez, 2012).

It's just a game, right?

Inclusion and exclusion extend far beyond mere purchasing choices and can have profound impacts on identity. Gaming sites serve as a useful example of this. In the past, video games and video gamers have received a relatively bad rap in both academic and popular discourse (Lorentz et al., 2015). However, with video gaming becoming a mainstream recreational activity, gaming is now being re-evaluated in terms of wellbeing, positive emotional and social functioning, and enhanced cognitive skill development. For example, one study found that participants who use multiple genders and ethnicities in online games develop a greater awareness of discrimination, and are able to develop critical thinking skills that enable problem-solving from multiple perspectives (Lee & Hoadley, 2007). Online multiplayer platforms allow for social development opportunities; relationships and friendships are formed, problems shared and skills developed (Earl, 2018). These outcomes are influential in encouraging users' participation in digital places concurrent with a sense of inclusion.

Despite these positive aspects, video games are also experienced as sites that reinforce gender stereotypes and exclude people from diverse communities. Video games tend to have heteronormative content, which is reflected in narrative-driven role-playing games (RPGs). The heteronormative content reinforces dominant social norms about gender that exclude or marginalise others. Game developers have traditionally been hesitant to include LGBQTIA+ options and narratives, mirroring mainstream media trends where socially disadvantaged, gender-diverse or ethnic minorities are less visible or are given problematic, stereotypical representation (Shaw, 2009).

Most game developers identify as heterosexual men, and therefore tend to produce games that reflect their own social location and gender relations. As a result, the dominant characters in RPGs tend to be hypermasculine, whereas female characters are often relegated to a subservient female role such as a sexualised 'damsel in distress' (Vorderer & Bryant, 2012). The subservient female role is often positioned as a 'prize' for the masculinised hero, whose task is to rescue her from the evil forces. These gender stereotypes exclude people whose personal identity threads don't conform to such bland representation.

In order to negotiate a sense of inclusion, LGBTQIA+ players strategise their game-playing (Krobová et al., 2015). Some gamers disconnect their LGBTQIA+ identity from their gaming identity, while others strategise to use the game queerly despite the dominant characters' gendered traits. This allows players to compensate for the lack of representation of LGBTQIA+ themes and thus identify with their characters more readily. Regardless of strategy, gender representation in gaming, and indeed in other digital places, remains an issue to be adequately addressed.

Belonging and participation in a digital world

Exclusion doesn't just happen in specific digital places such as gaming sites. Digital skills are a necessary part of contemporary life in Aotearoa New Zealand, and such skills are now often formed early in life. Growing up with digital access means some young people develop skills, information and experiences that may be advantageous to their belonging and participation in offline *and* online places. Others with restricted digital access may be excluded from this and thereby disadvantaged.

Research into the participation of 10–11-year-olds in the digital world in Aotearoa New Zealand suggests that participation in the digital world is both complex and evolving (Starkey et al., 2019). Three main issues emerge. First, access to the positive benefits of participation and skill development in digital technology is dependent on differential access. Gaps exist in household access, rural versus urban locations, and along ethnic groupings. Children can develop digital skills only if their educational and home environments provide access. Second, children at this age are strongly influenced by parents and teachers, so the contextual influences of these key figures have an impact on outcomes of digital participation. Third, participation is linked to outcomes such as access to benefits and inclusion in wider civic society.

Greater participation leads to greater feelings of familiarity and belonging. Children learn how to interact in digital places that cement their feelings of belonging, and this is reinforced by various aspects of digital life, such as gaming and interest groups, including community groups such as sports-club web pages and chat forums. Digital literacy can therefore enable users to access forums and groups online that may provide offline benefits. As a result, digital proficiency leads to a feedback loop that increases one's sense of belonging and participation in both offline and online contexts.

Similar data emerges from four large-scale surveys of New Zealanders from 2014 to 2018 (Digital Government New Zealand, 2021). The findings identify disparities in digital access across vectors such as age, ethnicity and disability. For example, in Aotearoa New Zealand internet access at home is relatively high at around 91 per cent of all households, but just 69 per cent of those in Housing NZ (now Kāinga Ora) or equivalent social housing, and just 71 per cent of those with disabilities, have access. These inequities matter: those without access tend to be more disengaged from civic engagement with society, have less sense of belonging, are less likely to vote or make submissions to government, and have a lower level of subjective wellbeing (Digital Government New Zealand, 2021).

When belonging goes bad

Digital culture has seen the proliferation of vast amounts of mediated content, catering for all kinds of niche communities and tastes. Whether you are interested in keto dieting, *Minecraft*, sustainable gardening or cute cat videos, there is a vast amount of material online to suit your interests, along with a community of people also interested in the same thing. These communities are distributed across the globe, and provide users with a ready supply of people to discuss, debate, comment and engage with you (Taffel, 2017). Access to information also facilitates access to like-minded people, and this can have positive benefits for community-building and allow groups to amplify their voice. The accessibility of information can be, and is, used for many positive purposes, such as social justice, ethics and efforts to mitigate climate change. Unfortunately, not all sites, nor all interests, are

ISTOCK

Video gaming

Gaming has variously been framed as time-wasting, non-productive or antisocial. However, academic study has demonstrated that video gaming can have a wide-ranging impact on wellbeing, from improving thinking skills to helping with pain management. It can also improve social connections, relieve stress and help players keep their minds active. The findings are not all positive, however. Concerns about gaming include sexualised depictions of women, bullying and harassment, sexual predators, and privacy and security issues.

benign. Access to information such as hate material incubates violence, harassment and terror, transcending digital places into physical places and impacting the lives of real human beings.

This was tragically demonstrated on 15 March 2019 when a terrorist walked into two mosques in Christchurch, opened fire with automatic weapons, and murdered 51 people and wounded 50 others. The terrorist live-streamed the murders on Facebook, and in advance had posted a 74-page 'manifesto' outlining his ideology and justification for the murders, which subsequently went viral on the dark web. He claims his identity as a white supremacist was formed on the dark web through connecting with others on internet chat groups, message boards and networks (Macklin, 2019). This example highlights how hate groups can shape identity and recruit members, with devastating consequences due to the scale and speed with which content can be uploaded and disseminated through digital places.

One consequence of this tragedy and the digital proliferation of offensive, violent or extremist content was an integrated cross-platform response called 'the Christchurch Call', initiated by Jacinda Ardern, prime minister of New Zealand. Initially spearheaded by New Zealand and France, the Christchurch Call is a commitment by governments, non-governmental organisations and tech companies to eliminate violent extremist content and terrorism online, and to limit the participation of extremist groups. The Call aims to address the circulation of hate propaganda while still maintaining the principles of 'free, open and secure internet, without compromising human rights and fundamental freedoms, including freedom of expression' (Christchurch Call, 2019). This is tricky ground to negotiate: freedom of expression in a digital sense has fewer constraints and more avenues than in the offline world, where adjacent social norms, rules and conventions shape behaviour and expressions of identity.

User-defined digital identities

One way in which digital identity is formed is by users' direct interaction with platforms. Video games provide an appropriate format to investigate user-defined digital identities, because gaming platforms provide a specific environment in which gamers can experiment and operationalise different identity markers. An estimated two out of three New Zealanders play some form of video game, over 98 per cent of homes with children have computer games, 73 per cent of players are aged over 18, and gendered use is more or less even, with 47 per cent of video gamers identifying as female (Brand et al., 2017).

For a more in-depth look at gaming and the New Zealanders who play, see the *Digital New Zealand Report, 2018*: https://www.igea.net/wp-content/uploads/2017/08/Digital-New-Zealand-2018-DNZ18-Full-1.pdf

Identity formation is evidenced through the ways that gamers use avatars. Avatars are digital representations of the gamer's virtual persona (Hébert et al., 2020). Gamers typically spend quite some time customising their avatar, which may include features such as gender, race, physical attributes, customisable voice tones, bodies and faces, and values. As such, avatars represent a range of possibilities for the self, and enable gamers to experiment with potential future outcomes of who they might become (aspirational avatars) or who they perceive themselves to be in real life (similarity avatars). The construction of self through avatars reveals that digital identity has the potential to shape offline identity and vice versa. The customisable aspect of avatars also provides avenues for gamers to learn about social interaction, discrimination and other social issues.

The curated self

Aside from avatars, digital identities are formed in other ways. Since the emergence of a technological innovation around 2006 called Web 2.0, users can create their own content on platforms with increased levels and improved degrees of interaction between parties (van Dijck, 2013). Prior to Web 2.0, the internet consisted of webpages that resembled glorified brochures. The functionality of Web 2.0 now allows users to upload personalised content and interact with others in real time across social media sites and communication technologies, in ways that allow users to feel as if they are in control of their representations. This innovation has had a profound effect on us in both explicit and implicit ways — and changes the ways that we experience life in the wider sense, not just the digital sense.

Occupational or work identity is an important aspect of individual identity. Increasingly, contemporary work life is characterised by precarity. This is often framed as flexibility, in the form of remote work, on-demand gig work, part-time and seasonal work, micro-entrepreneurship and contract work (Standing, 2011). Work flexibility has redefined the idea of 'freedom' in capitalist market terms (Fraser, 2016), and amplified the imperative to market one's *self* as a saleable commodity (Bauman, 2007).

This coincides with the rise of specific corporate and professional websites such as LinkedIn, where users curate and personalise their own work or professional identities. Because the job market is precarious, people use LinkedIn to promote themselves as a form of curriculum vitae. Moreover, because employers increasingly use LinkedIn to peruse suitable candidates' profiles, jobseekers are compelled to use LinkedIn to increase their visibility and attractiveness as a potential employee. This process is called 'network effects', referring to the state of enhanced competition that occurs when both sides of a market scale up to a point that to be viable the individual must be visible (Johnson, 2018). The effect of this is that sites such as LinkedIn become integral to the jobseeker. It becomes part of their 'place to stand' in the job market.

Earlier, I delineated between the concepts of place as being bounded, and space as being less constrained. A recent study of New Zealanders' use of LinkedIn highlights tensions between the understanding of digital *places* as distinct from digital *spaces* (Barnett, 2019). In some instances, the digital is perceived as a place; that is, bounded by conventions, norms and rules that shape expected behaviour and cater to specific occupants or audiences. LinkedIn is a good example of a digital place. In other instances, the digital is contrastingly experienced as 'space' — unbounded, disembodied and unregulated. Social media platforms such as Facebook or TikTok are examples of digital spaces.

Boundaries between social media *spaces* and professional *places* such as LinkedIn are permeable. People present different selves to different audiences on social media; how you interact on Facebook with close friends may be quite different to the socio-political conversations you engage with on Twitter, and different again to the polished professional profile you present on LinkedIn.

Digital places — because of their perceived boundedness, rules, norms and conventions — are inherently understood to be safe places. But because of the potential for personal data to leak across boundaries between place and space, digital places such as LinkedIn have also become sites of anxiety. On LinkedIn you are expected to adhere to the norms, rules and conventions that govern appropriate behaviour on the platform. However, LinkedIn users experience anxieties based on concerns around the personal and social risks associated with personal data that may be algorithmically linked to other digital spaces with little or no regulation or boundaries. You definitely don't want a potential employer to be confronted with images of that bawdy hens' night back in 2018! The point is not to highlight the differences between social media sites such as Facebook and LinkedIn, but to emphasise that context and boundaries are blurred in digital places in ways that do not often occur in physical places.

Despite these concerns, participants in the Barnett (2019) study spent considerable effort developing and curating their professional online identities.

Additionally, the imperative to network through LinkedIn (a global digital place) collides with the values of a particularly situated collective identity that is specifically connected to a physical place (Aotearoa New Zealand). The stereotypical New Zealand identity — or at least, the story we tell ourselves about our collective identity — is built on self-deprecating independence; we're not 'tall poppies'. We also draw collective identity values from 'the No. 8 wire attitude', indicating resourcefulness and a tendency to act independently. These values clash with the logics of networking as promoted by LinkedIn, which is based on self-promotion, tenuous but extensive connections to others, networking and leveraged support.

Platform-defined digital identities

As Ella outlines in Chapter 1, identity is both personal and social. In the same way that identity construction occurs by encounters with others in everyday life, the influence on identity by digital platforms is both powerful and pervasive. The evolution of digital technologies enables platforms to frame people as a set of discrete data points in ways that suit the logics of digital capitalism — that is, the logics of profit. Or, put another way, users (Deleuze's 'dividuals') become artefacts — products — of algorithmic data treatments (Pennell, 2019).

Digital places demand our uniqueness and specificity; we want, and are impelled, to stand out from the crowd (Dean, 2018). This underpins platform capitalism's demand for granular data, and is reinforced by platforms that enable users to track how many likes, comments or followers they have. (Hey, look how popular I am!) Think about this for a minute; Web 2.0 has allowed us to create and curate our digital selves — we upload text, blogs, photos, memes, YouTube videos and so on. While this may *seem* self-directed and 'free-choicy' what we're doing is *creating content*, and while you might think that you own your personal content, legally, you don't; the platform owns your information then disaggregates that data into categories. From that categorisation, digital platforms are uniquely placed to modulate user behaviours in subtle ways. As Beer (2008) outlines, the intrusion of digital technology leads 'to an increasingly mediated way of life with little if any unmediated room outside' (p. 521). In effect, digital technologies shape the behaviour of users into newly defined social norms in ways that blur the boundaries between offline and online identities.

An example of this modulation comes from Airbnb, a seemingly benign platform that connects hosts and guests in the holiday accommodation market. Airbnb positions its hosts as 'hospitality entrepreneurs' (Airbnb, 2019). Airbnb's subtext is that economic success is dependent on following the demands of the platform ever more closely in terms of availability, price, presentation and behaviour. Those that do are rewarded with a digital 'badge' naming them as a 'Superhost'; those that don't are subject to sanctions.

By framing hosts as entrepreneurs, Airbnb hooks into an emotive dimension of identity. Entrepreneurs are highly regarded in our society as exemplars of self-made success, understood to be innovative, to enjoy financial freedom and to deserve respect. As critical thinkers, you'll recognise that the trope of entrepreneurship is somewhat of a myth, but myths are just stories, and, as will be discussed in Part 4, stories carry enormous power. Unsurprisingly, Airbnb hosts buy into the myth of entrepreneurship. After all, who doesn't want to be successful, innovative, respected, financially free and a Superhost to boot? Except hosts don't own their business — Airbnb does — and they don't have financial freedom. The average Airbnb host in New Zealand earned a mere $4400 per year in 2018 (O'Mahoney et al., 2018). Scholars have named this type of work 'subsistence entrepreneurship', because of the precariousness of the work and the subsistence earnings (Ravenelle, 2017, p. 284).

Despite this (and nudged along by Airbnb), hosts work really hard to align with the identity of a 'Superhost' entrepreneur. In research conducted on 28 Airbnb hosts in Aotearoa New Zealand, participants describe a range of adjusted behaviours since becoming hosts (Pennell, 2019). Regardless of wide diversity among hosts (ages 30 to 70, varied personal circumstances, such as single, partnered, flatting, dependent children, a 70/30 female/male gender split and a range of ethnic identifications), hosts display remarkably similar behaviours that demonstrate how effectively they adopt the subjectivity of 'hospitality entrepreneur' at the expense of their previous ways of living.

For example, all hosts report that they don't let friends or family visit when they have guests, have spent considerable money upgrading the 'business' part of the house, offer free goods and services in addition to the room price in the hope of gaining good ratings from guests, self-identify as entrepreneurs or business owners, and report significant changes in their daily routines that privilege Airbnb over their personal or family needs. The privileging of the identity of host over other identity threads is evident; one hosting couple won't let their grandchildren stay overnight, 'ever', because it's 'not fair on the guests'. Another couple move out of their home into an old caravan so that guests have full use of the house, and another whose small historic cottage has one bathroom, sets up a portable toilet in her garage for her personal use so that guests have sole use of the bathroom facilities.

The direct influence of digital platforms is evident in the ways people change their behaviours to form attachment to specific identity markers. In other words, digital platforms can shape behaviour in specific ways. Often, the influence of digital technology is obscured because users (in the above case, hosts) willingly adopt the pre-configured identity traits set by the platform in pursuit of an idealised self. Platforms set specific guidelines to ensure that users participate in ways that suit the goals of the platform. Guidelines for participation are crafted around ideas of collective identity. Play by the rules and you're one of the team! In other words, digital platforms operate their own eco-systems of control, and hold the power to shape identity, participation, belonging and, indeed, citizenship.

Digital places, power and citizenship

Power is the capacity to bring about consequences (Boulding, 1989). The owners of data hold enormous power in society, yet that power is by and large hidden from view. The sheer velocity of information generated by users becomes collated into 'big data'. This big data, coupled with the ability of algorithms to spread and amplify certain messages, leads to the pervasive belief that information generated from this collected repository of user-generated data is some sort of *a priori,* unassailable fact or truth, yet these individual bits of data often represent ideas or opinions, not hard and fast 'facts'. Digital platforms have the power to control who sees what content, which messages gain mass circulation, and which ideas get amplified or suppressed. As Nick Srnicek (2017) has observed, 'far from being the mere owners of information, these companies are becoming owners of the infrastructures of society' (p. 92).

This is certainly the case with Facebook, which is one of the largest tech companies in the world. It has become 'the central bank of social capital' and encompasses individuals, cultural, political and commercial groups, resulting in a concentration of extreme power over social and political life (Schwarz, 2019, p. 123). Facebook has been likened to an empire — that is, more of a political and economic state than a company — and is already recognised as a security issue for many nation states because of its corporate and political surveillance, secrecy surrounding regulation, and monopoly business practice, including its current consideration of a move into cryptocurrency, thus threatening stock markets, banking systems and currency exchange globally (Andrews, 2020). As Leighton Andrews (2020) notes, the real power centre of Facebook is its vertical integration as a social media network, a media distribution company, a media buying company, an advertising exchange or platform, an advertising agency and a data analytics company; its horizontally integrated data exchanges between Facebook, WhatsApp, Messenger and Instagram; and the ability of advertisers to sell across the Facebook companies (p. 98).

Facebook governs its users by enforcing codes of conduct through surveillance methods. These methods include algorithmically monitored content coupled with users reporting on other users, algorithmic governance which censors content according to Facebook's own logics, and the threat of exclusion (Schwarz, 2019). As a result, Facebook's governance rules are secretive, subject to change without consultation, and unpredictable. The consequences are widespread. For example:

1. Political processes and elections are undermined through issues such as fake news.
2. It creates the potential for manipulation of digital media, such as occurred in the Cambridge Analytica scandal, which, aside from influencing the outcomes of multiple elections across the globe, potentially affected over 64,000 New Zealander's Facebook accounts (Reidy, 2018).
3. Social issues are amplified or suppressed (climate change, misinformation on political, social and health issues, Covid-19 vaccination information and misinformation).
4. Citizenship is undermined (through processes of inclusion and exclusion and the enactment of power).
5. Social life is commoditised (through targeted advertising, social media influencers and the mobilisation of followers).

Additional consequences of power in digital places are evident in data discrimination that exacerbates social problems and entrenches inequalities, thus impacting opportunities for equal citizenship among users. Scholars dismantle the idea that search engines like Google are neutral repositories of information. For instance, white experiences are privileged over those experienced by people of colour (Noble, 2018). In particular, representations of women of colour are often sexualised or presented as evidence of criminality or poverty. These types of negative stereotyping perpetuate oppression and lead to racial and gender profiling.

Read the article and watch the presentation from Joy Buolamwini, whose own experiences of gendered facial (mis-)recognition led her to investigate gender bias in artificial intelligence (AI): https://news.mit.edu/2018/study-finds-gender-skin-type-bias-artificial-intelligence-systems-0212

Whenever cases of demonstrable data marginalisation emerge, the companies involved routinely claim that they are not responsible for the algorithms and accompanying harm, but are working to fix them (Noble, 2018). Even significant policy adjustments because of public pressure — such as Facebook's identity policy change to allow stage identities of drag queens — are framed as 'corrections' of enforcement mistakes (Andrews, 2020). This raises questions of why this marginalisation of groups occurs, how stereotypes are reproduced and amplified in the first place, and what the resulting harms are.

The mathematical formulae that underpin computer code are written by living, breathing people. People, as we know, come with all sorts of inherent biases and value systems that reflect their own worldviews. The implications of these types of inbuilt biases are profound, not least because the organisations that use information — from schools through to governments — are increasingly reliant on web-based technologies that are owned by powerful digital corporations, and, as discussed, big data is not neutral. As Giles Deleuze (1992) has said, 'We are taught that corporations have a soul, which is the most terrifying news in the world' (p. 6). This raises serious questions about the political, social and economic consequences of the use of such data without checks and balances.

A chilling example comes from research on data bias in artificial intelligence (AI), particularly facial recognition (Raji et al., 2020). This research tested three major platforms — Microsoft, Amazon and Clarifai — for accuracy in gender classification and facial recognition. The results demonstrate significant demographical bias in the algorithms, which consistently misrepresent or mis-identify people of colour; a bias that is even more evident for females of colour. Evidence of demographical bias in AI algorithms has moral and ethical implications for organisations that regularly use AI, such as law enforcement and immigration. The inherent biases in code that amplify discrimination of racial, ethnic, gender and political dimensions can expose entire groups of people to over-policing or additional profiling. These ramifications have serious implications for society as a whole and for distinct groups of society particularly, especially those who are already marginalised by structural disadvantage.

Conclusion

Thinking about digital places requires us to consider how our technologically mediated activities impact our ongoing performances of identity and sense of belonging. Development of digital skills and participation in digital places have crossover effects into civic, political and social engagement, and can enhance wellbeing and a sense of belonging. However, the blurring of boundaries between offline and online worlds means that barriers to inclusion, such as gender stereotypes and social biases, are also replicated in digital spaces.

Digital identity, much like offline identity, is both personal and social, and is both user-defined and shaped by the digital places that one inhabits. Users have the ability to curate their own identities through personalised content, while simultaneously digital platforms, through categorisations of individuals as 'dividuals', place users into pre-defined categories or populations, a process that enables platforms to create specific subject-positions that modulate and regulate behaviour.

Digital places are also sites of power that allow surveillance to penetrate aspects of our lives that were previously deemed to be private and personal, as well as influence social and political realms. The sheer scale of some digital tech companies, coupled with their secrecy around code and algorithmic analysis, means that these companies wield extreme power to shape the personal, social and political lives of citizens with minimal regulatory oversight. This has serious implications for issues of freedom, citizenship and social justice.

Awareness of how power operates in digital places, what influences the construction of identity, and the implications of these processes on the lived experiences of people enables us to make informed choices and ask probing questions of the ways in which place, self and society interact. Digital places then, are important sites for understanding key elements of identity, belonging and citizenship in the twenty-first century.

Chapter 9 — Digital places: Identity, participation and power:
http://turangawaewae.massey.ac.nz/ch9.html

Further reading

Cheney-Lippold, J. (2011). A new algorithmic identity: Soft biopolitics and the modulation of control. *Theory, Culture and Society, 28*(6), 164–181. https://doi.org/10.1177/0263276411424420

Dean, J. (2018). Collective desire and the pathology of the individual. *Journal for Cultural and Religious Theory, 17*(1), 36–49.

Fuchs, C. (2021). *Social media: A critical introduction* (3rd ed.). Sage.

References

Airbnb. (2019). *About us.* https://press.airbnb.com/about-us

Andrews, L. (2020). *Facebook, the media and democracy: Big tech, small state?* Routledge.

Barnett, S. J. (2019). Digital me in a virtual world: Identity construction on LinkedIn by Aotearoa/New Zealand entrepreneurial professionals. In *Proceedings of the IADIS International Conference on Web Based Communities* (pp. 333–343). IADIS Press.

Bauman, Z. (2007). *Consuming life.* Polity Press.

Beer, D. (2008). Social network(ing) sites . . . revisiting the story so far: A response to Danah Boyd & Nicole Ellison. *Journal of Computer-Mediated Communication, 13*(2), 516–529. https://doi.org/10.1111/j.1083-6101.2008.00408.x

Boulding, K. (1989). *Three faces of power.* Sage.

Brand, J., Todhunter, S., & Jervis, J. (2017). *Digital New Zealand report 2018.* http://www.igea.net/wp-content/uploads/2017/08/Digital-New-Zealand-2018-DNZ18-Full-1.pdf

Burr, V. (2015). *Social constructionism* (3rd ed.). Routledge.

Cheney-Lippold, J. (2011). A new algorithmic identity: Soft biopolitics and the modulation of control. *Theory, Culture and Society, 28*(6), 164–181. https://doi.org/10.1177/0263276411424420

Christchurch Call. (2019). https://www.christchurchcall.com/call.html

Dean, J. (2018). Collective desire and the pathology of the individual. *Journal for Cultural and Religious Theory, 17*(1), 36–49.

Deleuze, G. (1992). Postscript on the societies of control. *October, 59*, 3–7.

Digital Government New Zealand. (2021). *Digital inclusion and wellbeing in New Zealand.* https://www.digital.govt.nz/dmsdocument/161~digital-inclusion-and-wellbeing-in-new-zealand/html

Earl, R. (2018). Video game use as a tool for assessing and intervening with identity formation and social development in family therapy. *Australian and New Zealand Journal of Family Therapy*, *39*, 5–20. https://doi.org/10.1002/anzf.1282

Fraser, N. (2016). Contradictions of capital and care. *New Left Review*, *100*(July–August), 99–117.

Hébert, T. P., Wood, S. M., & Szymanski, A. (2020). 'The me I want you to see': The use of video game avatars to explore identity in gifted adolescents. *Gifted Child Today*, *43*(2), 124–134. https://doi.org/10.1177/1076217519898217

Johnson, N. (2018, 5 February). What are network effects? *Applico*. https://www.applicoinc.com/blog/network-effects

Krobová, T., Moravec, O., & Švelch, J. (2015). Dressing Commander Shepard in pink: Queer playing in heteronormative game culture. *Cyberpsychology: Journal of Psychosocial Research on Cyberspace*, *9*(3), Article 3. https://doi.org/10.5817/CP2015-3-3

Langley, P., & Leyshon, A. (2016). Platform capitalism: The intermediation and capitalisation of digital economic circulation. *Finance and Society*, *3*(1), 11–31.

Lee, J., & Hoadley, C. (2007). Leveraging identity to make learning fun: Possible selves and experiential learning in Massively Multiplay Online Games (MMOGs). *Innovate: Journal of Online Education*, *3*(6), Article 5. https://nsuworks.nova.edu/innovate/vol3/iss6/5

Lorentz, P., Ferguson, C. J., & Schott, G. R. (2015). Special issue: Experience and benefits of game playing. *Cyberspace: Journal of Psychosocial Research on Cyperspace*, *9*(3), Article 1. https://doi.org/0.5817/CP2015-3-1

Macklin, G. (2019). The Christchurch attacks: Livestream terror in the viral video age. *CTC Sentinel, 12*(6), 18–29.

Martinez, M. (2012). Communication, technology, temporality. *Communication +1, 1*(1), Article 5. https://doi.org/10.7275/R56H4FBZ

Mead, H. M., & Grove, N. (2003). *Ngā pēpeha a ngā tīpuna* (2nd ed.). Victoria University Press.

Noble, S. U. (2018). *Algorithms of oppression: How search engines reinforce racism*. NYU Press.

O'Mahoney, J., Meade, L., Hill, A., Kilkelly, M., Alvaro, E., & Burgess, B. (2018). *Economic effects of Airbnb in New Zealand*. https://press.airbnb.com/wp-content/uploads/sites/4/2018/05/dae-economic-contribution-Airbnb-new-zealand.pdf

Parker, G., Van Alstyne, M., & Choudary, S. (2016). *Platform revolution: How networked markets are transforming the economy — and how to make them work for you*. W. W. Norton.

Pennell, S. M. (2019). *Trouble in paradise: Contradictions in platform capitalism and the production of surplus by Airbnb hosts in regional tourist towns*. [Doctoral dissertation, Massey University]. Semantic Scholar. https://mro.massey.ac.nz/handle/10179/15803

Raji, I. D., Gebru, T., Mitchell, M., Buolamwini, J., Lee, J., & Denton, E. (2020). Saving face: Investigating the ethical concerns of facial recognition auditing. In *Proceedings of the 2020 AAAI/ACM Conference on AI, Ethics, and Society (AIES '20), February 7–8, 2020, New York, NY. USA*. ACM. https://doi.org/10.1145/3375627.3375820

Ravenelle, A. J. (2017). Sharing economy workers: Selling, not sharing. *Cambridge Journal of Regions, Economy and Society, 10*(2), 281–295. https://doi.org/10.1093/cjres/rsw043

Reidy, M. (2018). Cambridge Analytica 'misuse' may affect nearly 64,000 Kiwis, Facebook says. *Stuff*. https://www.stuff.co.nz/business/102928825/Cambridge-Analytica-misuse-may-affect-nearly-64-000-Kiwis-Facebook-says

Rouvroy, A., & Stiegler, B. (2016). The digital regime of truth: From algorithmic governmentality to a new rule of law. *La Deleuziana — Online Journal of Philosophy, 3*, 6–27.

Schwarz, O. (2019). Facebook rules: Structures of governance in digital capitalism and the control of generalized social capital. *Theory, Culture and Society, 36*(4), 117–141.

Shaw, A. (2009). Putting the gay in games: Cultural production and GLBT content in video games. *Games and Culture, 4*(3), 228–253. https://doi.org/10.1177/1555412009339729

Slee, T. (2015). *What's yours is mine: Against the sharing economy*. OR Books.

Srnicek, N. (2017). *Platform capitalism*. Polity Press.

Standing, G. (2011). *The precariat: The new dangerous class*. Bloomsbury Academic.

Starkey, L., Eppel, E. A., & Sylvester, A. (2019). How do 10-year-old New Zealanders participate in a digital world? *Information, Communication and Society, 22*(13), 1929–1944. https://doi.org/10.1080/1369118X.2018.1472795

Taffel, S. (2017). Digital places: Globalising identity and citizenship. In T. Cain, E. Kahu, & R. Shaw (Eds.), *Tūrangawaewae: Identity and belonging in Aotearoa New Zealand* (pp. 185–203). Massey University Press.

van Dijck, J. (2013). *The culture of connectivity: A critical history of social media*. Oxford University Press.

Vorderer, P., & Bryant, J. (2012). *Playing video games: Motives, responses, and consequences*. Routledge.

PART FOUR:
STORIES OF AOTEAROA NEW ZEALAND

Stories
Introduction

Ella Kahu

Welcome to the last section of the book, the key purpose of which is to critically engage with three major national narratives that make particular assertions about national identity in Aotearoa New Zealand, and examine the ways in which we New Zealanders represent ourselves both to each other and to the wider world.

About Part 4

In Part 1 we explored who makes up our nation, in Part 2 we looked at how those diverse peoples use their voices to participate and have a say in our communities, and then in Part 3 we explored how the places in which we interact with others shape our identities. Now we take a step back and look at how those identities, voices and places are shaped in part by the wider national narratives we tell ourselves (and others) about what it means to be a New Zealander.

Our national identity is more than just our history: 'The facts of history are the bare bones of nationhood; it is in the fleshing out of facts into narratives of meaning that a people are forged' (Liu et al., 2005, p. 13). As British sociologist Duncan Bell (2003) says, those narratives 'tell a particular type of story about the nation and its importance, a story that resonates emotively with people, that glorifies the nation, that is easily transmitted and absorbed' (p. 67). National narratives are important and powerful: they shape our social norms and our view of our world, they include or exclude certain groups, and perhaps most importantly, they impact on who feels they belong in this place and who feels they do not. National stories often grow from a kernel of truth, but, as the following chapters illustrate, that kernel is surrounded by layers of fiction.

Here in Part 4, we explicitly address three of our national narratives (or stories), and the ways in which individuals both reproduce (for example, through language, rituals and behaviour) and have their identities shaped by these stories. The conceptual template underpinning these chapters is as follows:

1. We look at the nature and origins of each narrative. What is the story, and what messages does each convey? Here we are interested in teasing out the historical, political, economic and social contexts from which our chosen narratives have emerged.
2. We ask: What are the purposes of the narratives? To what ends are they deployed?
3. We explore how these grand, sweeping national stories are propagated and maintained. How are they communicated and reinforced? What have been some of the past and present struggles over the claims to 'truth' and the degrees of accuracy contained within these narratives?
4. For each of the three national stories, we examine the material, social, political and economic consequences for people and for our shared national identity.
5. Finally, we compare the narrative with empirical evidence and circumstance, and explore alternative stories that are marginalised or masked by the dominant narrative. We will pose such questions as: Is the story 'real' for everyone? What (or who) has been left out of the national story?

Overview of chapters

So what are the stories that we tell about our nation? About this place? Any nation has multiple narratives, and choosing three was not easy. There are other stories that are just as strong and have equally important impacts on our national identity: 'New Zealand is a great place to raise kids' or 'We are all one people' are two such examples. We are confident, however, that the three narratives we have selected — New Zealand is an equal society, New Zealand is clean and green, and Anzac as our nation's creation story — will resonate, albeit in different ways, with many New Zealanders.

In Chapter 10, David Littlewood tackles the story that New Zealand is a country where everyone is treated equally. He traces the history of this view from the promises made to early British settlers, to the implementation of social security

STORIES: INTRODUCTION   225

systems by the Labour Government in the 1930s, to the reduction of those supports during the neoliberal reforms of the 1980s. Critically, David distinguishes between equality of opportunity and equality of outcome, and highlights that outcomes were not, and are still not, equal for all identities. Today, Aotearoa New Zealand is far from equal, with Māori and Pasifika peoples disadvantaged by most measures, massively uneven income and wealth distributions, and some of the world's worst rates of child poverty. For all that, the equality narrative persists, and is used to justify the argument that any differences between people are down to individual choices and responsibility.

Next, Juliana Mansvelt, in Chapter 11, looks at a story that is, among other things, the backbone of marketing campaigns aimed at selling New Zealand to the world: Clean and Green. Like equality, our clean, green image stems initially from early British settlers contrasting New Zealand to their homeland. Juliana highlights the multiple purposes of this narrative — as a source of national pride, and as an economic tool that supports both tourism and our agricultural export industry. She then looks closely at the evidence for the truth of the narrative: is New Zealand as clean and green as we like to think? Her conclusions remind us that national identity narratives are not always strongly grounded in fact.

Finally, we end this section on the shores of Gallipoli, where, according to some, our national identity was first founded. In Chapter 12, Helen Dollery and Carl Bradley explore the Anzac narrative. They look at significant engagements in New Zealand's military history, including those wars that took place here at home, and examine both how that history has been shaped by other aspects of our national identity, and what the Anzac story tells us about New Zealand. Crucially, they also ask what is missing from the story, and — paralleling the exclusions evident in the story of equality — highlight that this narrative has been dominated by masculine, monocultural views and experiences. However, the Anzac narrative is continuing to evolve, widening to give greater voice to the experiences of those who have been silenced, including pacifists and conscientious objectors.

Conclusion

Tūrangawaewae is intended to encourage you to think critically about the assumptions we all carry regarding identity and belonging in Aotearoa New Zealand. Our main focus in this final section is to explicitly develop your understanding of how non-material factors help shape the world. In earlier sections of the book we tended to look at the material dimensions of identity, such as demography, place, historical events and so forth. In this section we look at the profound influence that words can have when they are strung together into compelling stories.

There is a second and quite subtle purpose to this section. By studying how narrative (or storytelling) functions, we will directly address how we made sense of and attribute meaning to the content we covered in the earlier sections on faces, voices and places. That is, as you read through these final chapters, we encourage you to think critically about how those topics were framed through particular choices of words, and about the contestability and consequences of such framing.

This final section moves our lens wider and looks not just at individual identity but also at national identity. The three narratives we analyse provide examples of the ways in which the particular stories we tell about ourselves shape our collective sense of self and place. It is often taken as given that to be a New Zealander means to live in a nation that treats people fairly, that has a pristine environment and that has a proud history on the world military stage. Many of us wear these stories almost as badges of pride, particularly when we are overseas or talking about this place to others; they can literally define what it means to be a New Zealander. But these stories mask both the lived experiences of some groups in our society, and other narratives we might tell about ourselves. And what does *that* say about our national identity?

References

Bell, D. S. (2003). Mythscapes: Memory, mythology, and national identity. *The British Journal of Sociology, 54*(1), 63–81. https://doi.org/10.1080/0007131032000045905

Liu, J. H., McCreanor, T., McIntosh, T., & Teaiwa, T. (2005). Introduction: Constructing New Zealand identities. In J. H. Liu, T. McCreanor, T. McIntosh, & T. Teaiwa (Eds.), *New Zealand identities: Departures and destinations* (pp. 11–20). Victoria University Press.

10.
We're all equal here
Ideals of equality

David Littlewood

Mā mua ka kite a muri, mā muri ka ora a mua.
Those who lead give sight to those who follow,
those who follow give life to those who lead.

This whakataukī can be elaborated to say that a leader will not be a leader without those who are willing to trust them and listen to them. In Māori society, a rangatira (chief) has a responsibility to act on behalf of what is best for the collective, and if they are not acting appropriately they will come up against opposition from their people and may lose their social licence to lead. Therefore, everybody is an important part of the community, from those who are seen out in front to those who are working out the back.

He tirohanga Māori: A Māori perspective

Te Rā Moriarty

Now, let's talk about something a bit uncomfortable — equality. Or what is, for Māori, inequality. Many statistics highlight that Māori in Aotearoa do not experience equality. For instance, in the justice system: in 2014, Māori made up just over 45 per cent of total apprehensions by the police at 71,621 of 156,029 (Stats NZ, 2014) and over half of the total prison population at 52.5 per cent in 2021 (Department of Corrections, 2021). Yet Māori make up just 16.7 per cent of the population of Aotearoa. Māori life expectancy is 77.1 years for females and 73.4 for males. For non-Māori, it is 84.4 for females and 80.9 for males (Stats NZ, 2021). I could go on and cite differences in health outcomes, wealth and education, for example.

Being treated unfairly has been felt by Māori since the nineteenth century. During that time, a range of legislation was passed that specifically targeted and disadvantaged Māori. The Suppression of Rebellion Act 1863 and the Maori Prisoners Trials Act 1879 were discussed in Chapter 2. These were intended to confiscate land and to imprison Māori without trial indefinitely. The preamble to the Maori Prisoners Trials Act 1879 states 'that the ordinary course of law should be suspended and the trial for such Natives should take place under special legislation'. The Tohunga Suppression Act 1907 explicitly intended to outlaw a very important figure in Māori society, the tohunga. The tohunga was an expert in many kaupapa of te ao Māori. They were responsible for conducting important rituals, retaining whakapapa, teaching, healing, interpreting astronomy, and anything that required expertise. In the same year, the Native Land Settlement Act 1907 required Māori land considered by Government Commissioners to be 'unoccupied or not profitably occupied' to be vested in a Maori Land Board, whereupon half of that land was to be sold and the other half leased. Other more recent legislation has also impacted on Māori equality. For instance, the government's pepper-potting policy of the 1950s and1960s sought to assimilate Māori into Pākehā culture and to keep whānau separate from each other as they migrated from the countryside to urban centres (Durie, 2019).

What can be seen from the examples presented here is the targeting of Māori by the Crown through specific legislation and government policy, and through ongoing institutionalised bias. This inequality has a whakapapa starting from Crown attempts to alienate land from Māori to sell to the settler population. This, then, is also the whakapapa of the foundations of our nation, New Zealand.

Introduction

In his foreword to a recent centenary history of the New Zealand Labour Party, then leader Andrew Little (2016) asserted that the defining attribute of the party has been its efforts to 'promote greater equality of opportunity' for all New Zealanders (p. 9). Whether true or not, the fact Little chose to emphasise this particular ideal is highly significant. It demonstrates the continued resonance of one of the most influential narratives in Aotearoa New Zealand's post-1840 history: that this is a country where everyone is treated equally. However, formal definitions of 'equality' refer not just to the opportunities people have in life, but also to the outcomes they experience as a result — especially their income, wealth and power within society. As Little's wording suggests, New Zealanders have consistently attached more importance to a perceived equality of *opportunity* than to an equality of *outcome.*

This chapter examines the origins, accuracy and impacts of the notion that 'we're all equal here'. It begins by investigating why the concept first developed, before outlining three periods that enshrined it as a cornerstone of Aotearoa New Zealand's national identity. The chapter then looks at how the equality narrative has since been undermined, to the point where it now bears only a passing resemblance to reality. The final section considers the ongoing consequences of the narrative for different social and ethnic groups.

A foundational narrative

The idea that equality is a defining feature of Aotearoa New Zealand society emerged during the early stages of European settlement. After the signing of Te Tiriti o Waitangi in 1840, the new colony's administrators wanted to attract as many British immigrants as possible. Yet their efforts ran up against a major obstacle. Victorian Britain was one of the wealthiest and most industrialised nations in the world, whereas Aotearoa New Zealand was a long and expensive voyage away, had little European infrastructure, and faced competition for immigrants from the more established colonies in Canada and Australia. It quickly became apparent that Britons would only relocate to Aotearoa New Zealand in large numbers if doing so were made a more attractive proposition.

Over the ensuing decades, Aotearoa New Zealand's administrators arranged for a vast quantity of propaganda to be targeted at potential immigrants. While these publications refrained from suggesting the colony possessed an equality of income, it was marketed as being free from the extremes of wealth and poverty, and from the rigid class divisions, that had come to afflict Britain. By moving to New Zealand, the literature promised, individuals from all social backgrounds would be guaranteed a fair opportunity at 'getting on'. If they worked hard and acted responsibly, they would be able to obtain a better standard of living and achieve social advancement (Belich, 1996).

See the Te Ara encyclopedia section on 'British immigration and the New Zealand Company', which includes images of posters and adverts: www.teara.govt.nz/en/history-of-immigration/page-3

An enduring narrative

The maintenance of this narrative can largely be attributed to the policies enacted during three periods. From 1890, the Liberal Government sought to enhance the opportunities for ordinary people to improve their circumstances. This involved state interventions in the market and imposing restrictions on what some property owners could do with their possessions. By the time the Liberals lost power in 1912, they had broken up and redistributed several large land holdings; introduced a graduated income tax; provided low-interest loans to help settlers purchase their own land; and set up a state-administered old age pension. The Liberals' most famous measure was enacted in 1893, when Aotearoa New Zealand became the first country to grant women the right to vote in parliamentary elections (Hamer, 1988). This extensive programme of reforms helped to restore public faith in the equality ideal and became a source of considerable national pride. Aotearoa New Zealand again began to market itself as a 'workingman's paradise', and also adopted the mantle of the 'world's social laboratory' (Belich, 2001).

Equality became further cemented in the national psyche during the South African War and the First World War. These conflicts were the first time that large bodies of New Zealanders travelled overseas, and the first time they were able to compare themselves directly with their British counterparts. Many scorned the deference to authority displayed by some working-class British soldiers, and particularly loathed the pompous manners and attitudes of the upper-class British officers. Letters home frequently asserted that the Anzacs' 'superior' military performance was due to the more equal relationships that existed within their units (Harper, 2015). Such accounts illustrate the strong links between two of Aotearoa New Zealand's national stories — equality and the Anzac narrative.

The equality narrative received its strongest reinforcement during the late 1930s. To avoid any repeat of the hardship caused by the Great Depression, the First Labour Government was determined to manage the economy in a way that would allow healthy people to find work at wages that provided a 'decent' standard of living. The central plank of this agenda was 'full employment', to which end the government took control of monetary policy, and introduced guaranteed prices and import restrictions to protect domestic industries. A wide-ranging social security system of state-provided housing, free healthcare, free education and means-tested benefits was also made available to all citizens as of right (Franks & McAloon, 2016). On reviewing this raft of reforms and the attitudes they had fostered, American political scientist Leslie Lipson suggested that if the New Zealanders were to erect their own version of the Statue of Liberty on the Waitematā Harbour in Auckland, it would surely be named the 'Statue of Equality' (Lipson, 1948).

Equality has been an important part of Aotearoa New Zealand's self-identity ever since. Labour lost power in 1949 and enjoyed only two more terms in office over the next 35 years. Nonetheless, the intervening National governments accepted the major economic and social initiatives that had been introduced — particularly 'full employment' and extensive social security provisions — meaning they remained in place until 1984. Even after the profound changes initiated during that year, notions of equality have continued to find regular expression in politics, media and language. The National Party's 1990 election campaign banner signalled its intention to uphold 'A Decent Society', while the claim Pākehā and Māori enjoy 'the best race relations in the world' still holds considerable appeal. New Zealanders tend to portray themselves as inherently sceptical of authority figures, as disliking conspicuous displays of wealth, and as being scornful of anybody who 'talks themselves up' too much — the negative reaction to which is often referred to as 'tall poppy syndrome'.

The narrative qualified

However, some commentators assert that equality in Aotearoa New Zealand has always been a myth. One of the leading figures in European colonisation, New Zealand Company director Edward Gibbon Wakefield, explicitly desired the new society to be based around traditional rural classes, with a land-owning aristocracy supported by small farmers and labourers. A rigid hierarchy certainly existed on the ships that brought the first European immigrants, with cabins at the top for the richer passengers and steerage below for the working people who received assisted passage. If the social structures that developed in Aotearoa New Zealand

ALEXANDER TURNBULL LIBRARY, PUBL-0009

Selling paradise

The New Zealand Company was a commercial venture set up to colonise New Zealand, thereby helping relieve the burden of overcrowding in nineteenth-century industrial-era Britain. Investors were promised 100 acres of farmland, but they needed labourers to work the land. An advertising campaign sold New Zealand as 'a Britain of the South', free from class tension and with a good climate; the inconvenient fact that the land was already possessed by Māori or covered in bush was not mentioned. Free passage was offered to people with specific skills, such as mechanics and agricultural labourers, and the Company utilised paintings featuring idyllic scenery, like this one of Wellington Harbour by Charles Heaphy, to attract the new colonists.

were looser than both of these models, there were still significant income disparities and an identifiable commercial and agricultural elite (McAloon, 2002).

Even the reforms implemented during the 'golden eras' of equality were designed to produce better outcomes for certain people. As economist Brian Easton (2020) puts it, 'Jack may have been as good as his master, but what about Haki? What about Jill?' (p. 608). While the Liberal Government strove to enhance opportunities for Pākehā, it simultaneously acquired an additional 3.2 million acres of Māori land, often via underhand or coercive methods. When large numbers of Māori subsequently moved to urban areas following the Second World War, poverty and discrimination forced them into poor-quality accommodation and poorly paid work. Likewise, the First Labour Government's goals of 'full employment' and reasonable wages must be set against the fact that many women were still struggling to find jobs during the 1950s, and invariably received much lower pay when they did so (Nolan, 2007).

These caveats are undoubtedly significant. However, they should be viewed alongside the overall picture. From the 1950s to the early 1980s, the degree of income inequality in Aotearoa New Zealand declined, for Māori and women as well as for Pākehā and men, at a rate exceeding the global average. Indeed, the share of pre-tax income received by the top 1 per cent of earners reached an all-time low during 1984 (Rashbrooke, 2013). So, while Aotearoa New Zealand has never been an equal society, it did used to possess a *greater degree* of equality than most other countries.

The narrative undermined

By the 1980s, the economic and social structures established by the First Labour Government were coming under strain. The oil shocks of the 1970s proved particularly damaging to Aotearoa New Zealand, where they coincided with a reduction in agricultural exports to Britain when the latter joined the European Economic Community. As revenue fell and inflation surged, governments remained committed to subsidising domestic industries and funding expensive social security programmes. As a consequence, the country's debt ballooned and its reserves of foreign currency reached dangerously low levels.

These issues fuelled discontent within sections of society. Many bankers, professionals and large business owners were tired of Aotearoa New Zealand's web of regulations, and cast envious glances at the neoliberal agenda being implemented in the United Kingdom and the United States. This philosophy called for government expenditure and involvement in the market to be significantly reduced in favour of free trade and investment, low taxation on income, and the privatisation of state enterprises and government functions.

The tipping point came in 1984, when the Fourth Labour Government assumed power during a major financial crisis, and used the ensuing turmoil to begin dismantling the controls that had bound Aotearoa New Zealand's economy for so long. Driven by the neoliberal ideologies of both the Treasury and the Minister of Finance, Roger Douglas, the subsequent six years of 'Rogernomics' saw government priorities switch from full employment to reducing inflation. Financial markets were deregulated, price subsidies were removed, many state-owned assets were sold off, and income tax rates on high earners were cut in favour of a universal goods and services tax (GST).

The succeeding National Government extended the neoliberal revolution into social and employment policy. In late 1990, Finance Minister Ruth Richardson unveiled a mini-budget that replaced the wide-ranging principles hitherto underpinning social security — '*degree of need*' as the key criterion for assistance, and allowing recipients to 'enjoy a standard of living much like that of the rest of the community, and thus [be] able to feel a sense of *participation in and belonging to* the community' — with the much narrower goal to '*sustain life and health*' (Easton 2020, p. 281; Royal Commission on Social Security, 1972).

This new approach saw deep cuts to support levels and a pronounced shift in official rhetoric. Benefits were no longer described as a safety net that should be available to all, but as a drain on the country's finances that encouraged dependency and curtailed individual responsibility. The fact that invalid, sickness and unemployment benefits would now be set at different rates also reintroduced the nineteenth-century distinction between a 'deserving poor' (the sick and those with disabilities) and an 'undeserving poor' (those out of work). A further tranche of reforms — collectively dubbed 'Ruthanasia' by their critics — saw the introduction of 'user-pays' mechanisms for healthcare and education, together with a switch to individual employment contracts that dramatically reduced the negotiating power of trade unions.

In just nine years, the basis of Aotearoa New Zealand's economy and society had been altered. Some of the consequences can certainly be viewed as beneficial. With foreign companies and investors rushing to take advantage of the new financial freedoms, a surge in immigration stimulated ethnic diversity. The relaxing of controls also increased the availability of consumer goods, and provided people with greater choices in food, entertainment and services. Several exports carved out a niche in the international market, while Aotearoa New Zealand simultaneously began to promote itself as a tourist destination — complete with majestic scenery and a 'clean, green' environment.

STUFF LIMITED

Struggling in the land of milk and honey

A queue forms outside the City Mission in Hobson Street, Auckland. Many families are now reliant on access to food banks to feed their children, and demand is especially strong at Christmas. Many charitable organisations throughout New Zealand run food-bank systems, and across them all the number of food parcels being handed out is growing every year. Covid-19 only further exacerbated this trend as many people lost their incomes or had their work hours reduced. Often an unexpected bill now sees people turning to a food bank for the first time. For example, Auckland City Mission distributed 48,679 food parcels from June 2020 to June 2021, up from 34,124 the year before, and triple the numbers of 2017–2018. Beyond highlighting the wealth and security disparities within our society, this also rather puts paid to the idea that the pandemic has been 'the great equaliser'.

Yet the impact on equality was nothing less than catastrophic. According to journalist and researcher Max Rashbrooke (2013), 'In the two decades framing these changes, the gap between those at the top and bottom of the income ladder in New Zealand opened up more rapidly than in any other comparable society' (p. 27). Bankers, senior managers and property developers tended to do very well, thanks to the growth in the financial and speculative sectors of the economy. On the other hand, many lower-class people encountered tremendous difficulties. The stifling of trade unions allowed employers to reduce wages and compel longer hours, while the quest for 'efficiency' and the removal of guaranteed prices caused many businesses to close down. Unemployment soared from 4 per cent in 1984 to 11 per cent by the early 1990s, and, with benefits slashed and goods and services now subject to GST, increasing numbers of families were unable to make ends meet. It was not long before food banks reappeared in Aotearoa New Zealand for the first time since the Great Depression.

Substantial damage was also done to the country's social fabric. As the former state trading enterprises — particularly forestry, mining and the railways — were corporatised, restructured, and in many cases sold to private companies, the support and voluntary structures that had grown up around them withered away. Likewise, many family-owned businesses or farms proved unable to cope with the new era of competition and were forced to close after years of supplying irreplaceable jobs and networks within their provincial communities.

See Marcia Russell's documentary *Revolution* about the reforms of the 1980s and 1990s, which can be viewed in bite-sized chunks on the NZ On Screen website: www.nzonscreen.com/title/revolution-1996/series

The narrative today

Between 1984 and 1993, the advocates of neoliberalism maintained that the 'pain' of transitioning to a free-market society would prove worthwhile, as any short-term rise in inequality would soon be offset by a 'trickle-down' of prosperity. Such forecasts have proven emphatically wide of the mark. The evidence suggests that after inequalities spiralled upwards during the 'Rogernomics' and 'Ruthanasia' eras, there have been *no* significant shifts over the following three decades. In other words, income and wealth distributions had become massively uneven by 1993 and remain almost as uneven today (Easton, 2014).

The resulting statistics are staggering. In 2018, the highest-earning 10 per cent of adults owned fully 59 per cent of Aotearoa New Zealand's total wealth, the next 40 per cent of adults owned 39 per cent of the wealth, and the bottom half of adults owned just 2 per cent. Whereas the wealthiest 38,000 New Zealanders have a combined $141 billion held in trusts, three-quarters of a million others sit below the poverty line — defined as living in a household that earns less than 60 per cent of the median disposable income — and fully 41 per cent of families have insufficient food and cannot reliably provide a nutritious diet for all their members (Jackson & Graham, 2017; Rashbrooke et al., 2021). Aotearoa New Zealand also has some of the worst rates of child poverty and preventable disease in the developed world. Overall, this country slipped from being the fourteenth most equal of 34 economically developed countries at the start of the neoliberal revolution to the twenty-fifth most equal in 2014 (Easton, 2014).

Within these figures are a number of specific inequalities. Although the gaps have decreased over the past two decades, women still earn on average around 12 per cent less than men, and remain heavily under-represented on company boards and in senior managerial roles (Stats NZ, 2016). Booming property prices have also seen the rate of home ownership decline from around three-quarters of adults in 1991 to just 50 per cent in 2018 (although that figure climbs to nearly 65 per cent if homes held in family trusts are added), with every metric showing that the gap between income and house affordability is growing at a phenomenal rate. This trend has had a disproportionate impact on younger people, more and more of whom face living the whole of their adult lives in rented accommodation (Dean, 2015; Eaqub & Eaqub, 2015).

Aotearoa New Zealand's greatest points of inequality are along racial lines. Its Māori and Pasifika populations sit at the negative end of nearly every social indicator: from income to imprisonment, from education to employment, and from health to housing. Indeed, the 750,000 New Zealanders who are living in poverty comprise around one out of every 10 Pākehā households, but around one out of every five Māori and Pasifika households (Rashbrooke, 2013).

The narrative going forward

The continued influence of the equality narrative undoubtedly has some positive consequences. It has helped drive the evolution of Aotearoa New Zealand's democratic institutional structure, which is underpinned by equal voting rights and by a mixed member proportional (MMP) electoral system that ensures most people's votes have some impact on the result. Aotearoa New Zealand is also viewed as a world leader when it comes to legislation that protects human rights and promotes equal opportunities. The New Zealand Bill of Rights Act of 1990 outlined the rights and freedoms that should be enjoyed by every person who comes under Aotearoa New Zealand law. Discrimination on a wide variety of grounds — including sex, age, race, ethnicity, religion and sexual orientation — was formally outlawed by the Human Rights Act three years later. Finally, in 2013 Aotearoa New Zealand became just the fifteenth country to legalise same-sex marriage through the Marriage (Definition of Marriage) Amendment Act. It was largely on the basis of such progressive legislation that a United Nations Human Rights Council (2009) review described Aotearoa New Zealand (albeit with some crucial exceptions) as a country committed to protecting and upholding its citizens' rights.

Yet the narrative's ongoing influence also fosters problematic trends. On the one hand, opinion surveys consistently identify a commitment to ideals of equality, and a sense that the distribution of wealth has become too uneven. On the other hand, those same surveys indicate a majority of New Zealanders oppose government measures to redistribute that wealth. Such paradoxical findings appear to derive from the common prioritisation of equality of opportunity over equality of outcome. Support for greater government spending on health and education — thought to promote a universal enhancement of opportunities — is matched by resistance to targeted redistribution measures with a focus on outcomes, such as higher income taxes or increased benefit levels (Humpage, 2014).

Management academic Peter Skilling (2013) links these sentiments to a belief that outcomes are primarily determined by a person's own actions: 'equality of opportunity can be seen as a sort of equality quite consistent with individual responsibility and reward; a sort of equality able to provide a justification for inequalities of outcome' (p. 20). In other words, people are said to be poor due to laziness and a lack of willpower — they do not deserve support and instead need to be pushed to grasp the opportunities available through greater effort. Wealthy individuals, on the other hand, are said to be reaping the benefits of having capitalised on their natural abilities by working hard and seizing opportunities.

See this article about hardening public attitudes regarding equality and the poor: https://www.stuff.co.nz/business/118532029/why-new-zealand-is-unsympathetic-towards-the-poor

Such attitudes also manifest in debates surrounding the disparate living standards experienced by Māori and Pākehā. The notion that equality of opportunity exists, and must not be compromised, causes many New Zealanders to regard equity measures — giving certain groups of people different access to jobs, services, funding, etc. — with considerable hostility, even if they are designed to ameliorate a blatant inequality of outcome. Criticisms of so-called 'Māori privilege' have focused on several areas: the continued existence of the Māori electorates; the Treaty settlement process and activities of the Waitangi Tribunal; and the awarding of scholarships specifically intended for Māori students.

The most famous denouncement occurred in 2004, when the then National Party leader Don Brash lambasted the provision of government funding based on ethnicity. Brash (2004) explicitly appealed to the notion of equal opportunities by insisting there should be 'one rule for all' and that 'the Treaty of Waitangi should not be used as the basis for giving greater civil, political or democratic rights to *any* particular ethnic group'. These arguments have subsequently featured in debates over the establishment of Māori wards on local councils and over reforms to the Resource Management Act. The recent *He Puapua* report on the steps Aotearoa New Zealand should take to implement the United Nations Declaration on the Rights of Indigenous Peoples has also prompted allegations of a move towards 'tribal control' and the creation of a 'two-tier health system based on race' (Hobson's Pledge, 2021; National Party, 2021).

See Peter Meihana's *Dominion Post* article about 'Māori privilege': www.stuff.co.nz/dominion-post/comment/78559148/There-is-nothing-new-about-Maori-privilege

Attitudes like these can be critiqued on at least three interrelated grounds. First, opportunities are not abstract things waiting to be grasped by anyone, but rather concrete things like incomes, cars, houses and schools that both create *and* derive from outcomes in a cyclical relationship (Sharp, 1997). For example, children from poorer families tend to go to schools located in more socio-economically deprived areas than those from wealthier families, and are more likely to experience a lack of books and computers in their home, and a lack of funds for out-of-school activities. They are also more likely to suffer worse nutrition, less domestic stability and greater health problems during their formative years. All of this means children from poorer families have a reduced chance of succeeding within the education

Out of work and angry

The Great Depression had a devastating impact on thousands of New Zealanders, and many communities faced a desperate struggle to feed and clothe their families. In this photograph, taken in 1932, Jim Roberts — secretary of the New Zealand Waterside Workers' Federation (and sporting a bow tie) — is surrounded by unemployed men at a demonstration at Parliament.

system, which in turn means they are less likely to obtain a higher-paid job. These poorer adults then find it harder to provide opportunities for their own children, and so the cycle begins again.

For a powerful visual representation of how wealth is distributed in this country, see this graphic by Toby Morris and Max Rashbrooke: https://thespinoff.co.nz/society/31-07-2018/the-side-eye-inequality-tower-2018

Second, even if opportunities could be separated from outcomes, they are decidedly not equal. Social mobility does allow people to break out of the poverty cycle, but it occurs to only a very limited extent. Indeed, the figures for Aotearoa New Zealand show that 45 per cent of people who live in poverty are still there at least seven years later (Rashbrooke, 2013). This is hardly surprising, given the different treatment wealthier and poorer people receive. Claims that the wealthy attain their status primarily through 'hard work' ignore the fact New Zealanders on high incomes pay far less in tax than their counterparts in other economically developed countries, and that this country is almost unique in making little or no deductions from wealth, capital gains, inheritances or gifts. The wealthy are also much better able to engage the services of accountants and other financial experts, who can help structure their clients' affairs to minimise the tax they are required to pay.

At the opposite end of the spectrum, benefits are set at a very low level — one that is deliberately calculated to force people into work (Marriott, 2018). The standard unemployment allowance for a single person replaces just a third of the average wage, with Aotearoa New Zealand ranking thirty-second out of 34 developed countries in terms of generosity of unemployment benefits (Rashbrooke, 2015). Similarly divergent are the ways in which the justice system treats tax evasion and welfare fraud. The former, despite amounting to an estimated $6–$8 billion every year, is rarely investigated, hardly ever prosecuted, and usually only punished with a fine. In contrast, instances of welfare fraud, which amount to just $20–$50 million a year, are investigated more diligently, prosecuted more commonly, and often punished with a prison sentence (Marriott, 2018).

Third, it is far from clear that achieving an equality of opportunities would be sufficient to narrow the gaps between different groups. Moves to ensure Māori enjoy the same citizenship rights as Pākehā have been hugely important and long overdue. But such legal prescriptions alone have not, and cannot, create equal opportunities in any real sense, because the two groups are not starting from an equivalent position. For well over a century following Te Tiriti o Waitangi, Europeans dispossessed Māori of their economic base by alienating them from their land and resources, while also seeking to undermine their culture by assimilating them into European ways (Poata-Smith, 2013). In contrast, the economic and social structures established under colonisation deliberately gave British immigrants major advantages. That most of these policies have now been overturned, at least legally, does not negate their past and ongoing impacts — Māori land holdings currently amount to just 6 per cent of the Aotearoa New Zealand total. Therefore, rather than being attacks on equal opportunities, the Treaty settlement process and policies targeted at Māori are surely best viewed as a means of redressing past wrongs and creating a real degree of equity in the present.

Conclusion

Two conclusions emerge from this chapter. The first is that national narratives are integral to developing, or inhibiting, a sense of identity and belonging. Equality has been at the heart of this country's self-image for nearly 200 years and continues to influence notions of what it means to live in Aotearoa New Zealand. At a more tangible level, the belief that people are, or should be, 'all equal here' has driven some of the most profound social and economic changes in Aotearoa New Zealand's history, but has also been employed to justify the status quo. It still causes many New Zealanders to vehemently oppose equity measures, and to argue that people can improve their situation simply by working harder and embracing individual responsibility.

A second conclusion is that the idea of Aotearoa New Zealand being an equal society now has almost no basis in fact. This country does display a general respect for human rights and has a great deal of progressive legislation on the statute books. However, its Māori and Pasifika populations are disadvantaged in nearly every way, its income levels are highly stratified, it treats its wealthier individuals favourably and its beneficiaries punitively, and more and more of its young people are facing the likelihood of never owning their own homes. While the equality narrative continues to shape perceptions, policies and ideals in Aotearoa New Zealand, it is as far removed from reality as it has ever been.

Chapter 10 — We're all equal here: Ideals of equality:
http://turangawaewae.massey.ac.nz/ch10.html

Further reading

Dean, A. (2015). *Ruth, Roger and me: Debts and legacies.* Bridget Williams Books.

Easton, B. (2014). Economic inequality in New Zealand: Update to a user's guide. *New Zealand Sociology, 29*(3), 7–23.

Rashbrooke, M. (Ed.). (2013). *Inequality: A New Zealand crisis.* Bridget Williams Books.

Skilling, P. (2013). Egalitarian myths in New Zealand: A review of public opinion data on inequality and redistribution. *New Zealand Sociology, 28*(2), 16–43.

References

Belich, J. (1996). *Making peoples: A history of the New Zealanders from Polynesian settlement to the end of the nineteenth century.* Allen Lane.

Belich, J. (2001). *Paradise reforged: A history of the New Zealanders from the 1880s to the year 2000.* Allen Lane.

Brash, D. (2004, January 27). *Orewa 2004 — nationhood.* http://www.donbrash.com/national-party/orewa-2004-nationhood

Dean, A. (2015). *Ruth, Roger and me: Debts and legacies.* Bridget Williams Books.

Department of Corrections. (2021). *Prison facts and statistics — September 2021.* https://www.corrections.govt.nz/resources/statistics/quarterly_prison_statistics/prison_stats_september_2021

Durie, M. (2019). *Te āhua o te kāinga: Shaping the house.* [Paper presentation]. Māori Housing Network Seminar. Te Puni Kōkiri.

Eaqub, S., & Eaqub, S. (2015). *Generation rent: Rethinking New Zealand's priorities.* Bridget Williams Books.

Easton, B. (2014). Economic inequality in New Zealand: Update to a user's guide. *New Zealand Sociology, 29*(3), 7–23.

Easton, B. (2020). *Not in narrow seas: The economic history of Aotearoa New Zealand.* Victoria University Press.

Franks, P., & McAloon, J. (2016). *Labour: The New Zealand Labour Party, 1916–2016.* Victoria University Press.

Hamer, D. (1988). *The New Zealand Liberals: The years of power, 1891–1912.* Auckland University Press.

Harper, G. (2015). *Johnny Enzed: The New Zealand soldier in the First World War, 1914–1918.* Exisle Publishing.

Hobson's Pledge. (2021). *The issues.* https://www.hobsonspledge.nz/the_issues

Humpage, L. (2014). *Policy change, public attitudes and social citizenship: Does neoliberalism matter?* Policy Press.

Jackson, K. & Graham, R. (2017). When dollar loaves are all you have: Experiences of food insecurity in Hamilton, New Zealand. In S. Groot, C. van Ommen, B. Masters-Awatere, & N. Tassell-Matamua (Eds.), *Precarity: Uncertain, insecure and unequal lives in Aotearoa New Zealand* (pp. 76–87). Massey University Press.

Lipson, L. (1948). *The politics of equality: New Zealand's adventures in democracy.* University of Chicago Press.

Little, A. (2016). Foreword. In P. Franks & J. McAloon, *Labour: The New Zealand Labour Party, 1916–2016* (pp. 9–10). Victoria University Press.

Maori Prisoners Trials Act 1879. http://www.nzlii.org/nz/legis/hist_act/mpta187943v1879n3389

Marriott, L. (2018). Governing the poor: Evidence from New Zealand's tax and welfare systems. *Journal of New Zealand Studies, 27,* 110–129. https://doi.org/10.26686/jnzs.v0iNS27.5179

McAloon, J. (2002). *No idle rich: The wealthy in Canterbury and Otago, 1840–1914.* Otago University Press.

National Party. (2021). *Demand the debate on He Puapua.* https://www.national.org.nz/demand-the-debate-on-he-puapua

Native Land Settlement Act 1907. http://www.nzlii.org/nz/legis/hist_act/nlsa19077ev1907n62329

Nolan, M. (2007). The reality and myth of New Zealand egalitarianism: Explaining the pattern of labour historiography at the edge of empires. *Labour History Review, 72*(2), 113–134. https://doi.org/10.1179/174581807X224560

Poata-Smith, E. T. A. (2013). Inequality and Māori. In M. Rashbrooke (Ed.), *Inequality: A New Zealand crisis* (pp. 148–158). Bridget Williams Books.

Rashbrooke, M. (2013). Inequality and New Zealand. In M. Rashbrooke (Ed.), *Inequality: A New Zealand crisis* (pp. 20–34). Bridget Williams Books.

Rashbrooke, M. (2015). *Wealth and New Zealand.* Bridget Williams Books.

Rashbrooke, M., Rashbrooke, G., & Chin, A. (2021). *Wealth inequality in New Zealand: An analysis of the 2014–15 and 2017–18 net worth modules in the household economic survey* (Working Paper 21/10). Victoria University of Wellington Institute for Governance and Policy Studies.

Royal Commission to Inquire into and Report on Social Security. (1972). *Social security in New Zealand: Report of the Royal Commission of Inquiry.* Government Printer.

Sharp, A. (1997). *Justice and the Māori: The philosophy and practice of Māori claims in New Zealand since the 1970s* (2nd ed.). Oxford University Press.

Skilling, P. (2013). Egalitarian myths in New Zealand: A review of public opinion data on inequality and redistribution. *New Zealand Sociology*, 28(2), 16–43.

Stats NZ. (2014). *Apprehensions for the latest 24 calendar months (ANZSOC)*. http://nzdotstat.stats.govt.nz/wbos/Index.aspx?_ga=2.245864196.1236587753.163640%205023-1291840256.1636405023#

Stats NZ. (2016). *Measuring the gender pay gap*. www.stats.govt.nz/assets/Uploads/Retirement-of-archive-website-project-files/Methods/Measuring-the-gender-pay-gap/measuring-gender-pay-gap.pdf

Stats NZ. (2021). *National and subnational period life tables: 2017–2019*. https://www.stats.govt.nz/information-releases/national-and-subnational-period-life-tables-2017-2019

Tohunga Suppression Act 1907. http://www.nzlii.org/nz/legis/hist_act/tsa19077ev1907n13353

United Nations Human Rights Council. (2009). *Report of the working group on the Universal Periodic Review: New Zealand*. https://www.ohchr.org/EN/HRBodies/UPR/Pages/Highlights7May2009AM.aspx

11.
Clean and green
A myth that matters

Juliana Mansvelt

He oranga taiao, he oranga tangata.
A healthy environment results in a healthy community.

This whakataukī is a reminder that the health of humanity and our communities is dependent on a healthy environment. It also informs the need for people to be kaitiaki of our environment so that it can then support us into the future.

He tirohanga Māori: A Māori perspective

Te Rā Moriarty

Affiliations to the natural environment are an important part of Māori identity. As I explained in Chapter 2, pepeha are an oral expression of identity and belonging to the physical landscape. One from my iwi Ngāti Koata follows:

Ko Maungatapu te maunga	Maungatapu is the mountain
Ko Maitahi te awa	Maitahi is the river
Ko Te Aorere te tai	Te Aorere is the tide
(Ngāti Koata Trust, n.d.)	

Papatūānuku, the earth, and Ranginui, the sky, are considered to be the primal parents of the world everyone inhabits (Mead, 2016). Through their union came all of the natural features of the environment: for example, the water, plant growth, animals and humans. From a Māori perspective, the descent of humanity from the environment informs the view that identity and belonging are closely associated with geographical features in the landscape, as evident in the above pepeha.

Through the continuous occupation of specific areas, a particular hapū, or iwi, becomes the mana whenua; the group that has mana in association with their whenua — and this informs their collective duty to be kaitiaki. Kaitiakitanga can include cleaning waterways, planting trees, looking after the whenua, and anything that works to promote and keep the environment alive and well. Ahikā is another relevant concept: it means the 'long burning fires', which refers to the continual occupation of an area where there is a fire burning constantly to provide warmth, light and fire for cooking. The whānau, hapū or iwi that maintain this fire become the ahikā of the area. This association also informs the concept of tūrangawaewae as a whakapapa connection to ancestral lands, allowing a person to feel that they belong with, and can stand alongside, their whānau, hapū and iwi.

All of these aspects of identity contribute to a Māori sense of conservation. The practice of placing a rāhui (a restriction for a certain time) on certain environmental features, such as a forest, an ocean or a river, allows the life in those spaces to regenerate. It is a custom that was practised by ancestors and is still done in modern times. Harvesting of food and natural resources from the environment was determined by the seasons when those resources were able to be sourced without depleting them. Once the harvesting season was over, a rāhui was placed on gathering those products until they were in a state healthy enough for another harvest at the right time. This ensured that the resource would flourish for future generations.

Introduction

Perhaps one of the most pervasive and powerful narratives surrounding Aotearoa New Zealand is based on the representations that have become attached to place and environment: the narrative of being 'clean, green' and over recent decades '100% Pure New Zealand'. Although contested, this story remains powerful because it has a role in shaping individual and collective identities that surround being and belonging in Aotearoa. The clean and green narrative also influences how New Zealanders understand what constitutes 'natural' environments. It has become a part of how New Zealand as a nation state represents itself to the world.

Although understandings of natural environments as 'non-human surroundings' (Simmons, 1993, as cited in Clayton & Opotow, 2003, p. 6) may indicate a separation between 'nature' and 'culture', this separation is a fallacy. Natural environments are socially constructed and understood through a human lens. Perspectives on what comprises a 'natural' environment will differ across people, place and time. Relationships to, and attachments with, the natural environment may be intense, whether these are material, affective or spiritual in form. Accordingly, some individuals may have deep-seated but unexamined values and beliefs concerning the environment, while others may hold explicit preferences and positions about the environment and environmental change (Clayton & Opotow, 2003). These differing values, beliefs and understandings of environment can result in varying attachments to place, and may act as a basis for individual and group identification and action. Consequently, the different voices, stories and place meanings that circulate about the nature of Aotearoa New Zealand's natural environment influence encounters between people, resulting in outcomes which may range from strong collective affinities to place to land-use conflicts.

How one such story about Aotearoa New Zealand's natural environment came to signify place meanings, national identity and the construction of Aotearoa New Zealand's place in the world is the focus of this chapter. Moving from its colonial origins, I explore how the 'clean and green' story was created and propagated through a range of agents and organisations, from early scientists and writers to tourism and business firms. The purpose of the narrative is discussed, and the effects of this narrative for individual and collective identifications explored. Finally, the chapter examines contestations of the clean and green narrative through the rising prominence of alternative stories of Aotearoa New Zealand's environment. In doing so I reflect on the consequences of deploying this narrative and the challenges to its existence in the context of uncertain environmental futures.

Nature and origins of the narrative

In this book, we have suggested that places can shape individual and collective identities. The clean, green narrative has been significant in how a range of individuals and agencies (in tourism, business, media, marketing, and local and national governments) portray New Zealand's national identity globally. Although the catchphrase 'Clean, Green and 100% Pure' comes from the promotion and tourism marketing campaigns of the late 1990s, the origins of the clean, green and pure story can be found in New Zealand's colonial heritage. This narrative became vested in the economic and utilitarian valuation of land based on private ownership and economic productivity. As this narrative grew in dominance, it rendered less visible Māori people and place stories embedded in concepts of tūrangawaewae, whakapapa mana whenua, and kaitiakitanga (care and guardianship of the land).

Nineteenth-century colonial artists, poets and writers produced a vision of nature that strongly emphasised its centrality to the nation (Clark, 2004). Nature was frequently presented as spectacular, unspoiled and beautiful (McClure, 2004). Geologists and botanists disagreed with their European colleagues that New Zealand was immature and degenerate, and instead focused on the rarity, uniqueness and wondrous nature of landforms, flora and fauna (Clark, 2004). With the rapid conversion of lowland ecosystems to farming in the nineteenth and twentieth centuries, tensions between, and histories of, Māori, Pākehā and other new settlers over land use were obscured in the attribution of 'green' to the newly emerging pastoral landscapes. Over the past two centuries, notions of clean and green have extended beyond pristine natural landscapes to encompass agricultural land uses, with both scenery preservation and human transformations of rural places emphasising a natural affinity to the land and healthiness of life lived close to nature (Clark, 2004; Pawson, 1997).

During the 1980s, clean and green also became associated with New Zealand's anti-nuclear stance (Coyle & Fairweather, 2005; Tucker, 2017). This association arose through protests against French nuclear testing in the Pacific, the bombing and sinking of the Greenpeace ship the *Rainbow Warrior* in Tāmaki Makaurau in 1985, and the passing of nuclear-free-zone legislation in 1987.

What purpose does the clean and green narrative serve?

The clean and green narrative has become central to the invention of New Zealand, shaping a sense of national consciousness and national pride; a story that is reproduced by citizens, civil society and the state (Bell, 1996). The narrative incorporates elements of nostalgia (Pawson, 1997), based on frontier culture and images of a healthy life in concert with access to nature — a story that still has meaning today, even though only 13.3 per cent of New Zealanders dwell in a rural area (World Bank, 2021).

For more on New Zealand's changing urban population, see: http://www.tradingeconomics.com/new-zealand/urban-population-wb-data.html

Clean and green is part of New Zealanders' individual and social identification, a construction that can be a source of pride and wellbeing. For many New Zealanders, 'getting away from it all' may mean leaving New Zealand's urban areas to experience the natural environment — sea, mountain and bush. Engaging with and experiencing clean and green environments has long been associated with active and outdoor pursuits (Cloke & Perkins, 1998), such as tramping, hunting, fishing, climbing, mountain biking and kayaking.

Although the explicit narrative of 'clean and green' had emerged through colonial and Pākehā constructions of the environment, for Māori, a natural environment was and continues to be a significant part of how whakapapa, hauora (wellbeing) and tūrangawaewae are expressed. The concept of mana whenua — the mana and authority to manage environments and exercise kaitiakitanga and tino rangatiratanga — also stems from this connection and preceded any colonial constructions of clean and green. Landscapes and environments (and the entities which comprise them, e.g. rivers, mountains, lakes, flora and fauna) provide a source of material, social and spiritual wellbeing and tūrangawaewae. This can be created through the deep affective and whakapapa (ancestral) connections to place, and through activities such as dwelling, growing and harvesting kai, using the land to create a living, or practising rongoā.

For a great case study of kaitiakitanga, read how Motiti Island tangata whenua campaigned for marine protection controls following the grounding of the container ship *Rena* in 2011 (scroll down to Chapter 3: The MV *Rena*): https://interactives.stuff.co.nz/2018/11/motiti

Country of dreams

Happy, fit young people, sparkling water, green hills . . . one of the iterations of the 100% Pure New Zealand campaign. Despite the slogan's contentious relationship with reality, marketing and tourism experts highlight the 50 international awards it has won, naming it 'a brand that still leaves most other international tourism promotions for dead' (Carter, 2019).

Sitting alongside these personal and collective connections to the environment for tangata whenua and tangata tiriti is the emergence of clean and green as a narrative that serves wider economic purposes. Although representations of clean and green were integral to the romanticised image of New Zealand portrayed in order to attract immigrants and visitors from the 1890s, the idea of New Zealand as a utopian environmental paradise was explicitly marketed by the New Zealand Tourist Board in their '100% Pure' tourism campaign (Yeoman et al., 2015). The 1999 campaign, developed by M&C Saatchi, heralded a specific imagineering of New Zealand, connected with the personal pride New Zealanders might feel in beautiful landscapes and places, and was intended to attract overseas tourists and increase visitor spending.

For a more recent incarnation of the campaign, see the Tourism New Zealand website: http://www.newzealand.com/int

The campaign uses images of unspoilt natural environments, magnificent vistas and green pastoral landscapes, with visitors both gazing on and actively engaging with these spaces (Cloke & Perkins, 1998), portraying a sense of New Zealand's uniqueness and bounty, as well as an affinity with nature and a relaxed pace of life (Yeoman et al., 2015). The 100% Pure brand has served Aotearoa New Zealand well, and has come to stand for many aspects of national identity. The brand is elastic, in the sense that it has stretched to encompass elements of the experience of visiting New Zealand (exhilaration, discovery and relaxation, for example) and has been taken up by a range of firms promoting both themselves and their commodities to the world.

In recent years, the rhetoric of clean and green has moved well beyond tourism and found its way into a range of other products, and therefore into the relationships that consumers and investors have with New Zealand firms. Clean, green and pure narratives have been aligned with the marketing of agricultural products as environmentally friendly, untainted, safe and fresh (particularly dairy, meat and horticultural produce), a representation which includes the 'pure discovery' of our export-quality New Zealand wines (Cloke & Perkins, 1998; Lewis, 2011).

Used alongside the silver FernMark (registered as a trademark in 1991), the 100% Pure brand also portrayed the personality of a vibrant country seeking to market itself to the world. Brand, place and lifestyle qualities became fused in the marketing of goods and services and how New Zealanders do business, with clean, green and pure underpinning political and economic constructions of Aotearoa New Zealand's identity in a global world. 'The New Zealand way' encapsulates a young, fresh, innovative country comprising quiet achievers seeking contemporary solutions to a range of issues (Insch, 2011).

Brands such as Steinlager Pure, Anchor, 42Below Vodka, The Clean Green Shirt Company and Living Green have capitalised on these associations. By the mid-2000s the clean and green narrative was linked to the 'New' New Zealand Thinking campaign designed by New Zealand Trade and Enterprise, which was premised on high technological capability and scientific achievement, including biotechnologies. Clean and green had become a central part of 'Brand New Zealand' (Lewis, 2011).

How is the narrative propagated and maintained?

Clean and green is a narrative that represents a particular and partial story about the relationship between people and places in Aotearoa New Zealand. It is a story that has gained momentum as it has been reproduced, accepted, talked about and acted upon by groups and individuals over time. Connections between identity and the environment are reproduced through talk (consider, for example, why New Zealanders living or visiting overseas might choose to talk about New Zealand's environment and landscape in terms of its spectacular scenery).

Social practices also reinforce identity threads connecting people and environments people engage in. 'Going bush' or taking a trip to the beach, engaging in an environmental campaign, adhering to state and local governments' environmental regulations or staging a protest — any of these activities may help perpetuate or challenge depictions of Aotearoa New Zealand as clean and green.

Environmental meanings and narratives are also reproduced through stories, waiata, whakataukī, the performing and visual arts, and through popular culture and the media. They can provide a source of pleasure, pride, identity and belonging. Images of mountains, rivers, beaches, and rugged and agricultural landscapes portrayed on television, for example, may encourage citizens to see and understand landscapes and the practices associated with them as clean, green and pristine.

Tourism New Zealand continues to draw on clean, green and pure, through its slogans and images, to market the country as a destination for overseas tourists through multiple media: websites, print images, posters, trade shows and magazines. Kaefer (2014) notes that mass media have played a critical role in promulgating these narratives in the context of a world in which environmental credentials have become a critical part of the global competitiveness of nations. Media and film have been significant in publicising 'Brand New Zealand' — albeit with tongue firmly in cheek in the case of the highly successful comedy series *Flight of the Conchords,* which aired on HBO in the United States between 2007 and 2009.

Check out the posters on Murray's office wall in *Flight of the Conchords*: https://www.youtube.com/watch?v=uPYQNqc8OGY

The *Lord of the Rings* (2001–2003) and *Hobbit* film trilogies (2012–2014) have been significant vehicles for promoting Aotearoa New Zealand's clean, green narrative. The creation of maps, tours and sites of Middle-earth provided an extension of the clean, green New Zealand brand for overseas film audiences, and opportunities for the further commodification of place, with one tourism poster proclaiming New Zealand as the 'Best supporting country in a Motion Picture'! Many New Zealanders also seem to have embraced Aotearoa as the home of Middle-earth (Organ, 2013).

The creation of a whole new raft of New Zealand places as Middle-earth tourist destinations, including Matamata (rebranded Hobbiton), was an opportunity not lost on Air New Zealand. At the height of the films' popularity, the airline adorned its planes with film images and produced a safety video drawing on characters from the movies (Jutel, 2004). Before Covid-19 curtailed international travel, many visitors to New Zealand had some form of 'hobbit' experience, contributing to New Zealanders' local economies and livelihoods across a range of 'Middle-earth' sites and destinations. In 2019, Hobbiton, near Matamata, employed 300 staff and had approximately 600,000 international and domestic visitors annually, contributing $78 million to the Matamata–Piako district annually (Hope, 2019). Successive New Zealand governments have also been keen to provide incentives for overseas film makers to produce movies and television series here, many of which feature New Zealand's rugged landscape and pristine natural environments.

It would be easy to assume that global marketing and media campaigns, and the reworking of New Zealand's natural and constructed landscapes as the home of Middle-earth, are simply the framings of organisations and firms keen to promote commodified landscapes and commodities to the world; but these constructions are also intimately connected to the meanings, experiences and practices of individuals. The Keep New Zealand Beautiful Society (2021), for example, argues on their website that their activities are focused on 'ensuring a greener, more climate conscious future for Aotearoa', noting that their ' "Be a Tidy Kiwi" and "Do the Right Thing" campaigns are now an intrinsic part of New Zealand's DNA'.

Thus, the practices and narratives of governments, firms and organisations promoting clean and green intersect with individual and collective meanings and experiences of environment and landscape to produce a dominant version of national identity which is reproduced by individuals. The consequences of this clean and green story for New Zealand and its citizens are explored in the following section.

Consequences

'Clean, green and pure' has been taken up as a rhetoric of government and industry bodies such as Fonterra, ENZA and New Zealand Wine. As mentioned previously, the 100% Pure campaign has been strongly aligned to the FernMark, and the promotion of 'Brand New Zealand' by New Zealand Trade and Enterprise (Lewis, 2011). Parliamentary speeches and government reports (e.g. Ministry for the Environment, 2013; Ministry for the Environment & Stats NZ, 2015) mention the significance of clean and green to economic revenue. A Ministry for the Environment (2001) report noted that 'if New Zealand were to lose its clean green image it would have an enormous effect on the economy' (p. 4), with an estimated loss of a minimum of $241 million to the dairy sector and $530–$938 million in terms of tourism.

The maintenance of a clean and green environment is also important to the quality of life of New Zealanders, whose livelihoods, recreational pastimes and emotional attachments may draw from that environment. Public health researchers Elizabeth Butcher and Mary Breheny (2016) note that for Māori place attachment is vital, and that the 'loss of these connections may have a damaging effect on identity' (p. 50). Loss of such people and place connections through degraded natural environments that affect livelihoods and the harvesting or hunting of kai may be significant, but it is not just whenua (land) or connections to Papatūānuku (Earth Mother) that are significant in te ao Māori. Tina Ngata (2018) describes the centrality of life-giving water in the genealogy of te ao, stemming from Wainuiātea, the huge expanse of water that was the first partner of the Sky Father, Ranginui. Aside from the practical need for clean water as part of food systems, Ngata (2018) notes that wai (water) is used in customary rituals as a means of physical and spiritual cleansing imbuing mauri and mana. As a significant contributor to waiora (sense of wellbeing), clean water is also enshrined in kaitiakitanga.

Clean and green is thus a story that is reproduced by individuals both resident and living outside of Aotearoa, and by a variety of public and private sector agencies that aim to promote New Zealand places and products for consumption. Yet, as Morgan and Pritchard (1998) suggest, the imagery reveals as much about the power relations that curate it as it does about the places and commodities that it promotes. Clean and green is a shifting social construction which encompasses a diverse range of identity, place and product constructions. The narrative provides a partial and temporal story about New Zealand as a nation, its history, landscape, identity and aspirations. Yet, despite limits to its representational claims, this narrative has remained a dominant story in shaping the identity of a nation and its people. I turn now to look at how the utopian representation of New Zealand as a clean, green paradise is being challenged.

Is New Zealand really clean and green? Fractures in 'paradise'

This chapter has suggested that New Zealand landscapes and orientations to nature have been socially constructed by a range of public and private sector agencies, creating an indivisible link between environment and the production of New Zealand and its economy in a global arena (Werry, 2011). The construction of the environment as clean and green has been tied up in the creation of nationhood and belonging (Clark, 2004), influencing how New Zealanders might see their nation's place in the world and their own place within Aotearoa New Zealand. Consequently, it is important to ask: Is the narrative that Aotearoa New Zealand is clean and green a myth?

As sociologist Corinna Tucker (2017) argues, the answer to this question depends on how we look at it. Based on a lower population density and the environment's capacity to cope with current practices, and compared to other nations, she suggests an argument could be made that we are clean and green. However, she also notes that taking per capita consumption of resources and current land-use practices into account means New Zealand's environmental integrity can be questioned. A study by Bradshaw and colleagues (2010) — which examined population and resource availability, and measured countries' loss of native vegetation, native habitat, the number of endangered species and water quality — showed that, per capita, New Zealand was ranked the eighteenth worst country in the world for its environmental impact. Chris Howe, director of WWF (the World Wildlife Fund for

Nature) in New Zealand, notes that 'Aotearoa, the land of the long white cloud, is now a land of polluted rivers and lakes, rising greenhouse gas emissions, pressured marine ecosystems and disappearing bird and mammal species' (WWF, 2012).

On many environmental indicators, New Zealand is less than 100% clean, green and pure. The removal of indigenous forests and the destruction of natural environments also make for grim reading. Almost one-third of New Zealand's landscape has less than 10 per cent of its indigenous cover remaining, while 46 per cent of New Zealand's land area has less than 20 per cent remaining. Of New Zealand's original wetlands, fully 90 per cent are gone (Ministry for the Environment & Stats NZ, 2015). In addition, nearly 40 per cent of New Zealand's indigenous vascular plant species are at risk or are threatened with extinction.

Human activities are impacting on New Zealand's landscapes and environments. For example, population growth and urban expansion are putting increased pressure on the environment to provide for the food, housing and recreational demands of urban dwellers (Ministry for the Environment & Stats NZ, 2021). The same report found 80 per cent of sites monitored for soil quality in Aotearoa New Zealand failed to meet at least one soil quality indicator. Forty-six per cent of lakes larger than 1 hectare (1758 lakes) are in poor or very poor ecological health, 67–77 per cent of lakes in urban, pastoral and forestry areas are polluted by nutrients, and 95–99 per cent of river length in urban, pastoral and exotic forest areas do not meet water quality guidelines (Ministry for the Environment & Stats NZ, 2020). The use of land for intensive agriculture affects soil and water quality, and also contributes to climate change. In 2018, 53 per cent of New Zealand's greenhouse gas emissions by volume were nitrous oxide and methane, with the bulk of these gases deriving from agriculture. Emissions from livestock made up 86 per cent of methane emissions and 93 per cent of nitrous oxide emissions (Ministry for the Environment & Stats NZ, 2021).

The situation with wildlife in Aotearoa New Zealand also makes for grim reading. Introduced pests, such as possums, rats and stoats, are found in over 94 per cent of the country, and other native bird and animal species are threatened, including more than 80 per cent of New Zealand's living bird species and 90 per cent of our lizard species (Ministry for the Environment & Stats NZ, 2015). In 2017, 76 per cent of our native freshwater fish (39 of 51 species) were either threatened with or at risk of extinction (Ministry for the Environment & Stats NZ, 2020). Seven of New Zealand's 10 official indicator species for measuring biodiversity status are threatened. The kōkako, for example, has suffered a 90 per cent contraction in its range since the 1970s (Ministry for the Environment & Stats NZ, 2015).

These are sobering statistics, and many of them are produced by the government's own departments. More than two decades ago, environmentalist Cath Wallace

STUFF LIMITED

Dirty and disappearing

Beyond simple degradation of river water quality, we are starting to witness the disappearance of rivers altogether exacerbated by human activity. In one of Canterbury's iconic braided rivers, the Ashley–Rakahuri River, the naturally low flows of the river have been compounded by climate change, as well as the increased drawing up of surface and groundwater in the area for drinking and irrigation. This threatens the survival of 16 species of fish and 25 species of native bird. The over-allocation of water consents has been pointed to as a key issue by activists, and this has not been rectified despite a swathe of freshwater regulations introduced in 2017. This degradation could even impact on tourism should things deteriorate further, as the high country's most valuable attractions are water and natural scenery (Vance, 2021).

(1997) argued that we cannot rely on the clean and green mantra to pretend we do not have 'deep-seated and complex environment problems' (p. 29). Yet despite these counter-narratives, empirical evidence of environmental degradation and a decline in biodiversity, it remains difficult to challenge the dominance of the clean and green narrative because of its significance as part of national identity and the way in which it has come to be intertwined with the country's economic fortunes. Although successive governments have long acknowledged the potential costs of not living up to the reality of clean and green (Ministry for the Environment, 2001), little has been achieved in terms of environmental protections (Joy & Canning, 2021).

However, alternative stories and contestations are gaining momentum and are beginning to challenge the dominance of clean, green and pure as an environmental story. Over the past two decades, a focus on New Zealand as an entrepreneurial knowledge economy has seen clean (non-polluting) digital and bio technologies identified as part of Brand New Zealand. As a biotechnology, the application of genetic engineering (GE) techniques to solve issues such as crop failure and animal diseases helps support the narrative of a clean and green New Zealand free of unwanted pests or pesticides (Coyle & Fairweather, 2005). But these GE techniques also occupy an ambivalent role in relation to the narrative, with GE-free campaigners arguing that genetic modification may put the clean, green 100% Pure branding at risk, leaving New Zealand behind in the organic marketplace and threatening the 'natural' environment (Henderson, 2005).

In addition, the development of biotech, digital and advanced technology companies may no longer easily align with representations of New Zealand. The association of these companies with a progressive, high-tech and forward-thinking nation does easily align with the images of idyllic pastoral greenery founded in a previous era. Brodie and Sharma (2011) suggest that New Zealand's business community members are concerned that New Zealand's national identity might be overly reliant on nature, prejudicing the reputation of more 'sophisticated' export industries (p. 10). 'The New Zealand Story', a government-led business growth initiative, was established in 2013 to frame a narrative of what Aotearoa New Zealand has to offer to world. Current director Rebecca Smith notes that the clean and green image doesn't necessarily convey the kind of images that technology, export education or assistance services want to portray to the world (Kaefer, 2021).

Perhaps the most visible contestation of the narrative thus far has been in the writings of Mike Joy, a freshwater ecologist and senior research fellow in the School of Governance at Victoria University of Wellington. Joy (2011; 2014; 2015; 2018; Joy & Canning, 2021) has drawn attention to the fragility of claims associated with '100% Pure' in articles drawing on his own research and highlighting New Zealand's poor environmental record with regard to increasing water pollution, the negative effects of intensive land use (particularly in relation to dairying), and the decline in biodiversity.

Joy's comments have attracted international attention. He was cited in *The New York Times* as saying, 'There are almost two worlds in New Zealand. There is the picture-postcard world, and then there is the reality' (Anderson, 2012), contrasting the landscapes (many of them from New Zealand's pristine national parks) presented to tourists and visitors with the reality of environmental degradation experienced elsewhere. Joy was later quoted in a *New Zealand Herald* article as saying 'We don't deserve 100% Pure. We are nowhere near the best in the world, we are not even in the top half of countries in the world when it comes to being clean and green' (Preston, 2012). He also argued that in 'five decades New Zealand has gone from a world-famous clean, green paradise to an ecologically compromised island nation near the bottom of the heap of so-called developed countries' (Joy, 2011).

While there was media commentary both in support of and against Joy's views when he initially voiced them in 2011, the economic significance of an individual publicly contesting the narrative was not lost on businesses and tourism industry representatives, with some suggesting that it was irresponsible to refute the myth. Joy was accused of tourism industry sabotage, with the advertising agency FCB's managing director, Derek Lyndsay (cited in Preston, 2012), claiming that 'a lot of tourists, particularly the big spenders, came from the USA, so having writers for *The New York Times* contradict the campaign's claim could be potentially damaging for tourism'.

Joy (2011), in another *New Zealand Herald* article, flagged 'The dying myth of a clean, green Aotearoa', noting that there had been a subtle shift in New Zealand Tourism's 100% Pure New Zealand campaign from the pristine nature of New Zealand's natural environment to branding connected with individual experience. Claims based on experience (e.g. magical, relaxing, authentic and spectacular experiences) are much less easily contradicted by the facts and statistics of New Zealand's environmental degradation. Despite the weight of evidence about the costs of the rhetoric of clean and green not aligning with the reality, Joy sees little evidence of a desire to shore up the narrative through regulation that would require individuals, organisations and firms to act in ways that will prevent environmental degradation.

In this 2021 talk, Mike Joy focuses on environmental degradation of our waterways and the proposed Taumata Arowai Three Waters Plan for reorganising New Zealand's infrastructure and water management: https://www.youtube.com/watch?v=ajiUjL3O2eM

On 18 February 2021, Joy directed his attention at a new target in a seminar given as part of the Public Health Summer School at the University of Otago, Wellington (see link above). In it, he focused on the environmental degradation of our waterways and why he believes the proposed Taumata Arowai Three Waters Plan (https://threewaters.govt.nz) for reorganising New Zealand's infrastructure and water management doesn't go far enough in addressing the key sources of water pollution.

Over time, his has not been a lone voice. The groundswell of data emerging from academics, advocacy groups and successive governments' own reports has troubled the clean and green narrative, critiquing its legitimacy and highlighting the need for environment protections, improved waste minimisation and management practices, and better environmental performance. Debates about mining/prospecting licences, intensive forms of agriculture, 1080 poisoning, genetic modification, climate change inaction, greenhouse gas emissions, animal cruelty and intensive irrigation further muddy the coherence of clean and green as a metaphor for New Zealand's future economic growth, and as a symbol of its products and forms of production (see Coyle & Fairweather, 2005; Henderson, 2005; Joy, 2014; Knight, 2011; Pearce, 2009; Rudzitis & Bird, 2011; Tucker, 2011). Publicity around the effects of contaminated groundwater and increased human and animal health issues (such as cyanobacterial growth in rivers, unswimmable lakes and rivers and the unsafe harvesting of kaimoana) also confront visions of New Zealanders' healthy and active engagement with land and water.

For a conception of land and nature as something beyond a tool for ownership and resource extraction, see the case of Te Awa Tupua (Whanganui River) being legally recognised as a legal person: https://www.tepoutupua.nz/te-awa-tupua

For scholars and protestors, acknowledging and confronting the clean and green narrative can provide an effective means of giving voice to environmental concerns, particularly when these are reported in the international media. Scientific data and debates around New Zealand's future environmental sustainability draw attention to the concern about the consequences of the rhetoric of the narrative not meeting the reality, raising the issue of the extent to which clean, green and 100% Pure can continue to have traction as a means of shaping identity, economy and place.

Conclusion

A study by Gendall (1993, cited in Coyle & Fairweather, 2005) showed that even nearly 30 years ago less than half of the population surveyed believed that the clean, green concept was a true representation of Aotearoa New Zealand. Despite this, the narrative endures, both as a medium for the economic promotion of New Zealand and its products, and as a foundation for the shaping of national identity. As sociologist Claudia Bell (1996) argues of the clean, green and pure narrative, we 'sell it to tourists as national identity; and half believe it ourselves' (p. 48). Aside from economic concerns about a potential decline in agricultural and tourist revenues, and the impact on rural and urban communities of any reduction in export incomes, if the reality of Aotearoa New Zealand's environmental record doesn't match the rhetoric, then much more than economic revenue is at stake.

In addition to health and livelihood concerns surrounding environmental degradation, loss of biodiversity, pollution and unsustainable land-use practices, a key source of national identity is troubled. Clean and green has been significant as a basis for material, emotional and spiritual attachments to place and national pride. Indeed, efforts to protect the environment led by a range of non-governmental organisations have long been a part of Aotearoa's history. If the meanings, attributes and experiences of encounters with Aotearoa New Zealand's natural landscapes are changed as a consequence of environmental degradation, then a central foundation for belonging, wellbeing and identity formation for New Zealand citizens is lost.

Kaefer (2014) argues New Zealand is at a critical juncture in terms of the credibility, legitimacy and sustainability of this narrative. Consequently, 'clean, and green' is a contested narrative that requires urgent and intentional efforts to sustain, through a range of state, business and civil society interventions. For while it is a story that still has currency, unless practical action is taken to shore it up, 'clean and green' is a narrative with an uncertain future.

Chapter 11 — Clean and green: A myth that matters
http://turangawaewae.massey.ac.nz/ch11.html

Further reading

Anderson, C. (2012, November 16). New Zealand's green tourism push clashes with realities. *The New York Times.* http://www.nytimes.com/2012/11/17/business/global/new-zealands-green-tourism-push-clashes-with-realities.html

Joy, M. (Ed.) (2018). *Mountains to sea: Solving New Zealand's freshwater crisis.* Bridget Williams Books.

Tucker, C. (2017). Clean, green Aotearoa New Zealand? In A. Bell, V. Elizabeth, T. McIntosh, & M. Wynyard (Eds.), *A land of milk and honey? Making sense of Aotearoa New Zealand.* Auckland University Press.

References

Anderson, C. (2012, November 16). New Zealand's green tourism push clashes with realities. *The New York Times.* http://www.nytimes.com/2012/11/17/business/global/new-zealands-green-tourism-push-clashes-with-realities.html

Bell, C. (1996). *Inventing New Zealand: Everyday myths of Pakeha identity.* Penguin.

Bradshaw, C. J. A., Giam, X., & Sodhi, N. S. (2010). Evaluating the relative environmental impact of countries. *PLoS ONE, 5*(5), e10440. https://doi.org/10.1371/journal.pone.0010440

Brodie, R. J., & Sharma, R. (2011). National branding for New Zealand exports: Developing distinctive meanings. *University of Auckland Business Review, 14*(1), 6–17.

Butcher, E., & Breheny, M. (2016). Dependence on place: A source of autonomy in later life for older Māori. *Journal of Aging Studies, 37*, 48–58. https://doi.org/10.1016/j.jaging.2016.02.004

Carter, C. (2019, July 30). 20 years of 100% Pure New Zealand controversy. *Stuff.* https://www.stuff.co.nz/business/opinion-analysis/114576906/20-years-of-100-pure-new-zealand-controversy

Clark, N. (2004). Cultural studies for shaky islands. In C. Bell & S. Matthewman (Eds.), *Cultural studies in Aotearoa New Zealand. Identity, space and place* (pp. 3–18). Oxford University Press.

Clayton, S. D., & Opotow, S. (2003). Introduction: Identity and the natural environment. In S. Opotow & S. D. Clayton (Eds.), *Identity and the natural environment: The psychological significance of nature* (pp. 1–24). MIT Press.

Cloke, P., & Perkins, H. C. (1998). 'Cracking the canyon with the awesome foursome': Representations of adventure tourism in New Zealand. *Environment and Planning D: Society and Space, 16*(2), 185–218.

Coyle, F., & Fairweather, J. (2005). Challenging a place myth: New Zealand's clean green image meets the biotechnology revolution. *Area, 37*(2), 148–158. https://doi. org/10.1111/j.1475-4762.2005.00617.x

Henderson, A. (2005). Activism in 'Paradise': Identity management in a public relations campaign against genetic engineering. *Journal of Public Relations Research, 17*(2), 117–137. https://doi.org/10.1207/s1532754xjprr1702_4

Hope, S. (2019, June 22). From rural town to film fame: How Matamata has changed since the boom of Hobbiton. *Stuff.* https://www.stuff.co.nz/business/113460102/from-rural-town-to-film-fame-how-matamata-has-changed-since-the-boom-of-hobbiton

Insch, A. (2011). Leveraging nation branding for export promotion — 100% sustainable? In R. Fletcher & H. Crawford (Eds.), *International marketing: An Asia-Pacific perspective* (5th ed., pp. 616–619). Pearson.

Joy, M. (2011, April 25). Mike Joy: The dying myth of a clean, green Aotearoa. *The New Zealand Herald.* http://www.nzherald.co.nz/business/news/article.cfm?c_id=3&objectid=10721337

Joy, M. (2014). Cool, clear water. In D. Cooke, C. Hill, P. Baskett, & R. Irwin (Eds.), *Beyond the free market: Rebuilding a just society in New Zealand* (pp. 102–107). Dunmore Press.

Joy, M. (2015). *Polluted inheritance: New Zealand's freshwater crisis.* Bridget Williams Books.

Joy, M. (Ed.) (2018). *Mountains to sea: Solving New Zealand's freshwater crisis.* Bridget Williams Books.

Joy, M. K., & Canning, A. D. (2021). Shifting baselines and political expediency in New Zealand's freshwater management. *Marine and Freshwater Research, 72*(4), 456–461. https://doi.org/10.1071/MF20210

Jutel, T. (2004). *Lord of the Rings:* Landscape, transformation, and the geography of the virtual. In C. Bell & S. Matthewman (Eds.), *Cultural studies in Aotearoa New Zealand: Identity, space and place* (pp. 54–65). Oxford University Press.

Kaefer, F. (2014). *Credibility at stake? News representations and discursive constructions of national environmental reputation and place brand image: The case of clean, green New Zealand* [Doctoral dissertation, University of Waikato]. https://hdl.handle.net/10289/8834

Kaefer, F. (2021). Rebecca Smith on country branding in New Zealand. In F. Kaefer, *An insider's guide to place branding* (pp. 253–257). Springer. https://doi.org/10.1007/978-3-030-67144-0_046

Keep New Zealand Beautiful. (2021). *Our story.* https://www.knzb.org.nz/about-us

Knight, J. G. (2011). *New Zealand's 'clean green' image: Will GM plants damage it?* University of Otago.

Lewis, N. (2011). Packaging political projects in geographical imaginaries: The rise of nation branding. In A. Pike (Ed.), *Brands and branding geographies* (pp. 264–288). Edward Elgar.

McClure, M. (2004). *The wonder country: Making New Zealand tourism.* Auckland University Press.

Mead, H. M. (2016). *Tikanga Māori: Living by Māori values* (2nd ed.). Huia.

Ministry for the Environment. (2001). *Our clean green image: What's it worth?* https://www.mfe.govt.nz/sites/default/files/clean-green-aug01-final.pdf

Ministry for the Environment. (2013). *Freshwater reform 2013 and beyond.* http://www.mfe.govt.nz/publications/fresh-water/freshwater-reform-2013-and-beyond

Ministry for the Environment & Stats NZ. (2015, October). *Environment Aotearoa 2015.* http://www.mfe.govt.nz/publications/environmental-reporting/environment-aotearoa-2015

Ministry for the Environment & Stats NZ. (2020). *Our freshwater 2020* (New Zealand's Environmental Reporting Series). https://environment.govt.nz/publications/our-freshwater-2020/

Ministry for the Environment & Stats NZ. (2021). *Our land 2021* (New Zealand's Environmental Reporting Series). https://environment.govt.nz/publications/our-land-2021

Morgan, N., & Pritchard, A. (1998). *Tourism promotion and power: Creating images, creating identities.* John Wiley & Sons.

Ngata, T. (2018). Wai Māori. In M. Joy (Ed.), *Mountains to sea: Solving New Zealand's freshwater crisis* (pp. 6–11). Bridget Williams Books

Ngāti Koata Trust. (n.d.). *Our history.* https://www.ngatikoata.com/our-history/

Organ, M. (2013). 'Please Mr Frodo, is this New Zealand? Or Australia?' . . . 'No Sam, it's Middle-earth.' *Metro, 177,* 56–61.

Pawson, E. (1997). Branding strategies and languages of consumption. *New Zealand Geographer, 53*(2), 16–21. https://doi.org/10.1111/j.1745-7939.1997.tb00494.x

Pearce, F. (2009, November 12). New Zealand was a friend to Middle Earth, but it's no friend of the Earth. *The Guardian.* http://www.theguardian.com/environment/cif-green/2009/nov/12/new-zealand-greenwash

Preston, N. (2012, November 19). Clean, green image of NZ 'fantastical'. *The New Zealand Herald.* http://www.nzherald.co.nz/entertainment/news/article.cfm?c_id=1501119&objectid=10848410

Rudzitis, G., & Bird, K. (2011). The myth and reality of sustainable New Zealand: Mining in a pristine land. *Environment. Science and Policy for Sustainable Development, 53*(6), 16–28. http://www.environmentmagazine.org/Archives/Back%20Issues/2011/November-December%202011/Myths-full.html

Tucker, C. (2011). The social construction of clean and green in the genetic engineering resistance movement of New Zealand. *New Zealand Sociology, 26*(11), 110–121.

Tucker, C. (2017). Clean, green Aotearoa New Zealand? In A. Bell, V. Elizabeth, T. McIntosh, & M. Wynyard (Eds.), *A land of milk and honey? Making sense of Aotearoa New Zealand* (pp. 278–289). Auckland University Press.

Vance, A. (2021, October 26). This Is How It Ends: 'We take staggering amounts from our waterways'. *Stuff.* https://www.stuff.co.nz/environment/300422378/this-is-how-it-ends-we-take-staggering-amounts-from-our-waterways

Wallace, C. (1997). The 'clean green' delusion: Behind the myths. *New Zealand Studies,* March, 22–29.

Werry, M. (2011). *The tourist state: Performing leisure, liberalism, and race in New Zealand.* University of Minnesota Press.

World Bank. (2021). *Rural urban population — in New Zealand.* http://www.tradingeconomics.com/new-zealand/urban-population-wb-data.html

WWF. (2012, May 27). *Paradise lost. New report shows 20 years of environmental inaction threatens NZ's natural heritage.* http://www.wwf.org.nz/?8941/Paradise-lost-New-report-shows-20-years-of-environmental-inaction-threatens

Yeoman, I., Palomino-Schalscha, M., & McMahon-Beattie, U. (2015). Keeping it pure: Could New Zealand be an eco paradise? *Journal of Tourism Futures, 1*(1), 19–35. https://doi.org/10.1108/JTF-12-2014-0017

12. Anzac

'Lest we forget' or 'Best we forget'?

Helen Dollery and Carl Bradley

Ko Tū a waho, ko Rongo a roto.
Tū is outside, Rongo is inside.

The whakataukī above mentions two atua, Tū and Rongo. Tū is the atua of conflict and humanity, Rongo is the atua for peace and agriculture. The reference to 'waho' (outside) and 'roto' (inside) relates to the marae where debate and serious issues may be discussed with vigour outside on the marae ātea, while inside of the whare the activities are more toned-down and friendly (Grove & Mead, 2001). As the Anzac narrative is the topic for this chapter, I have chosen this expression to reflect how we acknowledge our actions fighting wars overseas, and yet we strive to believe our country has been peaceful at home — a belief sustained by the amnesia of the wars against Māori in the nineteenth century.

He tirohanga Māori: A Māori perspective

Te Rā Moriarty

In light of the opening whakataukī, here I will focus on war at home in Aotearoa. In Chapter 2, I mentioned what have often been called the 'land wars', or the New Zealand wars, between the Crown and Māori in the second half of the 1800s. These took place throughout Te Ika a Māui, and were driven by the Crown's intention to dispossess land from Māori, which was to be settled instead by the incoming Pākehā population. The wars are an enduring reminder for Māori that the foundations of New Zealand are built on the deaths of their ancestors and the dispossession of their lands. A stark outcome of this is an environment where the lush forests of the past have been replaced by paddocks of pasture, where the waterways have been diverted, drained and polluted, and where the ancestral names of that land have been placed in the dusty back pages of history, waiting to be revived.

Following the wars, 3,490,737 acres of land were confiscated in Taranaki, Waikato and the Bay of Plenty (Keenan, 2021). Māori from Taranaki alone were dispossessed of 1,244,300 acres, and 1,217,437 acres were taken from Waikato iwi (Keenan, 2021). As was also mentioned in Chapter 2, much more land was subsequently lost through the Native Land Court process, and, in my 'He tirohanga Māori' of Chapter 10 on equality, I talk about other legislation that alienated even more land from Māori. As a result of these acts, Māori land holdings are now around just 5 per cent of Aotearoa.

So why am I telling you this? My intention is not to make you feel angry or guilty. It is to help you reflect on how New Zealand has been shaped, lest we forget. I'm deliberately using the name New Zealand here, as opposed to Aotearoa, to highlight how this country is seen in different ways. For Māori, Aotearoa is the name commonly used; a name which encompasses the past, present and future. Yet, for many people, New Zealand is the favoured name, one that has been imposed through our colonial history. Although relations between Māori and Pākehā were initially relatively peaceful, the wars of the nineteenth century fought at home were the antithesis of peace and are an uncomfortable reality that sits underneath the pillars of New Zealand's foundations.

Introduction

As a national narrative, the Anzac story carries considerable weight. For over a century it has been used — along with other narratives — to claim, explain or support New Zealand's national identity. This narrative, based on Aotearoa New Zealand's experience in the First World War, asserts that we punched above our weight; that we valued mateship when fighting overwhelming odds and poor (British) leadership; that we died protecting our way of life; and that it was on Gallipoli's shores that New Zealand's identity as an independent nation was born. Anzac Day services and war memorials caution us 'Lest we forget', yet inevitably there is much that is 'best forgotten' in our remembering. What does this Anzac narrative say about what it means to be a New Zealander, a citizen of this land in the twenty-first century? Is the story we feel we know accurate, or is it time to reassess the narrative in the light of what we have historically chosen to remember — or forget — from our collective past?

We have drawn Anzac connections into our lives in many ways over many years. In recent decades, attendance at Anzac Day dawn services in New Zealand has steadily increased, and attending Gallipoli dawn services is seen as a rite of passage during OE (overseas experience) pilgrimages. So, given this popular engagement, what does the Anzac story say about a New Zealand national identity? When we speak about Anzac — Anzac Day services, the Anzac spirit, traditions and myths — we draw upon a variety of views, beliefs and understandings about its history and origins. Anzac commemorations and the associated narrative extend well beyond the beaches of Gallipoli and into New Zealand's sense of self. How we understand the narrative is contextually bound not only to military engagements including New Zealanders over time, but to commonly claimed national values and aspirations. The Anzac legend begins in 1915, over a century ago, and for at least the first half of that time the collective Kiwi military experience was generally viewed as a unifying one. But is the Anzac story appropriate for some of the assertions attached to it, and does it tell the whole story of New Zealanders' wartime — or peacetime — nation-building experiences?

In the introduction to this 'Stories' section, Ella discusses the significance and power of national narratives to shape our sense of belonging as citizens; yet inevitably some stories are retold and valued more than others — sometimes to the extent that they are seen as sacred and therefore beyond critique. In this chapter, we will consider how the 'kernel of truth' at the heart of this particular narrative has been embellished over time to meet a need for an uncomplicated, cohesive national identity; and examine where truth and fiction have blended in that pursuit.

When a narrative is so well accepted, critiquing it can be seen as disrespectful; yet if it can withstand that scrutiny then its truths and fictions become more balanced. That requires us to hold to two important ideas at once: the place for respectful remembrance of New Zealand veterans' military contributions through public commemoration; and the importance of critically evaluating those events to better understand their performative value and power for nation-building.

This chapter will look at the nature and origins of the Anzac narrative using three major armed conflicts in New Zealand's history: Gallipoli, Vietnam and the New Zealand Wars. Imperial or strategic contexts shaped expectations and aims in each case, yet we have historically focused on overseas conflicts to support the narrative, choosing to forget significant conflicts on our own soil and their consequences for citizenship and belonging. From wars over whenua and tino rangatiratanga within Aotearoa New Zealand to New Zealand troops fighting for 'empire' overseas, we will examine the Anzac narrative's role in developing and maintaining threads of national identity. Whose stories do we hear and see, and whose have been allowed to slip, forgotten, from view, and why? Recently, historically marginalised voices are gaining more traction in having their stories heard, with consequences for the big picture of our national identity.

Gallipoli: The seed of the narrative

The Gallipoli landings form the foundation of the Anzac narrative for this country and Australia, against which all subsequent military contributions have been compared. Yet examining the statistics as well as the campaign's effectiveness invites us to consider our contribution more dispassionately — and less as triumph in adversity, gallant action against overwhelming odds, or honourable conduct and superhuman deeds. This section discusses the origin of this narrative and why it matters when considering national identity.

When New Zealand went to war in 1914, the New Zealand Expeditionary Force (NZEF) was not large enough to form a complete military division, so an agreement between governments joined the NZEF with the Australian Imperial Forces (AIF) to form a joint division. By the time they got to Egypt in late 1914, they had become the Australian and New Zealand Army Corps (ANZAC; Pugsley & Ferrall, 2015). The 1915 Gallipoli campaign became their first major test as a fighting force.

Initially, New Zealanders volunteered to serve, many buoyed by the opportunity to be part of an overseas 'adventure' which was commonly but naïvely anticipated to be 'over by Christmas'. New Zealanders at home 'thrilled to the news that their

MARTIN JONES, HERITAGE NEW ZEALAND POUHERE TAONGA

Memorialising the 'untidy soldier'?

Following the First World War, New Zealand towns and cities created local memorial sites as places to collectively grieve and remember their war dead appropriately and reverently. The design and construction of these memorials were often fiercely contested in competitions run by the various civic and municipal bodies. Nevertheless, almost all of the submitted designs focused on representing a combination of collective losses and symbolic values of New Zealand manhood that represented a burgeoning national identity, 'legitimat[ing] the cause for which so many had died' (Sheftall, 2009, pp. 142–143).

Sculptor Frank Lynch, who served at Gallipoli with the New Zealand Expeditionary Force, submitted this model for consideration. Lynch based his 'untidy soldier' on a photograph of his brother awaiting evacuation from Gallipoli, hat in hand, reflecting on those left behind. Jock Phillips (2016) describes Lynch's efforts to personify the Anzac soldier in bronze: 'The strong, bony face is instantly recognizable . . . [his] clothes are unkempt and his bootlaces undone.' This mythologised digger may have 'failed on the spit-and-polish, but was heroic in battle' (p. 156). Yet Lynch's archetypal battle-worn soldier found favour with only two civic selection panels, in Devonport (shown above) and Masterton.

First World War memorials featuring soldiers tended to favour the innocents who left for war, rather than those who had seen its worst. These memorials reflected the social conventions and widespread grief following the war; later memorials would reflect different social contexts.

country's forces were in action with the enemy, a sense of exhilaration that was tempered only by the long casualty lists which soon began to appear in the newspapers' (McGibbon, 1991, p. 1). By the end of the Gallipoli campaign, the price was staggering. New Zealand forces had suffered 7991 casualties, including 2779 dead, a 53 per cent casualty rate of the 16,000–18,000 New Zealanders who took part in the campaign (Ministry for Culture and Heritage, 2016). Australian losses were similarly high, with a casualty rate of between 47 and 56 per cent (Pugsley & Ferrall, 2015, p. 21). Gallipoli was, militarily and in terms of human cost, a disaster.

For more on the Gallipoli campaign, visit:
https://nzhistory.govt.nz/war/the-gallipoli-campaign/introduction

As a young dominion, New Zealand followed the imperial lead, aligning its developing political identity with the British motherland, in war as in peacetime. By the end of the war, this had changed somewhat. The cost to New Zealand in lives and casualties was proportionally higher than any other contributing member of the British forces, and the impact had lasting societal, cultural and military ramifications for the rest of the century. Yet the Anzac experience has sometimes been described as the start of a true New Zealand identity, what history scholar James Bennett (2003) calls an 'un-English' identity — a comparative positioning of ourselves as 'other' than just a British offshoot. A New Zealand officer, Lieutenant William Deans of the Canterbury Mounted Rifles, reflected:

> Gallipoli was a proper disaster. Nothing else but a disaster. It was caused through bad management and bad generalship . . . But if Gallipoli had gone right, it would've been worth it. I think it was worth it in the way that it proved the worth of New Zealand and Australian soldiers. I sort of feel that after Gallipoli we were New Zealanders, before that we were colonials. (cited in Pugsley & Ferrall, 2015, p. 297)

Historian Michael King (2003) referred to the development of the 'coming of age at Gallipoli' narrative and its subsequent commemorative forms as a 'necessary myth' (p. 300), as the scale of our First World War losses and the impact on New Zealand society meant that there had to be a deeper sense-making symbolism at work at a national level. The alternative — that the war was a prolonged and pointless waste of lives — was deeply unpalatable when so many families were personally affected.

Early Anzac Day services took the form of sombre collective memorial services for families who could never bury their loved ones, and the language used reflected sacrifice and heroism. These commemorations evolved over time, becoming opportunities to promote desirable national identity threads. Jock Phillips (2014), writing of 1920s Anzac Day services, argued:

> Even the chaos and disaster of Passchendaele were turned into inspiration for moral duty. Anzac Day and Armistice Day became opportunities to teach moral lessons to children about the value of self-sacrifice and the glory of war. And increasingly, these moral lessons were focussed on the problems of the present rather than the horrors of the past. (pp. 235–236)

So the view that war has contributed to our national identity is not limited to the Gallipoli campaign. John McLeod (1986) noted that New Zealand's contribution to the two world wars contributed greatly to 'stirring our national consciousness and promoting the development of a national identity' (p. 190). This statement says something about collective identity in wartime, but also about drawing on Anzac values and commemorative formats in a national narrative — a process that continues to the present day.

Diverse wartime identities and experiences — heroes all?

Given the human costs of war, there is an understandable tendency to valorise all those who served in New Zealand's name. Yet a more nuanced reading of their motivations, experiences and voices provides a richer appreciation of how the Anzac narrative has been promulgated over time. How did they fight, conduct themselves and reflect their country of origin? This section discusses both the heroic and the less laudable actions and expressions of identity by New Zealand forces, muddying the simpler 'heroes all' narrative by revealing a more nuanced picture.

New Zealanders enlisted in the Great War for various reasons, either voluntarily or, from 1916, through state conscription. Some resisted conscription for ideological, religious or political reasons, wanting no part of it. As Shoebridge (2016) explains:

Conscripted men who refused military service were known as 'conscientious objectors', because their refusal to serve was based on their personal beliefs (or consciences). About 600 men declared conscientious objections, of whom around 286 were ultimately imprisoned in New Zealand as an example to other would-be objectors (others accepted non-combatant service or were exempt[ed]). Fourteen imprisoned objectors were forcibly despatched overseas in July 1917, with some ultimately transported to the Western Front and subjected to military punishments and incarceration. The broad question of dissent — and the specific experiences of 'the 14' — remain among the most controversial legacies of New Zealand's First World War. (p. 2)

Some of the conscientious objectors refused to compromise or to serve in non-combatant roles (Grant, 1986). Only two, Archibald Baxter and Mark Briggs, refused to give in to the military's concerted efforts, often harsh and brutal, to make them comply (Grant, 1986). Baxter, a committed socialist pacifist, unsuccessfully applied for conscientious objector classification and instead was sent to the Western Front, before being sent home after a dubious diagnosis of insanity (McGibbon & Goldstone, 2000). In 1939, Baxter's compelling account of his wartime treatment, *We Will Not Cease*, was published in the United Kingdom, with a New Zealand edition only coming out nearly 30 years later, in 1968.

The last New Zealander imprisoned for their conscientious objection was released in 1920 (once the last of the soldiers had returned home). Those who served prison sentences as defaulters lost the right to vote for 10 years, and were barred from working for the government or local bodies (Shoebridge, 2016). This loss of voting rights and employment exclusion constituted a breach of fundamental citizenship rights; their voices were effectively silenced for transgressing wartime rules and social norms in a social context that strongly supported the war effort.

Māori responses to the imperial bugle call also represented diverse views and voices. This reflected the dual traditions of reform and protest in Māori political organisations, which had crystallised in the years from 1890 to 1910. While Māori participation is now an important part of Anzac commemorations, their First World War experiences were no simple story of inclusion. Bennett (2003) tells us that some Māori leaders saw a willingness to fight for 'King and Country' as leverage for reducing discrimination by Pākehā, but more significantly to also allow them to 'claim the status of equality for Māoridom in New Zealand society' (p. 32).

A significant source of opposition to Māori conscription came from the Kīngitanga movement. It was highly resistant to fighting for an empire that had, within living memory, dispossessed them of large tracts of whenua and affected their tino rangatiratanga in the New Zealand Wars of the 1860s (O'Malley, 2016). Waikato's Te Puea Hērangi stated: 'They tell us to fight for King and Country, well that's all right. We've got a King. But we haven't got a country. That's been taken off us. Let them give us back our land and then maybe we'll think about it again' (King, 1977, p. 78). Principled dissent in a highly pro-war context showed many of the same qualities ascribed to those who fought; Māori soldiers who enlisted drew praise for their bravery and service throughout the war, despite unequal military citizenship conditions while away as at home. The conscientious objectors also displayed Anzac values of bravery, loyalty and resilience against the odds. Courage and comradeship took many forms.

The hero has been a significant element of this narrative. Heroic stories of individual bravery shape our collective view of ourselves as the narrative evolves. Do you recognise the three New Zealanders in the photographs on the opposite page? New Zealanders' perceptions of these men's bravery, alongside how they might have seen themselves, shows how masculine, individual and national identity threads have developed in line with Anzac values of mateship and humility.

The first, Cyril Bassett, was a signalman, and the only New Zealander to win a Victoria Cross at Gallipoli. 'When I got the medal I was disappointed to find I was the only New Zealander to get one at Gallipoli, because hundreds of Victoria Crosses should have been awarded there . . . All my mates ever got were wooden crosses' (Harper & Richardson, 2006, pp. 87–88).

The second, Charles Upham, is the only combat soldier to be awarded the Victoria Cross twice. He was a man of few words, and decidedly uncomfortable about receiving this ultimate gallantry award on two occasions. Harper and Richardson (2006) write that Upham was 'embarrassed at receiving the [first] Victoria Cross and felt that he had only been part of a much larger team effort' (p. 170).

The final soldier depicted is Willie Apiata, who received his Victoria Cross for gallantry in 2007, although the action had taken place in Afghanistan three years earlier. The then prime minister, Helen Clark, said Apiata had displayed stunning courage; but when pressed by the media shortly after the announcement, he showed similar characteristics of humility, stressing the importance of camaraderie and mateship that Bassett and Upham had espoused much earlier.

These three heroes, and their responses to their awards, highlight an important incongruity in New Zealand's national identity. While bravery and sacrifice are part of that identity, as depicted in the Anzac narrative, so is humility and the belief that individuals should not be singled out for praise — the 'tall poppy syndrome' as it is colloquially known. McLeod (1986) highlights, too, the importance of having a more realistic view of soldiers at war:

FROM LEFT: ATL, PACOLL-6001-05; ATL, DA-06918; NZ ARMY NGĀTI TUMATAUENGA

Our heroes

Military decorations reflect the martial, political and social contexts in which they originate and are awarded. The Victoria Cross is the highest decoration awarded to members of the British Commonwealth armed forces in official recognition of 'valour in the face of the enemy'. It was introduced in 1856, although was not initially available to colonial troops. In the 1990s, New Zealand amended its honours system and in 1999 instituted the Victoria Cross for New Zealand, expanding the criteria to include New Zealand forces' peacekeeping work. Twenty-three New Zealanders have been the recipients of the Victoria Cross, including the three soldiers pictured: one in the New Zealand Wars, one in the South African War, eleven in the First World War, nine in the Second World War and one in Afghanistan. A common thread amongst these New Zealand recipients has been downplaying their own courageous acts and talking up those of their peers, who they felt equally deserving of this recognition. Bravery and humility, as valued contemporary national identity threads, were thus represented both on and off the battlefield. Pictured here are (from left) Corporal Cyril Bassett, Captain Charles Upham and Lance-Corporal Willie Apiata.

AIDA TAVASSOLI

Surafend

The Surafend Massacre in December 1918 was a war crime against Arab civilians perpetrated by Anzac soldiers. After the war had ended, the troops were encamped near Surafend, Palestine, and tensions between the soldiers and the villagers soon began to build over race and incidents of disorderly and unlawful behaviour. These finally erupted when a soldier's kitbag was stolen. Giving chase, the soldier was shot and killed by the thief. His New Zealand comrades, along with Australian and Scots soldiers, organised their own vigilante reprisal against the nearby village, beating and killing between 40 and 100 Palestinian Arab men, and burning down their entire village and a nearby Bedouin camp. Military authorities investigated, but the troops closed ranks, and no one was held accountable. General Allenby, commander of allied forces in Palestine, was blunt in his address to the paraded men: 'I was proud to command you, but now I'll have no more to do with you. You are cowards and murderers' (Harper, 2015, p. 534). This massacre — and Allenby's strong reproof — showed the antithesis of the brave, fair Anzac ideal, and was thus until recently little known to most as part of the Anzac story.

This image shows Carl Bradley and Aida Tavassoli laying a wreath for the Surafend villagers at the Wellington Cenotaph 100 years later. Their actions that day were not well received by some others who were in attendance: even the ability to mark other victims of war in this way — and to question the official narrative — has at times been restricted by Anzac Day service organisers.

We are not natural soldiers and we are not immune to all the failings of men at war. At times our men were as good, if not better, than allies and enemies alike; at other times, they were just as bad or even worse. We have much to gain by understanding this reality of our men at war . . . I think if the lessons are going to be of any benefit to future generations, they must first realise that ex-servicemen and women were a cross section of ordinary New Zealanders and were not either: (a) heroes or (b) warmongers. (p. 191)

At the time McLeod wrote these cautionary words, New Zealanders were, however, much more likely to hear stories of military heroism than those that fitted less well with claimed national identity values of courage, mateship and compassion shown by those on active service. Whether shown in the inequalities experienced by Māori servicemen, the rough 'justice' meted out to conscientious objectors, or the swift and brutal reprisals against civilians in occupied territories, McLeod's more nuanced view of this cross-section of New Zealanders is worth noting as part of a fuller Anzac narrative and more rounded national identity.

McLeod's words also hint at something else; another part of the experience of war that rarely features in the official Anzac story — which is that many soldiers detested war. That fact is easily lost in the bravado typically associated with the hero narrative, but you do not have to go too far into the archival records to find evidence of it. Here is just one example, taken from the diary written by 20-year-old Alfred Cameron, a farmworker from Canterbury, who (as did William Deans, about whom you've just read) served with the Canterbury Mounted Rifles. Shortly after enlisting, Cameron began his diary, hoping that 'these lines . . . will be of interest to those at home' (cited in Owen, 2021, p. 110). However, the descent of his 'journey from home and adventure into hell' is graphically illustrated in the final entry he wrote from Gallipoli: 'Anyday. It's just hell here now no water or tucker only 7 out of 33 in no 1 troop on duty not either dead or wound. Dam the place no good writing any more. My cobber George Ilsley dead. Killed August 7th. bullet through the head. buried Taylor's Hollow' (Owen, 2021, p. 110). Shortly after Cameron put his pen down, he was blown up and buried alive. He was a long way from Canterbury in every respect.

Every Anzac Day, people gather at local war memorials throughout New Zealand and Australia; overseas, expatriates do the same. At Gallipoli, Australians and New Zealanders converge on Anzac Cove. All this for a relatively small and insignificant battle that was a military disaster, but important to us because it conveys something about who we are. It defined our identity as connected to but distinct from Britain and also from Australia.

NEW ZEALAND HERALD/NEWSPIX.CO.NZ

Angry years

New Zealand soldiers who served in Vietnam returned home to little fanfare. Only one official national homecoming parade took place, in Auckland on 12 May 1971, to mark the return of Battery 161 and 4 Troop NZSAS. It was an uneventful affair until the parade reached the Auckland Town Hall. There, a number of protestors drenched in fake blood burst out through the crowd in an attempt to halt proceedings, while others threw firecrackers and red paint bombs onto the road. Even so, the number of protesters there that day fell short of the thousands witnessed at other anti-war protests (both before and following this parade), and there was only a short period of disruption before police removed the protestors.

Many veterans discounted the parade as a formal welcome home – a factor in their decision to organise their own parade in 1998. Even 50 years on, there remains disagreement between returned veterans and protestors regarding the event, although some veterans were appeased by Crown apologies in 2008 and 2009 (delivered by then-Prime Minister Helen Clark, herself a former anti-war protester) and the resulting 'Tribute 08' official welcome-home march in Wellington.

New Zealand's Second World War experiences reinforced those of the First World War in endorsing the dominant narrative of capable and respected soldiering, and of duty done. These servicemen and -women gave impetus to the Anzac tradition, and to the Returned and Services Association's (RSA) guardianship of this Anzac ideal and its public commemorations. In contrast, the conflict in South Vietnam, and New Zealand's commitment (as an Anzac unit) to that war, tested the ideals of New Zealand veterans and notions of Anzac.

Vietnam

As in the First World War, the decision to send combat forces to Vietnam initially appeared to enjoy reasonably high levels of public support. However, New Zealand's military involvement in Vietnam was later overshadowed by wide-ranging debate about the conflict, which erupted at home (and internationally) following the rise of an organised anti-war movement. As Ella discusses in Chapter 5, the 1960s and 1970s were a time of significant social change, including anti-war protests. The anti-war movement attracted increasing popular support, especially during the closing stages of the Vietnam War, aided by unprecedented levels of televised media coverage. The Vietnam War ultimately polarised public opinion, provoking questioning of the government's defence alliance commitments and policies, particularly by young people in higher education.

So how does the Vietnam War fit into the Anzac story? Did the image of the Anzac soldier in Vietnam stir similar feelings of bravery and heroism as the popularly idealised Anzac soldier who fought at Gallipoli — and has that changed over time?

The website Vietman War was created as part of the Vietnam War Oral History Project and brings together interviews, photographs and essays on New Zealanders' experiences in the war: vietnamwar.govt.nz

Psychologist Veronica Hopner (2014), analysing the oral histories of returning New Zealand servicemen, has found that, when compared with veterans from the two world wars, rejection featured heavily in the Vietnam veterans' stories. McGibbon (2010) describes expressions of community hostility as being confined to 'activist anti-war protesters, who represented only a small minority of those opposed to New Zealand's involvement in Vietnam' (p. 525), but many veteran testimonies dispute this view. In their experience, they came home to an environment that was 'unsupportive, unwelcoming and on occasion openly hostile' (Hopner, 2014, p. 148).

For many this was deeply wounding, and it raises questions of how inclusive the Anzac story of patriotism and pride actually is. In so doing, it also throws a shadow on the assumption that the purpose of Anzac Day is to acknowledge *all* war veterans equally. Might it not be, rather, that only those who served in wars deemed consistent with the wider narrative get to fit this particular bill? If so, the presumption that the state extends its duty of care to all war veterans also needs probing.

One example that highlights such rejection was offered by a Vietnam veteran who had been asked to speak to a Scout group one Anzac Day:

> I was quite happy to because remember I was a member of an ANZAC unit on active service in Vietnam, which was the most stupid thing I could possibly have said, because man alive, all hell broke loose. 'Oh you are a baby killer, one of those mercenaries' and they were going to take their kids out of Scouts not to have them anywhere near a mongrel like me so I quit right there on the spot . . . and that was very, very hurtful . . . they were the sort of things that struck you everywhere. (Hopner, 2014, p. 153)

National identity and citizenship ideally guarantee inclusion (Biles & Spoonley, 2007). For many Vietnam veterans this was not so, and their exclusion by society was seen as punishment for their involvement in an unpopular and unwinnable war (Challinor & Lancaster, 2000). These Anzac soldiers did not enjoy the respect granted to earlier generations of soldiers on active service overseas, with anecdotal evidence that local RSAs refused membership to Vietnam veterans on the grounds that the Vietnam War was unlike the two world wars (*Otago Daily Times*, 2008). This contextual use of power and dominant social norms to include or exclude has been a feature of the Anzac narrative over time, yet officeholders at RSAs around the country now include Vietnam veterans shaping what is deemed appropriate at Anzac Day services.

We turn now to another historical, political and social context to examine how identity and belonging are affected when some of our history is excluded from the Anzac narrative. The battles fought on New Zealand soil have remained in the 'best we forget' category for most of the narrative's life cycle.

Best we forget or time we remembered? The New Zealand Wars — Ngā Pakanga o Aotearoa

The 'kernel of truth', which Ella discusses in the 'Stories' introduction as the heart of a national narrative, is altered by subsequent retellings, and some voices and perspectives become more powerful in the narrative's development. Gallipoli as the crucible of New Zealand identity formation has become so well known that it is often seen as simply factual; yet another birthplace, much closer to home, has been historically discarded or silenced as irrelevant, too contested — or just an uncomfortable fit — for a national story. Why have we framed overseas wars as nationally significant when so little attention is given to the New Zealand Wars that have fundamentally shaped the development of New Zealand and its national identity? In 2015, a century on from the Gallipoli landings and in the midst of many public commemorations sited around monuments, Morgan Godfery (2015) wrote:

> No one has built a tomb of the unknown toa. We don't keep a cenotaph for the defeated tauā. There isn't an obelisk for great rangatira. And, while we build and care for monuments to the men and women who perished in wars on foreign soil, as well as dedicate a day to those who fell at Gallipoli, we continue to ignore the lives lost in the New Zealand Wars.

Godfery's voice is one of many in the past decade increasingly asserting the importance of remembering New Zealand's colonial wars — in school curricula, and in terms of our national identity and Māori citizenship in Aotearoa New Zealand. Vincent O'Malley (2016), writing of the 'huge impact' of the Waikato War of 1863–64, sets it alongside the First World War in significance — not ranking them, but recognising both.

As Te Rā discusses in Chapter 2, Māori lives and citizenship were severely affected by the colonial wars and the resulting loss of whenua, yet public knowledge of this period and the preservation and commemoration of significant sites are minimal when compared with those of European battle sites and campaigns. O'Malley (2016) states that 'the Waikato War, especially with its accounts of British atrocities committed against women and children at Rangiaowhia, Ōrākau and elsewhere, offers cold comfort for those seeking reassuring tales of patriotism' (p. 13). Given that history, he argues that some may think it best to forget the Waikato War, and to look instead to stories where we fought with, rather than against, each other; yet his point is that 'a mature nation needs to own its history, warts and all' (p. 13).

That was also the stance of iwi leaders and Ōrākau heritage groups in the 2010s. In 2015 Ōtorohanga College school students Waimarama Anderson and Leah Bell presented the government with a 13,000-signature petition seeking a national day on which to commemorate the New Zealand Wars, and for this history to be part of the school curriculum. Their collective voices were heard, and the first Rā Maumahara for those who made sacrifices in wars within Aotearoa New Zealand was held on 28 October 2018. What and how we remember is not fixed, but it is contextually linked to generational agendas and power.

See how school students lobbied to successfully push for change to learn about their own national histories and stories: www.theguardian.com/world/commentisfree/2021/nov/02/new-zealands-children-will-all-soon-study-the-countrys-brutal-history-its-not-before-time

Questioning the Anzac narrative: Inclusion and exclusion

While the Anzac narrative talks up the inclusiveness of New Zealanders banding together as equals — as evidenced in the extremes of battle — that inclusion has since been tempered with exclusive practices that have predicated some identities over others. This section discusses examples of the tension between the narrative's inclusionary ideal and its application as a tool to ring-fence socially constructed exclusionary citizenship.

Academic critique of the narrative includes its domination by a male, monocultural demographic (Greener & Powles, 2015; Hoverd, 2015). Constructing a particular masculine New Zealand identity, and the accent on imperial unity, served clear political objectives in the early twentieth century (Bennett, 2003). Today, Anzac commemorations are highly influenced by the RSA and military heritage groups, reflecting this influential demographic which prioritises Pākehā, and sometimes Māori, over other groups.

For instance, inequitable and punitive citizenship parameters for Chinese people in New Zealand at the time of the First World War made their enlistment problematic. Nonetheless, between 50 and 150 soldiers of Chinese ethnicity fought for New Zealand; yet their voices, until recently, have been excluded from the Anzac narrative (Stone, 2014). Similarly, the 458 Pasifika men who served have also been marginalised (Walker, 2012). New Zealand's First World War centenary commemorations, lavishly state-funded, provided an opportunity to incorporate some of the forgotten Anzacs' stories. However, there is still a risk of simply rewriting or reinforcing the dominant narrative of Anzac and celebrating questionable aspects of New Zealand's history while continuing to marginalise others.

Hoverd (2015), in reflecting on the Anzac narrative, states the need 'to ask New Zealand to think reflectively about the consequences of how we memorialise our conflict' and 'to think about an Anzac discourse that is inclusionary rather than exclusionary' (p. 2).

The Anzac narrative reinvents a First World War-era New Zealand, a society where the legal dimensions of Te Tiriti o Waitangi were absent, and where Māori experienced only partial citizenship. Despite having fought as equals, most Māori returned servicemen were denied equal access to the war pensions and rehabilitation assistance offered to Pākehā returned servicemen after the conclusion of the First World War. Even so, Sir Āpirana Ngata argued in 1943 that Māori contributions in the Second World War were the 'price' of full post-war citizenship for Māori, a century on from the Te Tiriti o Waitangi partnership. While significant moves aimed to eradicate blatant paternalism and inequalities, fuller attempts to embed adequate policies and practices in the Māori affairs area left a legacy of post-war problems that constrained equal and genuine inclusion (Orange, 2000).

In a more inclusive contemporary social context, the previously silenced dissenters' stories — those of the conscientious objectors and pacifists — are now heard more clearly, but are still contested. In Chapter 6, Rand and Trudie discuss the temporary statues protesters erected showing conscientious objectors in the torturous field punishment No. 1 position, as a voice for the silenced dissenters and their peaceful intent. Yet the statue outside Te Papa ('Our Place') was quickly removed (Hunt, 2016). The protest's goal was to 'end the romanticisation of war and the militarisation of Anzac Day' (Peace Action Wellington, 2016). And while a permanent manifestation of this, the Archibald Baxter Memorial Peace Garden in Dunedin, was opened in late 2021, even this was not without controversy, with resistance from some Dunedin groups, including the RSA, who objected to the initial site on Anzac Avenue. Resistance to broadening the narrative was also evident when Dunedin mayor Aaron Hawkins reported receiving a white feather (an accusation of cowardice commonly used in the First World War) anonymously after he wore a white poppy (for peace) alongside the official red poppy on Anzac Day (McNeilly, 2021).

As another example of the tension between inclusion and exclusion at play, the 2019 Tītahi Bay Anzac Day dawn service organiser, Afghanistan veteran Major Simon Strombom, received violent threats when he proposed adding a Muslim prayer to acknowledge the recent Christchurch mosque shootings and show solidarity. He was disappointed at the belligerent defensiveness shown at a time of national trauma, while some ex-servicemen defended a traditional Anzac Day focus on veterans instead and reiterated the dawn service's perceived sacredness. The Muslim prayer was not recited (Livingston & Kenny, 2019). So while there is growing awareness of the need for inclusiveness, there are still those who see Anzac Day commemorations as 'rightly' exclusive in tone.

Women's roles in the Anzac narrative similarly raises questions of how representative this narrative is for all New Zealanders. Former Australian prime minister Tony Abbott referred to the 'splendid sons of Anzac' at the Pukeahu National War Memorial Park opening in Wellington in 2015. Greener and Powles (2015) argue that in this statement he 'marginalised the good efforts made on both sides of the Tasman to advance the role of women in the military'. Further, Greener and Powles assert that 'Abbott's comments speak to the heart of gender issues, but also hint at a broader issue that we need to begin to address; that is, what "ANZAC" represents and how we want to remember war and conflict'.

Recent Anzac Day services now include more women's voices, showing the influence of changing dominant social norms; and, influenced in part by the state's WW100 centenary funding, more materials on women's diverse war experiences are being published (Tolerton, 2017). Inclusivity, and the concern surrounding exclusion, are both fundamental issues for consideration, given the importance we attach to the Anzac story's connection to national identity. The changing sense we make of events that are now more than a century behind us, especially our understanding of identity and belonging, continues to evolve — and is manifestly sharpened by the way we 'do' Anzac Day today.

Just another holiday?

New Zealand has many national holidays with significant meaning associated with them. Although its significance and remembrance have remained as continuous threads since 1916, our public performances of Anzac Day have taken many forms during that time. A day of collective grief and sombre reflection has now evolved to also include a much broader public, and at times vocal, discussion of war, conflict and identity. Veterans may spend the day reminiscing with peers or sharing their experiences with family. Many current and former servicemen and -women will attend dawn services or visit cemeteries, or quietly reflect alone. Families of these veterans, and other members of the community, will choose to do similar things, too.

Sometimes, choices come through external events. Covid-19 lockdowns in New Zealand made us look again at Anzac observance, with householders standing at their gates at dawn instead of gathering at cenotaphs, while others publicly showed their support by attaching homemade poppies to fences. The impetus to participate remains, although the forms may differ.

In addition to attendance at services, media commentary can both influence and reflect public opinion. Māori Television's broadcasting role has been significant in promoting more diverse Anzac stories and voices since 2004. In 2010, Sir Jerry Mateparae, then head of the New Zealand Defence Force (NZDF) and subsequently a governor-general, gave the Anzac address on the channel, asserting Māoritanga as central to the Anzac story through Māori conceptions of war, the NZDF and the wider political citizenship of contemporary Aotearoa New Zealand.

Rowan Light (2020) discusses the development of Māori Television's Anzac Day broadcast as a weaving together of the bicultural identity threads of the nation — 'Nō tātou te toto/The blood we share'. The broadcast's first decade, he states, 'was "a weighty Anzac Kaupapa", as Wena Haupiri put it — the price of citizenship . . . that spreads beyond the shores of Gallipoli to other wars that have shaped the history of Aotearoa New Zealand' (pp. 471–472). Its inclusiveness and reinvention of Anzac coverage has created space to reconsider the way we think not just about Anzac Day and Gallipoli, but a fuller sense of both past and future.

While some changes are evident, other aspects of the Anzac narrative in action have been slower to reflect wider New Zealand society. Following the historical mistakes made with returning soldiers, particularly Vietnam veterans, and the absence of women, Māori and minority groups in the Anzac narrative, issues of returned service personnel's inclusion and exclusion remain. Despite New Zealand personnel serving on a series of United Nations-mandated peacekeeping missions since 1973, some peacekeepers received similar treatment from their local RSAs as had their Vietnam counterparts. Aaron Wood, a veteran of service in East Timor, Somalia and Afghanistan, believes that recent veterans have been treated with apathy and indifference by those same veterans who experienced similar exclusion on returning home from Vietnam ('Veterans from wars', 2016). We need to ensure that the narrative that we use to explain our military and national historical identity also acknowledges our current social and political contexts, and is capable of future adaptations.

Conclusion: Anzac — history and myth

As Ella explained in her introduction to this section of the book, one of the functions of official stories is to shape people's understandings of events which — as in the case of Anzac — have become central to many (but not all) people's sense of what it means to be in and of this country. But the thing about these narratives is that they always obscure other, competing interpretations of events, times and actions. This chapter has demonstrated some of the ways in which the orthodox Anzac narrative performs this kind of emotional and political labour. It is important to keep in mind, too, that such work does not happen by accident. There is always a point to it. In the case of the Anzac story, part of that point is to ensure that certain less noble engagements — such as the 1918 Surafend Massacre — are forgotten. Thus, a powerful narrative does two things at once: it tells a compelling story *and* makes sure that things which might disrupt that story slip out of sight. As New Zealand historian and archivist Rachel Buchanan (2012) puts it: 'Forgetting is rarely innocent. People have to work hard not to know, not to recall, not to see, to be truly ignorant' (p. 11).

Ending this sort of forgetting involves working hard to reach new understandings of things long taken for granted. In this regard, Australian historian Martin Crotty (2009) argues that war 'is often difficult and emotive for historians and history teachers to traverse' (p. 14), because in order to understand exactly what happened, and why, we need to unpack the narrative, to strip away the 'veneer of myth' and deal with the harsh realities of conflict. Examining the past can unearth stark realities that may not reflect our traditional understanding of an event, creating uncomfortable questions for individuals, families, organisations or states.

Crotty suggests that historians have collectively exposed gaps between 'Anzac the mythology and Anzac the reality' (p. 14). When the realities of conflict and war are examined, we see the death and destruction, hardships and trauma caused, and perhaps that is why such a history can be particularly grim for many of us. This may explain why many veterans came home and rarely spoke of their experiences, and why it fell to others to describe it for us in official history or constructed narrative.

Australian cultural historian Graham Seal (2007) states that, 'like all cultural constructs, Anzac is a conflation of history and myth' (p. 136). History gives us the opportunity to examine why and how certain Anzac narratives — be they myth or legend — have developed over time. Critical inquiry lets us consider where the Anzac legend came from and how it became so cemented in the national psyche. We can also examine those who challenge the narrative and think about why that matters. As Crotty (2009) puts it:

NZDF

Adapting to Covid: #StandatDawn Anzac commemorations

As New Zealanders complied with the restrictive Covid lockdown conditions in early 2020, the New Zealand Defence Force (NZDF) and the RSA launched a media campaign to show people how they could honour the spirit of the dawn service from their homes. The wording invoked Anzac values of courage, mateship and ingenuity in finding ways to participate on 25 April, but also suggested that these values were important in collectively facing the lockdown. RNZ broadcast the official service so people could stand at their gates, within their 'bubbles', listening to the service on their radios and so still feeling connected. Children were also encouraged to make poppies and attach them to their fences, as part of the family activities suggested on the NZDF website.

It is instructive to consider Anzac as a set of sometimes complementary and sometimes competing discourses — many voices, and many versions of Anzac, some of which are privileged, and others of which are silenced. But we need to remember in our teaching that Anzac is about much more than competing discourses. We need also to recognise that the Anzac legend cannot be so easily divorced from the realities that underlie it and which gave rise to it. Those very real human experiences, those moments of heroism and triumph, tragedy and farce, success and failure, deserve consideration for what they are — meaningful and profound human experiences worthy of recognition in their own right. (p. 15)

We may come to better understand the Anzac story by considering it from many perspectives — from soldiers and politicians to families, community groups and the state as a whole. Crotty (2009) adds that our understanding of war and conflict is incredibly important, 'just too important for us to not get it right' (p. 17), and we have a responsibility, as critical thinkers, to look beyond what we might see in newspapers and television, or hear from politicians, or indeed others — including the RSA — with interests in emphasising particular elements of the story at the expense of others.

Biles and Spoonley (2007) argue that national identities are mutable and should not be protected from change for nationalist ends. 'In a world of change,' they state, 'there is something decidedly unsettling about a cohesionist or nationalist approach that seeks to prevent or minimise change or diversity' (p. 195). Lest we forget, best we forget . . . or best we choose to remember more fully?

This chapter began by inviting you to reflect on the nature and meaning of Anzac. Its major aim was to consider the nature and origins of the Anzac narrative, and how it has evolved to meet the contextual needs of generations of New Zealanders. While its origin was in New Zealand's First World War experience, the narrative continues to evolve as it takes into account other conflicts, and embraces an idea of including those who hitherto have been deliberately removed or carelessly left out of the story.

We sometimes assert that New Zealand's identity as an independent nation was born at Gallipoli, yet it is contestable that commemorating Anzac Day today reflects a growing recognition of all our citizens. Does the commemoration accept that the idea of Anzac and its place in our nation's story is as varied as the people who make New Zealand what it is? We can choose to look at our history and use this foundation 'myth' to define our wider society beyond its military origins today. The Anzac story is transitioning to a more inclusive and accurate chronicle that not only acknowledges where we have come from in the recent past, but also looks at our current place in the world, and perhaps at what our identity as New Zealanders might look like in the future.

Chapter 12 — Anzac: 'Lest we forget' or 'Best we forget'?
http://turangawaewae.massey.ac.nz/ch12.html

Further reading

Light, R. (2020). 'No tātou te toto'/ 'The blood we share': Māori Television and the reconfiguring of New Zealand war memory, *Journal of Australian Studies, 44*(4), 457–472.

Littlewood, D. (2017). Personal, local and enduring: Masculine citizenship in First World War Britain. In A. Brown & J. Griffiths (Eds.), *The citizen: Past and present* (pp. 171–195). Massey University Press.

O'Malley, V. (2016). *The Great War for New Zealand: Waikato, 1800–2000*. Bridget Williams Books.

Phillips J. (2014). Lest we forget: Remembering and forgetting: New Zealand's First World War. In C. Ferrall & H. Ricketts (Eds.), *How we remember: New Zealanders and the First World War* (pp. 228–240). Victoria University Press.

References

Baxter, A. (1968). *We will not cease.* Caxton Press. (Original work published 1939.)

Bennett, J. (2003). 'Massey's Sunday School picnic party': 'The other Anzacs' or honorary Australians? *War and Society, 21*(2), 23–54.

Biles, J., & Spoonley, P. (2007). National identity: What it can tell us about inclusion and exclusion. *National Identities, 9*(3), 191–195.

Buchanan, R. (2012). Beating shame: Parihaka and the very long sorry. *Te Pouhere Kōrero, 6*, 1–23.

Challinor, D., & Lancaster, E. (2000). *Who'll stop the rain? Agent Orange and the children of New Zealand's Vietnam veterans.* HarperCollins.

Crotty, M. A. (2009). Teaching Anzac: Fraught territory, teachable moments and professional responsibility. *Agora, 44*(2), 13–17.

Godfery, M. (2015, April 26). Why do we ignore the New Zealand Wars? *E-Tangata.* https://e-tangata.co.nz/history/why-do-we-ignore-the-new-zealand-wars

Grant, D. (1986). *Out in the cold: Pacifists and conscientious objectors in New Zealand during World War II*. Reed Methuen.

Greener, B. K., & Powles, A. R. (2015, May 5). The 'sons — and daughters — of ANZAC'? *The Strategist*. http://www.aspistrategist.org.au/the-sons-and-daughters-of-anzac

Grove, N., & Mead, H. M. (2001). *Ngā pēpeha a ngā tīpuna*. Victoria University Press.

Harper, G. (2015). *Johnny Enzed: The New Zealand soldier in the First World War 1914–1918*. Exisle Publishing.

Harper, G., & Richardson, C. (2006). *In the face of the enemy: The complete history of the Victoria Cross and New Zealand*. HarperCollins.

Hopner, V. (2014). *Home from war* [Doctoral dissertation, Massey University]. Semantic Scholar. https://mro.massey.ac.nz/handle/10179/6235

Hoverd, W. (2015, April 22). *Rethinking Anzac Day: The dangers of an exclusionary discourse*. http://www.esocsci.org.nz/rethinking-anzac-day-the-dangers-of-an-exclusionary-discourse

Hunt, T. (2016, April 27). Peace action group behind guerrilla Wellington sculpture of Archie Baxter. *Stuff*. www.stuff.co.nz/national/last-post-first-light/79341719/peace-action-group-behind-guerilla-wellington-sculpture-of-archie-baxter

Keenan, D. (2021). *Wars without end: Ngā pakanga whenua o Aotearoa*. Penguin Random House.

King, M. (1977). *Te Puea: A life*. Hodder and Stoughton.

King, M. (2003). *The Penguin history of New Zealand*. Penguin.

Light, R. (2020). 'No tātou te toto'/ 'The blood we share': Māori Television and the reconfiguring of New Zealand war memory. *Journal of Australian Studies, 44*(4), 457–472.

Livingston, T., & Kenny, L. (2019, April 4). Muslim prayer at Anzac Day service scrapped over security concerns. *Stuff*. www.stuff.co.nz/national/last-post-first-light/111797046/muslim-prayer-at-porirua-anzac-day-service-scrapped-over-security-concerns

McGibbon, I. C. (1991). *The path to Gallipoli: Defending New Zealand, 1840–1915*. GP Books.

McGibbon, I. C. (2010). *New Zealand's Vietnam War: A history of combat, commitment and controversy*. Exisle Publishing.

McGibbon, I. C., & Goldstone, P. (Eds.). (2000). *The Oxford companion to New Zealand military history*. Oxford University Press.

McLeod, J. (1986). *Myth and reality: The New Zealand soldier in World War II*. Reed.

McNeilly, H. (2021, October 29). 'Stigma can stick': End to decade-long battle as NZ's first memorial to conscientious objectors is unveiled. *Stuff*. www.stuff.co.nz/national/education/126828253/stigma-can-stick-end-to-decadelong-battle-as-nzs-first-memorial-to-conscientious-objectors-is-unveiled

Ministry for Culture and Heritage. (2016, March 22). *New research dramatically increases the numbers of New Zealand soldiers at Gallipoli.* http://www.mch.govt.nz/new-research-dramatically-increases-numbers-new-zealand-soldiers-gallipoli

O'Malley, V. (2016). *The Great War for New Zealand: Waikato, 1800–2000.* Bridget Williams Books

Orange, C. (2000). The price of citizenship? The Māori war effort. In J. Crawford (Ed.*), Kia kaha: New Zealand in the Second World War.* Oxford University Press.

Owen, D. (2021). 'It's just hell here'. In M. Keith & C. Szekely (Eds.), *Te Kupenga: 101 Stories of Aotearoa from the Turnbull* (p. 110). Massey University Press.

Peace Action Wellington. (2016, April 25). *Remembering the conscientious objectors.* https://peaceactionwellington.wordpress.com/2016/04/25/remembering-the-conscientious-objectors/

Phillips, J. (2014). Lest we forget: Remembering and forgetting. New Zealand's First World War. In C. Ferrall & H. Ricketts (Eds.), *How we remember: New Zealanders and the First World War* (pp. 228–240). Victoria University Press.

Phillips, J. (2016). *To the memory: New Zealand's war memorials.* Potton & Burton.

Pugsley, C., & Ferrall, C. (2015). *Remembering Gallipoli: Interviews with New Zealand Gallipoli veterans.* Victoria University Press.

Seal, G. (2007). ANZAC: The sacred in the secular. *Journal of Australian Studies, 31*(91), 135–144.

Sheftall, M. D. (2009). *Altered memories of the Great War: Divergent narratives of Britain, Australia, New Zealand and Canada.* I. B. Taurus.

Shoebridge, T. (2016). *Conscientious objection and dissent in the First World War.* http://www.nzhistory.net.nz/war/first-world-war/conscientious-objection

Stone, A. (2014, August 16). 100 Kiwi stories: Chinese soldier a hero to mates. *The New Zealand Herald.* http://www.nzherald.co.nz/nz/news/article.cfm?c_id=1&objectid=11309675

Tolerton, J. (2017). *Make her praises heard afar: New Zealand women overseas in World War One.* Booklovers Books.

Veterans from wars since Vietnam 'treated with indifference'. (2016, April 24). *NBR Weekend Review.* http://www.nbr.co.nz/article/veterans-wars-vietnam-treated-indifference-188138-ck?u

Vietnam veterans remain divided. (2008, December 15). *Otago Daily Times.* https://www.odt.co.nz/news/national/vietnam-veterans-remain-divided

Walker, F. (2012). 'Descendants of a warrior race': The Māori contingent, New Zealand Pioneer Battalion, and martial race myth, 1914–19. *War and Society, 31*(1), 1–21.

Conclusion

Identity and belonging in Aotearoa New Zealand

Richard Shaw

Introduction

This book has been about what it means to be in and/or of this place, Aotearoa New Zealand, at this particular juncture in history. We haven't ventured a definitive response to the question of what that meaning might be for any given individual — that would have been more than a little arrogant — but we have sought, to quote from the introductory chapter, to provide you with the opportunity 'to probe, prompt and . . . reflect on aspects of your own sense of self, and of the ways in which we collectively make sense of who we are, which might otherwise continue to enjoy the status of received wisdom'.

In that spirit of reflection and curiosity, in this concluding piece we offer our own thoughts on many of the issues raised in the chapters you have just read, and consider some of the challenges and opportunities posed to our individual and collective sense of identity by the trends, events and developments covered by those who have contributed to this book.

The faces, voices, places and stories of Aotearoa New Zealand

There is a temptation for each generation to assert that the times in which it lives are more momentous, the challenges it faces of a greater magnitude, and the changes it is going through more sweeping than any which have come before. As editors, we are aware that by focusing throughout this book largely on things that are changing we risk overlooking the extent to which there is also constancy in Aotearoa. If this book is an account of change, it is also one of continuity: migration has always been part of the story of this place; today's protests are motivated by many of the same things (a wish to have one's voice heard, to right a wrong or to change minds) that compelled people to take to the streets in times past; and much as they have done since the University of New Zealand was created in 1870 (a year after the establishment of Otago University), our universities continue to create and disseminate knowledge.

All the same, at the end of this book the four of us are left with an unavoidable sense that things are *happening* here. Establishing whether or not those things — the 'trends, events and developments' referred to immediately above — are of greater (or lesser) significance than those of earlier eras is not the point. What matters is that they are consequential, and therefore need to be made sense of.

Faces

At the risk of stating the obvious, one of the most striking things going on is the extent to which the individual and collective faces of this place are changing. Think back to Trudie and Tracey's chapter in Part 1, for instance, and you will recall that the proportion of the population aged 65 years or older is climbing steadily. While much of the public debate occasioned by this trend is couched in the language of costs and burdens (it can't have escaped your attention that older people are typically described in terms of one or the other, or both), we think that it is important also to acknowledge that there is much to celebrate in an ageing population. It is worth noting, for example, that the European Commission (2015) estimates that the so-called Silver Economy — the value of public and private sector spending on older people — comprises the third largest economy in the world. Amidst the economic costs, in other words, there also lie opportunities. Moreover, older people contribute their experience and knowledge in paid and voluntary capacities, are important repositories of wisdom, and can provide an historical context for current events that is a valuable complement to the tyranny of the immediate.

There is, of course, a different demographic story unfolding among Māori. In 1856, the decimation of the tangata whenua population was such that Dr Isaac

Featherston, a physician and politician, felt moved to observe that Pākehā had a duty to smooth the pillow of a dying race (Buck, 1924). Featherston's observation has not come to pass: instead, Māori have picked up the pillow and hurled it across the room. Today a third of all Māori are 15 years of age or younger. This poses its own demographic, political and social challenges and opportunities, a number of which Te Rā referred to in Chapter 2, and it is important that these are not drowned out in the growing public discourse occasioned by an ageing non-Māori population.

Change of a different kind is reflected in the fact that there are now more ethnicities in this country than there are nations in the world (Hayward & Shaw, 2016). It is worth emphasising once again just how quickly things are shifting in this respect: it is estimated, for instance, that the percentage of the population identifying as European or New Zealander will fall from 70 per cent (at the 2018 census) to 64 per cent by 2043, while the proportion identifying broadly as Asian will grow from 16 percent in 2018 to 26 percent by 2043 (Stats NZ, 2021b).

These sorts of developments have consequences for other aspects of the ways in which things are done in Aotearoa. In short — and you have encountered this point repeatedly throughout the book — look closely enough and you will see that our different identity threads, at both the individual and collective levels, are always intricately interwoven: changes in one typically echo in another.

Voices

Demographic (and cultural, religious, linguistic, musical, sartorial, culinary and so on) diversification has altered the sounds, tone and tenor of the voices now heard in the public domain. There was a time in this country when a few voices regularly dominated at the expense of others, but — at the risk of sounding naïve — our view is that that epoch is gradually passing into history. This is not to deny that challenges remain: as Ella pointed out in her chapter on protest, and as David explained in his on inequality, there are voices which — for reasons of exclusion, often on the basis of identity — remain muted or entirely unheard. Nonetheless, to some degree at least, the ever-growing inclusion of previously marginalised groups as legitimate members of the national community — most recently, perhaps, through attempts to ban gay conversion therapy — is consistent with one particular characterisation of the history of democracy as 'the collapse of one exclusion after another' (Dunn, 2005, p. 136).

We are cautiously optimistic that this collapsing of exclusion will continue, not because the benign march of progress is inevitable (there is plenty of evidence to the contrary), but because people who care about such things will continue to agitate, protest, push and argue for change. But reflecting on Stella's chapter in particular (which enjoys many connections with the chapters on voice, even though it is ostensibly about places), we would also strike a cautionary note associated with the astounding growth in the number and variety of platforms from which voices can now be expressed (or suppressed).

In the context of a book interested in who gets to contribute to public debates (and who does not), and how they do so, this diversification presents both challenges and opportunities. Few of us, surely, would wish to revert to a world lacking the extraordinary opportunities the internet affords us to talk with, listen to, engage with and learn from others.

Yet in an increasingly cluttered, chaotic and noisy digital environment, there are no guarantees that our particular voice will be heard — much less listened to — by others. (Arguably, the reverse is more likely.) The distinction between voicing one's views and being listened to is critical. Expressing voice does not in and of itself lead to dialogue: the former can very well occur in the absence of the latter, such that people talk past each other and are eventually reduced to (or actively choose) shouting into a void. Bluntly, it is difficult to learn from others or to disagree well when the volume has been ratcheted up to 10.

Clearly, this is not restricted to online environments: as Ella explained in Chapter 5, one of the chief reasons people take to the streets in protest is because they feel they are not being listened to. However, the intemperate nature of much of what passes for discourse in online environments does throw into especially sharp relief just how important the capacity to listen to others — especially to those with whom we disagree — is to fostering an inclusive, tolerant society. But that, of course, requires encountering those others in the first instance, and the temptation to frequent gated digital communities inhabited by like-minded people can diminish the likelihood of ever encountering these 'Others'.

Perhaps this sounds dystopian (and certainly not everyone hangs out in digital echo chambers). All the same, our sense is that the exercise of voice in digital environments does present a conundrum. Certainly, we have many more forums in which we can seek to voice our views and to participate in various communities. But it is also the case that, if we opt to circulate online exclusively with those whose voices we find congenial, or indeed are (more worryingly) limited to those voices by the algorithms underpinning the digital tools we use, we reduce our contact with those with whom we might disagree or who live lives that differ to our own — and are therefore increasingly poorly placed to understand them. At its most extreme, of course, this can contribute to violent horrors such as those visited upon the Muslim community during the Christchurch mosque attacks on 15 March 2019.

Places

The places in and on which we stand are not immune from the sorts of phenomena covered in the initial sections of the book: they, too, are shifting. We do not necessarily mean that in a literal sense, although as those of us who live in Christchurch (and in other places, of course) know only too well, the potential for tectonic activity in our islands is such that this, too, is the case, and sometimes with devastating effects. Rather, our sense is that if we were able to take a large step back and literally look into the nation's homes, many of the day-to-day routines and rituals through which people now live their lives would be different to those of the homes of, say, 30 or 40 years ago.

Think of the developments we have touched on or alluded to in this book alone (and they are far from exhaustive): a young and growing Māori population; the advent of sophisticated digital technologies; migration within New Zealand (including from rural to urban centres, although to a degree this trend is now reversing); the arrival of new migrant and refugee families; and inequalities in the distribution of wealth and income. Now think of the myriad ways in which those and other developments might play out in people's homes, and you get some sense of how rich and varied must be the conventions, norms and rules that shape all of the lives lived in all of our homes.

But, as Trudie and Juliana highlighted in Chapter 7, for some people home is not a nurturing or caring environment; it is a place in which damage is done and from which scars are carried. Others do not have homes at all. If variety and richness are part of the story we tell of life at home in Aotearoa New Zealand, then we must also tell of those forced to sleep at night in cars, or live 10 to a room, or who are constantly moving from house to house in search of a home. These stories, too, must be narrated. This country can indeed be a great place in which to raise kids — but that seems unlikely to be the case for some or all of the 210,000 (fully 20 per cent) of our children who, in 2020, lived in households that earned less than 50 per cent of the median disposable household income (after removing housing costs) (Stats NZ, 2021a).

Insecurity of a different kind besets the nation's universities. They continue to perform the important statutory work of speaking truth to power, but their capacity to do so is under threat. The challenge has in part to do with the mounting cost of securing a university education (which Richard and Matt walked you through in their chapter); it also stems from the increasingly entrenched view that the primary purpose of a university education is to enhance students' employment prospects. Apropos the former, we may already have passed the point at which the price of attending university has become a significant deterrent to some. And while the employment narrative is, in and of itself, not necessarily a bad thing, if employability becomes the *only* basis on which the worth of universities is assessed, we risk doing damage to our institutions of higher learning that will be very difficult to repair.

Jointly, both developments have the capacity to significantly alter the nature of the university (if they have not already done so). We are certainly not suggesting that New Zealand's universities are in imminent danger of abandoning their historic mission to act as critic and conscience of society. However, if Harvard professor Michael Sandel (2012) is correct in arguing that when a price is charged for something then 'market norms will crowd out nonmarket norms' (p. 78), at the very least we should be asking whether or not recent developments are hampering the universities' ability to foster free and independent thought.

Stories

Notwithstanding that they contain kernels of truth, it is no surprise that some of the received wisdoms that may once have applied in this country no longer hold true (or are, at least, coming under stress). Put another way, certain of the narratives we have collectively constructed over the years as a means of explaining ourselves both to each other and to the wider world need to be questioned.

In Chapter 10, David demonstrated that — both empirically and rhetorically — the fabric of the broadly egalitarian society constructed across the better part of the twentieth century has been rent by over three decades' worth of reform. Much the same point — that material circumstances and the stories told about them are drifting apart — was made by Juliana, and Helen and Carl in the chapters on the environment and the Anzac story.

This general principle is not limited to the narratives that feature in this book. For instance, the increasingly multicultural character of the national population is thought by some to pose a risk to biculturalism. In recent decades, considerable investment has been made in clarifying and setting in place the foundations of a bicultural nation. That project has been greeted with differing degrees of enthusiasm, and is some way from completion. For some, the prospects of completion are challenged by the arrival of people from elsewhere who have not been part of the process thus far. Clearly, migration need not be anathema to biculturalism, but it does generate challenges that need careful political management if the bicultural project is not to slip into irrelevance.

What happens when we are confronted by such discrepancies? When confronted with something — an event, a person, a smell or a sight — that challenges the narrative tools we habitually deploy as sense-making devices, we have two main choices. One is to hold on to the stories with which we are familiar and feel comfortable, even when these are demonstrably at variance with material developments. The other is to not default to these orthodox narratives, but instead to 'use our intelligence freely' (Small, 2013, p. 74), and to adjust the story such that it is consistent with the new or emerging state of affairs.

This does *not* mean we have to repudiate that which is dear to us. The point collectively made by David, Juliana, Helen and Carl in Part 4 is that we cherish certain narratives in part because they contain truths and embody aspirations of who we would like to be. More than that, as British writer Lisa Appignanensi (2011) puts it: 'We are narrative creatures, and the stories we tell friends and ourselves occupy our consciousness for longer than the acts we engage in' (p. 69). Recruited to the purposes of this book, Appignanensi's point is that we recount and reproduce stories of national identity because they provide the co-ordinates through which we locate ourselves in this place; they give us a sense that we belong to a larger community; they help us recognise others like ourselves (which is helpful when you are far from home); and they furnish us with a sense of New Zealand exceptionalism.

For these reasons, it can be intensely unsettling when these foundation stories are called into question. All the same, we know that our grand narratives of national identity are partial and mask other inconvenient truths. For what it may be worth, our own view as editors is that, as circumstances change and new historical interpretations are reached, it is both healthy and necessary to question and revise these narratives. And defensiveness is not the only alternative. Rather, especially when change arrives from the outside (via migration, for instance, and the threats this allegedly poses to 'the New Zealand way of life'), it is possible to remain rooted in our personal understandings of our own cultural context but also to appreciate that 'what is foreign to that culture can . . . still be worthy of thought and respect' (McCumber, 2016). We are, in short, entirely capable of crafting refurbished national stories that are less partial and more inclusive than the ones they supersede.

Conclusion: Don't leave town 'til you've seen the country

The sorts of patterns and trends we have explored in this book beg a question that has been implicit in the chapters you have read, but which we wish now to make explicit. How do we respond, both as individuals and as a wider national community, to these things that are *happening* around us? How do we react — emotionally, personally, politically — to the changes taking place, and which, depending on one's stance, might be construed as either a threat to an existing way of doing things or an opportunity to do those things a little differently (and perhaps a little better)? The four of us would like to end this book with an explicitly normative response to such questions, using Aotearoa New Zealand's reputation as a much-travelled nation as a device for doing so.

That the gap year, or OE (overseas experience), is — or at least was, before the advent of Covid-19, but will be again — a rite of passage for young New Zealanders is another of our national truisms. Most of us have experience of or know someone with tales to tell of how they were received by others in far-off lands. Of how they were made welcome when their face was first encountered. Of how their voice — with its notoriously flattened vowels — was listened to by someone who became a friend. Of how they explored others' places — and perhaps made a home in them for a time. And of how their stories of rugby, beaches and baches were listened to with curiosity by others.

As with all such discourses, the OE or gap-year narrative provides only a partial description of reality, but it exercises considerable sway over our collective imagination nonetheless — perhaps even more so than was the case before the global pandemic reached our shores, temporarily curtailing international travel. Part of its appeal lies in what it says about our better nature: that travel opens our minds and broadens our understanding of the world and those in it. Much the same can also be achieved through the intellectual travel we engage in through reading. Of course, the reverse may equally apply: exposure to new faces, unknown voices, exotic places and unfamiliar stories can reinforce rather than revise one's existing views, beliefs and preferences. For instance, Janine Wiles (2008) has written of the ways in which New Zealanders in London try to recreate a sense of home while overseas by living, socialising and working with other migrant New Zealanders.

The Front Lawn song 'Tomorrow Night' has the immortal lyrics: 'On the [London] Underground she'd ride / talking loud in a Kiwi accent / talking about . . . tomorrow night': https://www.youtube.com/watch?v=ZC8-yvHm1io

But at the very least, when we travel we put ourselves in the way of potential encounters with others that can shape how we make sense of what we come across when (or if) we return to Aotearoa New Zealand. Importantly, and as the authors whose work you have read have portrayed, the conditions for developing this sort of reflexive identity via encounters with unfamiliarity also exist here in this place. In the 1980s, the then New Zealand Tourist and Publicity Department ran a highly successful advertising campaign, the punchline of which was — delivered just as our intrepid Kiwi traveller in the ad was about to paddle over the Victoria Falls — 'Don't leave town 'til you've seen the country'. (It remains a source of amazement to the four of us that someone didn't dust these ads off and run them again during 2020 and 2021.) In a sense, this book has offered the opportunity to travel that country, to explore some of its human, physical and historical contours, and — above all — to greet its people, listen to its voices, explore its places and learn its stories.

Watch the New Zealand Tourist and Publicity Department ad here: https://www.youtube.com/watch?v=PVH7uBzQX7I

References

Appignanensi, L. (2011). *All about love: Anatomy of an unruly emotion.* W. W. Norton.

Buck, P. (Te Rangi Hīroa). (1924). The passing of the Māori. *Transactions and Proceedings of the Royal Society of New Zealand, 55,* 362–375.

Dunn, J. (2005). *Setting the people free: The story of democracy.* Atlantic Books.

European Commission. (2015). *Growing the silver economy in Europe.*

Hayward, J., & Shaw, R. (Eds.) (2016). *Historical and political dictionary of New Zealand.* Rowman & Littlefield.

McCumber, J. (2016, October 2). How humanities can help fix the world. *The Chronicle of Higher Education.* http://www.chronicle.com/article/How-Humanities-Can-Help-Fix/237955

Sandel, M. (2012). *What money can't buy: The moral limits of markets.* Farrar, Straus and Giroux.

Small, H. (2013). *The value of the humanities.* Oxford University Press.

Stats NZ. (2021a). *Latest release of child poverty statistics — corrected.* https://www.stats.govt.nz/news/latest-release-of-child-poverty-statistics

Stats NZ. (2021b). *Population projected to become more ethnically diverse.* https://www.stats.govt.nz/news/population-projected-to-become-more-ethnically-diverse

Wiles, J. (2008). Sense of home in a transnational social space: New Zealanders in London. *Global Networks, 8*(1), 116–137.

About the contributors

Carl Bradley — an outstanding family man, colleague and wonderful friend to many — died suddenly in May 2021, before his chapter could be completed. Carl was a man of many talents. He came to academia following a career in private sector leadership and management, and held a PhD from the School of Humanities and Social Science (Classics Department), University of Newcastle, Australia. He had extensive tertiary teaching experience at Massey University, Victoria University of Wellington, and the Australian College of Applied Psychology in Melbourne, and his research interests ranged over criminology, leadership, warrior societies, Māori warfare, and responses to military imperialism. Carl brought all of that deep, wide knowledge to his scholarship: his book *Outlaw bikers and ancient warbands: Hyper-masculinity and cultural continuity* was recently published by Palgrave, and we are delighted and honoured that we still have his voice — joined by that of Helen Dollery — in the chapter in this publication on the Anzac narrative: '"Lest we forget" or "Best we forget"?'

Trudie Cain is a senior lecturer in the School of People, Environment and Planning at Massey University. She has particular expertise in qualitative research methodologies and ethics, and her research interests include gendered, sized and migrant identities; identity and belonging in a local context; and the materiality of everyday lives. She is currently involved in a number of collaborative research projects, including an examination of older adults' constructions of home, place and community; a study with tenants of public housing; and an ethnography of the impact of Covid-19 for migrants.

Helen Dollery teaches citizenship at Massey University as part of the Bachelor of Arts core courses. She is an Aotearoa New Zealand historian, whose PhD focused on the relationship between the New Zealand Scouting and Guiding movements and their role in developing youthful citizenship. Her research reflects her interest in how twentieth-century New Zealanders engaged in civil society, and she recently contributed to a social history of Palmerston North.

Rand Hazou is a Palestinian-Kiwi theatre practitioner and scholar. His research explores theatre engaging with rights and social justice.

His research interests lie in applied theatre, refugee theatre, and decolonial theory and practice. In 2004, he was commissioned by the United Nations Development Programme to travel to the Occupied Territories in Palestine to run workshops for Palestinian youths. In Aotearoa, he has led teaching and creative projects engaging with prison, aged-care and street communities.

Ella Kahu is a senior lecturer in the School of Psychology at Massey University, and also holds an Adjunct Senior Research Fellow position with the University of the Sunshine Coast in Australia. Her disciplinary background is social psychology, and her primary research focus is student experiences in higher education with a particular interest in student engagement. She has published widely in higher-education journals, and her conceptual framework of student engagement, developed in 2013 and extended in 2018, is used to inform both research and practice at universities around the world. Her primary teaching is the first-year inter-disciplinary course on identity and citizenship which saw the creation of this book.

David Littlewood is a lecturer in history in the School of Humanities, Media and Creative Communication at Massey University. He teaches on New Zealand's political and social history, and on topics relating to the world wars. His research focuses on how involvement in the two global conflicts impacted on New Zealand and British society, with particular reference to the implementation of conscription. His first book was *Military service tribunals and boards in the Great War: Determining the fate of Britain's and New Zealand's conscripts* (Routledge), and he is currently working on a book about New Zealand's experience of conscription in the Second World War.

Juliana Mansvelt is a professor in the School of People, Environment and Planning at Massey University. A social geographer, she is interested in the ways people understand and relate to one another in place. Her research interests centre on landscapes and practices of consumption, particularly with regard to the everyday lives of older New Zealanders.

Te Rā Moriarty is a descendant of Ngāti Toa Rangatira, Ngāti Koata, Rangitāne and Ngāti Kahungunu. He is an assistant lecturer in Te Pūtahi a Toi, the School of Māori Knowledge, at Massey University. His main areas of teaching are te reo Māori, tikanga Māori and te ao Māori. Currently, he is completing a doctorate focusing on karakia practitioners in the modern world.

Tracey Nicholls is a senior lecturer in the School of People, Environment and Planning at Massey University. She teaches in politics and international relations, predominantly in political theory. Her areas of research interest include decolonisation theory, feminist peace studies, ethics and politics of care, and theorising improvisatory elements of grassroots political movements. Her current research focus is gendered inequities within tertiary institutions, and the restructuring possibilities suggested by feminist ethics of care.

Stella Pennell is a lecturer in the School of People, Environment and Planning at Massey University. Her research interests include digital identities, platform capitalism, digital labour, biopolitics and qualitative research methodologies. She is an associate editor of *New Zealand Sociology* and is currently co-developing an international network of researchers interested in addressing the theoretical-empirical gap in relation to digital labour, capital accumulation, and the relationship between power and the reproduction of the symbolic order.

Matt Russell has been a tutor in the Tūrangawaewae citizenship course at Massey University since 2016. He is currently completing a doctorate in sociology, which looks at how science is politicised within resource management conflicts in Aotearoa New Zealand. Matt's research has been published in the *Journal of Tourism Research*, *Thesis Eleven* and *New Zealand Sociology*, but he has a particular interest in the relationship between science and politics. Prior to beginning his PhD, Matt had a long association with Massey University Students' Association.

Richard Shaw is a professor of politics at Massey University. He is author of *The forgotten coast* (Massey University Press), and has also authored or edited several books on public policy and executive government, most recently *The Edward Elgar handbook on ministerial advisers* (Edward Elgar; with Chris Eichbaum) and *Core executives in comparative perspective* (Palgrave; with Kristoffer Kolltveit). With Janine Hayward, he is co-editor of the *Historical and political dictionary of New Zealand* (Rowman and Littlefield), and his research on political advisers has been published in leading international journals, including *Governance*, *Public Administration*, *Public Management Review* and *Parliamentary Affairs*.

Acknowledgements

Books like *Tūrangawaewae: Identity and belonging in Aotearoa New Zealand* are called into existence through the efforts of many people, only some of whom are contributors to this edition. In that spirit we would like to thank our friends and colleagues who authored or co-authored chapters in the first edition of the publication — Te Rina Warren, Marg Forster, Veronica Tawhai, Ann Dupuis, Sy Taffel and Rhys Ball. Particular thanks are due to Catherine Rivera and Rosalie Alter-Shaw, whose research sits behind the blue pages and QR codes found in the first and second editions of *Tūrangawaewae*, respectively.

This book would not exist without the parallel course of study at Massey University. Since the first edition was published in 2017, the publication has been central to teaching the course over 10 semesters and three campuses to over 5000 students. Our thanks go to our students and our colleagues on those teaching teams whose questions, discussions and thinking have undoubtedly influenced this second edition.

We also wish to extend our gratitude to Nicola Legat, Anna Bowbyes and the team at Massey University Press, who have turned our words into the beautiful object you are holding. And finally, we would like to dedicate this book to our friend and colleague, Carl Bradley.

Index

100% Pure New Zealand 249–54, **252**, 256, 260–62

A

Abbott, Tony 286
ACT Party 190
advertising 32, 216, 231, 233, 261, 302
age 70–75, 296
agriculture & countryside 226, 250, 251, 253, 260–61
   see also land-use
     communities & workers 53, 112, 124, 232–34, 237, 263
ahikā 248
Aho, Huriana Kopeke-Te 138–40
Air New Zealand 255
Airbnb 213–14
Alderton, Chloe 161
algorithmic identity *see* data collection & mining; digital
Allenby, General 278
Altman, Dennis 114
Amazon 203, 217
Anderson, Waimarama 284
Andrews, Leighton 215–16, 271
Angus, Rita 132, 133
Anzac 15–16, 136–38, 225, 226, 231, 268–91 *see also* First World War; Gallipoli
   memorials & services 270, 272, **272**, 274, 279, 285–87, 289, **289**
Aotearoa, Māori arrival 44–46
apartheid 116–18, 120, 141 *see also* racism & race relations
Apiata, Willie 276, 277, **277**
Appignanensi, Lisa 301
application programming interfaces *see* data collection & mining
Aramoana 136
Archibald Baxter Peace Garden 137, 285
Ardern, Jacinda 130, 210
Armed Constabulary 52
the arts 15, 84–85, 129–47, 142
Ashley-Rakahuri River 259, **259**
assimilation *see* Māori
astronomy 201, 229
Athens 91, 109, 188

Auckland
   anti-Vietnam protest 280, **280**
   Auckland Arts Festival 130
   Auckland City Mission 236, **236**
   Auckland Council survey 67
   Auckland Pride Festival 66, **66**
   Bastion Point 53
   growth & diversity 65, 67, 74, 131, 134, 141
   Hero Parade 66, 114
   homes & housing 162, 166, **166**, 169, 170
   Lantern Festival 64, **64**
   Lighthouse/Tū Whenua-a-Kura 141–42
   Mt Albert state housing 166, **166**
   Northcote 162–63
   Pasifika Festival 144, **144**
   Pensioners Settlement electorate 98
   sculpture 141–42
   Takaparawhau 53
   Waiuku **71**
   Whakaako Kia Whakaora / Educate to Liberate mural 130, 131, 138–41, **139**
Australia 170–71
Australian and New Zealand Army Corps *see* Anzac
Australian Imperial Forces 271
avatars 210–11

B

baby boom & boomers 71, **71**, 73, 75
Ball, Claudia 263
Bastion Point 53, 118
Baxter, Archibald 137, 275
"Be a Tidy Kiwi" campaign 256
Beeby, Clarence 187
Bell, Duncan 224
Bell, Leah 284
Bellamy, Richard 34
Bennett, James 273, 275
Beyer, Georgina 69
biculturalism & multiculturism 16, 133, 135, 142, 287, 300–301
big data *see* data collection & mining
Big Gay Out 66
Biles, J. 290
bio technologies 260

biodiversity 258, 260–61

Births, Deaths, Marriages, and Relationships Registration Bill 70, 116

Black Panthers 130, 138–40

#BlackLivesMatter. 121, 123

Bradley, Carl 278, **278**

Bradshaw, C.J.A. 257

'Brand New Zealand' 254, 255, 256, 260

brands & environment 253–54

   100% Pure New Zealand 249–54, **252**, 256, 260–62

   Clean and Green 225, 226, 247–63

Brash, Don 240

Breheny, Mary 256

Briggs, Mark 275

Broadacre City 161

Brodie, R.J. 260

Buchanan, Rachel 288

Burr, Vivien 26, 29

Busby, James 47, 50, 51

Butcher, Elizabeth 256

C

Cain, T. 67

Cambridge Analytica 216

Cameron, Alfred 279

Canton, Alice 131, 134

Carroll, James 87

carving 129

Cass 132, **132**, 133

census 61, 64, 65, 168, 297

Chapple, Geoff 118

charity 236

Cheney-Lippold, J. 203–4

children 72, **72**, **166**, 169, 171, 208, 238, 299

  see also teenagers; youth

childcare 162–63, 165

Chinese 64, 67, 134, 284

Christchurch

Christchurch Call 210

Gap Filler 148, **148**

mosque attacks 13, 210, 298

Christianity 112–13, 114–15

citizenship 13–15, 23–26, **26**, 30–38, 89, 104, 155, 216

  see also communities

  Māori views 17

  universities 186–87

  & voice 84–85

Civil Union Act 2004 114–15

Clarifai 217

Clark, Helen 276, 280

Clean and Green 225, 226, 247–63

climate change 111, 123, 187, 258, 259

cloaks 129–30

Cole, Vanessa 169–70

colonisation *see* Māori; settlement

  & colonisation

communities 15, 29–30, 34, 84, 162–63

  see also citizenship

Concerned Citizens 136

conformity 70, 112, 207 *see also* gender

conscientious objectors 137–38, 275, 276, 285

  see also pacifism

conscription 137, 274–75

context 28–29 *see also* place

conversion therapy 66, 115, 297

Cook, James 50

Cook Islands 68

Cooper, Whina 48, **48**

Corrigall-Brown, C. 35

Cotton, Shane 133

Court of Appeal 108

Covid-19 171–72, 236, 255, 287, 289, **289**

  see also diseases & health

  & diversity 30, 65

  & education 183, 195–96

  & homes 158, 159, 170

  protests against 103, **103**, 123

Creative New Zealand 131

Crenshaw, Kimberlé 34

critical thinking 170, 179, 193–95, 197, 206

Crotty, Martin 288–89

cultural rights 43, 48, 53, 55–56, 60, 85, 129–47

Cyril Bassett 276, 277, **277**

D

dairy industry 256, 261

Daniels, Erina 143

data collection & mining 203–6, 212–13, 215–16

  see also digital

Dawn Raids 130, 138–41

de Beauvoir, Simone 32

Dean, Andrew 97

Deans, William 273, 279

  The Declaration of the Independence of

   New Zealand 47

Deleuze, Giles 204, 217

democracy 88, 90–91, 102, 109, 123, 204, 238–40, 297
& universities 170, 179, 188, 194
demographics 14, 22, 24
& age 73–74, 296–97 (*see also* diversity)
& ethnicity 32, 61, 63, 65
depression 131, 143
Depression, Great 166, 167, 232, 241, **241**
diet *see* food & diet
digital *see also* data collection & mining
access & literacy 207–10, 216–17
activism 120–23 (*see also* social media)
identities 203, 210–13, 215–17, 218
places 15, 155, 200–218, 298 (*see also* internet)
technologies 158, 183, 195
diseases & health 53, 74, 169, 238, 239, 240–41
see also Covid-19; mental health
diversity & superdiversity 22–23, 63–68
see also demographics; ethnicity
"Do the Right Thing" campaign 256
Dobbyn, Dave 162
domestic violence 171–72
Douglas, Emory 138–40
Douglas, Roger 235
Dupuis, Ann 167
Durie, M. 54, 55

E

Easton, Brian 234
education 72, **72**, 83, 169, 239 *see also* universities
Māori 54–55, 178, 201–2
Education Act 1989 193
egalitarianism *see* equality & inequality
elections & electoral systems *see* Māori; politics;
voting
Electoral Act 1893 96
emigration *see* immigration & emigration
employment & unemployment *see* labour market
entrepreneurs 213–14, 260
environment 15–16, 43–46, 225, 226, 247–63
ENZA 256
equality & inequality 15–16, 225–26, 229–43,
300–301 *see also* specific issues
ethnicity 61–68, 297 *see also* diversity
attacks & protests 13, 111, 116, 210, 298
ethnic precincts 65, 67
Māori 16–17
ethnoburbs 67–68
European Commission 296

European Economic Community 118, 234
exports 253–54, 256, 263

F

fa'afāfine 69
Facebook 70, 121, 203, 210, 212, 215–17
see also social media
fake news 216
families 162–65 *see also* homes & housing;
motherhood
domestic violence 171–72
farming *see* agriculture & countryside
fauna *see* flora & fauna
FCB 261
Featherston, Isaac 296–97
Federation of Aotearoa Migrants 88
FernMark 253–54, 256
fertility rates
festivals 65–66, **66**, 142, 144, **144**
Lantern festival 64, **64**
field punishment No. 1 **137**, 137–38, 285
films 82, 255
First World War 231, 272, **272**, 274–75 *see also* Anzac
flags 47, **47**, 50, 69, 121
flatmates *see* homes & housing
Fletcher Building 122
Flight of the Conchords 255
flora & fauna 258, 259
Fonterra 256
food & diet 67, 238
food banks 236, **236**, 237
Māori 46, 49, 248, 256
Foreshore and Seabed Act 2004 54, 108–9
forests 258
Fougere, Geoffrey 117–18
Frey, C. 193
Fridays for Future 123
Friedlander, Marti 117

G

Gallipoli campaign 271–74 *see also* Anzac
gaming & games 206–7, 209, **209**, 210–11
Gap Filler 148, **148**
Gay Day 66, 114
gay rights 68, 85, 112–14 *see also* LGBTQIA+
Gee, Maurice 159
Gendall 263

312   TŪRANGAWAEWAE

gender 69–70, 115–16 *see also* LGBTQIA+
  roles & norms 31, 112, 114, 164–65, 207
  see also conformity
Gisborne 65
Gleneagles Agreement 117
Godfery, Morgan 283
Goffman, Erving 158
goods and services tax (GST) 235, 237
government *see* politics; specific Parties
Greener, B.K. 286
greenhouse gas emissions 258
Greenpeace 250
Group Building scheme 168
Guy, Laurie 112, 113

H
hākari 49
hapū 46, 49 *see also* Māori, social structures
Harper, G. 276
HART (Halt All Racist Tours) 117
hate groups & attacks 13, 116, 210, 298
haukāinga 49, 60
Haupiri, Wena 287
Hawaiki 44, 55, 129
Hawkins, Aaron 285
Hay, Colin 104
Hay, Iain 197
Hay, Keith 110, **110**
He Puapua report 240
He tirohanga Māori 14, 16–17
He Whakaputanga o te Rangatiratanga o Nu Tireni
  47, 50–51, 87
health & disease 53, 74, 169, 238, 239, 240–41
Heaphy, Charles, painting by 233
Helen Ingram 94, 97
Hērangi, Te Puea 276
Hero Parade 66, 114
heroism 276–79
High Court 108
hīkoi 108–9
Hineahuone 42–43
Hine-te-Aparangi 44
Ho, Amber 191
Hobbit 255
Hobbiton 255
homes & housing 71, **71**, 73, 154, 156–72, 238, 299
  see also families
  ethnoburbs 67–68

homelessness & sleeping rough 170–71
  meaning 159–63
  ownership 167–68, 169, 172
  renting & flatting 162, 168–70, 181
  state 166, **166**, 168, 170
homosexual law reform, protests 110, 111, 112–16
Homosexual Law Reform Act 1986 66, 68–69,
  110, 111
Homosexual Law Reform Bill 114
homosexuality 66 *see also* LGBTQIA+
Hong, Celina 191
Hongoeka 49
Hopner, Veronica 281
Hotere, Ralph 136
housing *see* homes & housing
Housing NZ 208
Hoverd, W. 285
Howe, Chris 257–58
Hubbard, Laurel 69, 116
Human Rights Act 1993 68, 114, 115–16, 239
Human Rights Commission 115–16
Hunter, Alexis 136
Huntington, A. 29

I
identity
  collective 17, 24, 35, 37
  digital 203, 210–13, 215–17, 218
  personal 27, 32, **33**, 34
  social 27–28
  threads 23, 25–38, **26**
Ihumātao 122, **122**
Ilsley, George 279
immigration & emigration 63, 65, 120, 162, 235, 300
  see also settlement & colonisation
income 70, 73, 100, 186, 191
  family income 163, 165, 167–69
inequality & equality 93–94, 112, 169, 226, 230,
  234–37
inequality *see* equality & inequality; specific issues
Instagram 203, 216
internet *see* digital; media; social media
the internet of things 205, **205**
intersectionality 34
Islam & Muslims 115, 285–86
iwi 27, 41, 60 *see also* Māori, social structures

J

Jackson, Natalie 74
Jasper, J.M. 35, 112
Johnson, A. 32
Joy, Mike 260–62
justice system 31, 108, 229, 242

K

Kaefer, F. 254–55, 263
kaharoa 49
kāinga 156, 157
Kāinga Ora 208
kaitaka 129–30
kaitiakitanga 248, 250, 251, 257
kaupapa 49, 201, 229, 287
kawa 49
kāwanatanga 51
Kawharu, Hugh 51
Keep New Zealand Beautiful Society 256
Kember, David 191
King, Michael 273–74
Kīngitanga 47, 87, 275–76 *see also* monarchy
korowai 129–30
koru motif 133, 135
kotahitanga 60, 87
Kupe 44
Kura-mārō-tini 44

L

Laaksonen, Annamari 145
labour market 74, 88, 187, 211–12
    & education 191, 193–95, 299–300
    equality & inequality 232, 234, 235, 237
Labour Party & Governments 48, 92, 166, 186, 232,
    234, 235
    equality & inequality 226, 230
    gender & sexuality 70, 114–15, 116
Lacey, Anita 111
Land March *see* Māori Land March
landscape **132**, 132–33, 233, **233**, 254–56, 258
    Māori narrative 44–45, 248
land-use practices 249, 250, 257–58, 261, 263, 269
    see also agriculture & countryside
languages 29, 31, 35, 65, 67, 72, 109 *see also* Māori
Lantern festival 64, **64**
leadership 228
lesbians 68, 113
Leslie Lipson 232

LGBTQIA+ 66, 68–70, 110, 112, 115–16, 207
    see also gender
    gay rights 68, 85, 112–14
    homosexuality 66
    lesbians 68, 113
    sexuality 68–70
    transgender 66, 69–70, 112, 116
Liberal Government 231, 234
Light, Rowan 287
Lighthouse/Tū Whenua-a-Kura 141–42
Lincoln, Abraham 90
LinkedIn 211–13
Little, Andrew 230
Living by the Stars 201
Loomio 124
Lord of the Rings 255
Lowy Institute 102
Lynch, Frank 272
Lyndsay, Derek 261

M

MacKenzie, Numa 138–40
Mackley-Crump, Jared 65, 142
MacLean, Malcolm 118
Man Alone 133
mana 41, 43–4, 47
mana atua 43–44
mana i te whenua 47
mana tangata 43–44
mana tūpuna 43–44
mana whenua 43–44, 60, 122, 248, 250, 251
manaakitanga 44, 60
Mandela, Nelson 120
Māori 14, 23, 40–56, 60, 226
    & the arts 129–30, 133
    assimilation 36, 53, 229
    colonisation 50–54
    creation narrative 41–43, 248
    demographics 73, 74, 229, 296–97
    education 54–55, 178, 201–2
    equality & inequality 229–43, 238, 240, 242–43
    ethnicity 16–17
    & homosexuality 68
    identity & belonging 23–24, 27
    journeys to Aotearoa 44–46
    kaitiakitanga 248, 251, 253, 256–57
    land ownership 35, 48, **48**, 51–53, 108–9, 122, 229,
        234, 243, 269

language 35, 36, 53, 54–55, 60, 65, 120, 178, 201, 225

Māori Land March 48, **48**

& media 201–2

perspectives 14, 16–17

politics & parliament 35, 87, 97–98, 240

protests 35, 48, **48**, 53–54, 108–9, 118, 122, **122**

social structures 41, 45–46, 49–55, 60

tangata whenua 40–56, 42, 60

urbanisation 53, 229, 234

voting 35, 87, 97–98

& wars 51–53, 269, 275–76, 283–85, 287

Māori Council 87

Maori Land Board 229

Māori Land Court 108

Maori Prisoners Trials Act 1879 53, 229

Maori Representation Act 1867 97

Māori Schools **36**

Māori Sexuality Project 69

Māori Television 287

Māori Women's Welfare League 53, 87

marae 49–50, 54–55, 129, 178, 268

Marine and Coastal Area (Takutai Moana) Act 2011 108

markets, free 101–2, 237 *see also* neoliberalism

marriage 70, 110–13, 115, 116, 239

Marriage (Definition of Marriage) Amendment Act 239

Marriage (Definition of Marriage) Amendment Bill, 2013 112, 115

Marx, Anthony 111

Massey University 130, 180, **180**, 189, **189**, 192, **192**

Matahourua 44

Matamata 255

Matamua, Rangi 201

Mataora 129

Mātene Te Whiwhi 87

Mateparae, Jerry 287

Māui Pōtiki 41, 45

Māui Tikitiki a Taranga 41, 45

Maungapōhatu 53

M&C Saatchi 253

McArdle, Megan 194

McBride, Chris 138–40

McCahon, Colin 133

McCombs, Elizabeth 98

McGibbon, I.C. 281–82

McIntosh, Peggy 34

McLean, Donald 97

McLeod, John 274, 276, 279

Mead, H.M. 43

media 201–2 *see also* internet; social media

men, roles & norms *see* gender

mental health 131, 143 *see also* diseases & health

Microsoft 217

Middle-earth 255

mihimihi 160

millennials 74–75

Mills, C. Wright 102

Ministry for the Environment 256

Mixed fortunes: The geography of advantage and disadvantage in New Zealand 74

mixed member proportional (MMP) system 92, 238–39

The Model's Revenge 136

Mokaraka, Rob 131, 143

monarchy 92, 102 *see also* Kīngitanga

Morgan, N. 257

Morris, Toby, cartoon by **33**

motherhood 28–29, 71, **71**, 165 *see also* families

movies 82, 255

Muldoon, Robert 117

Mulgan, John 133

multiculturism *see* biculturalism & multiculturism

Murirangawhenua 45

Muslims & Islam 115, 285–86

N

narratives, national 224–27

National Party & Governments 118, 232, 235, 240

nationalism 290

nationality *see* citizenship

Native Land Court 51, 53

Native Land Settlement Act 1907 229

Native Schools **36**

Native Schools Act 36

neoliberalism 186, 196, 226, 234–35, 237–38

see also markets, free

Ness, Tigilau 138–41

'New' New Zealand Thinking campaign 254

The New York Times 261

New Zealand Bill of Rights Act 1990 123, 239

New Zealand Company 232, 233

New Zealand Defence Force 287, 289

New Zealand Expeditionary Force 271

New Zealand Herald 261

New Zealand Rugby Union 117

New Zealand Settlements Act 1863 108

'The New Zealand Story' 260

New Zealand Tourist and Publicity Department 302–3

New Zealand Tourist Board 253, 261

New Zealand Trade and Enterprise 254, 256

New Zealand Wars 51–53, 269, 271, 283–84

New Zealand Wine 256

Ngā Kete o Te Wānanga 177

Ngā Tamatoa 48, 53

Ngata, Āpirana 87, 285

Ngata, Tina 256–57

Ngāti Apa 108

Ngāti Koata 108

Ngāti Kuia 108

Ngāti Rārua 108

Ngāti Tama 108

Ngāti Toa 108

Ngāti Toa Rangatira 46, 87

Niwareka 129

No. 8 wire attitude 213

nuclear & anti-nuclear 250

O

oil shocks 234

O'Malley, Vincent 283

Osborne, M. 193

Otago goldminers electorate 98

Otago University 296

OTHER [chinese] 134

overseas experience, OE 270, 302

P

pacifism 226, 285 *see also* conscientious objectors

painting 133, 136

Painting No. 1 133, 135, **135**

Pākehā 118, 133, 232, 242, 284–85 *see also* settlement & colonisation

   cultural framework 17, 52, 62, 112

   statistics 32, 238

Papatūānuku 41–42

Parekowhai, Michael 141–42

Parihaka **52**, 52–53, 111

Parihaka Peace Festival 52

parliament 83, 88, 90–93 *see also* politics; specific Parties

participation 15, 34–35, 37, 65, 83–88, 91, 104, 109–11 *see also* specific issues

Pasifika 130, 131, 138–41, 226, 284

   demographics 73

   equality & inequality 238, 240

Pasifika Festival 65, 142, 144, **144**

Paterangi 107

Patté, Max 141–42

Peace Action Wellington 136–38

peacekeeping 277, 287

Pensioners Settlement electorate 98

pensions & superannuation 73, 98, 231, 285

   see also welfare & benefits

pepeha 41, 45–46, 55, 160, 248

Phillips, Jock 165, 272, 274

photography 136

place 152–218 *see also* context

politics 15, 84–85, 86–104, 89–90, 100–102

   see also parliament; voting

   anti-politics 100–102

Polletta, F. 35, 112

Polynesian Panthers 117, 130, 131, 138–41

Pōmare, Māui 87

Pooley, Leanne 120

population statistics *see* demographics

poupou 129

poverty 230, 234–35, 238, 242 *see also* welfare & benefits

pōwhiri 49, 60

Powles, A.R. 286

Pritchard, A. 257

privacy 172, 205, 209

privilege 32–34, 63, 83–84, 98, 216, 240, 290

Proposals Against Incitement of Hatred and Discrimination 116

protests 15, 84–85, 108–24, 298

   homosexual law reform 110, 111, 112–16

   Ihumātao 122, **122**

   Māori 35, 48, **48**, 53–54, 108–9, 118, 122, **122**

   Springbok tour, 1981 111, 116–20, **119**

   Wellington, 2022 103, **103**

Public Health Summer School 262

Pupuke Te Wānanga 201

Q

The Quarter Acre Dream 161, **161**

R

Rā Maumahara 284

racism & race relations 32, 34, 117–18, 120, 121, 123, 162 *see also* apartheid; rugby

Raglan 53

rāhui 248

rainbow community *see* LGBTQIA+

Rainbow Warrior 250

Rakiura 45

rangatira 47, 50, 228, 283

rangatiratanga 41, 47, 48, 50–51, 55, 251, 271, 276

Ranginui 41–42

Rangitāne 108

Rashbrooke, Max 237

Rātana 87

Red Peak flag 121

religions *see* specific religions

renting *see* homes & housing

Resource Management Act 240

returned service personnel 276, **280**, 280–82, 287, 288 *see also* RSA

Richardson, C. 276

Richardson, Ruth 235

'River Wind' 136

Roberts, Jim 241, **241**

Rogernomics 235, 237

Rongo 268

Rose, G. 159

Royal Commission of Inquiry into the terrorist attack on Christchurch masjidain on 15 March 2019 13

Royal Society of New Zealand Te Apārangi 63, 65

RSA 284, 285, 287, 289 *see also* returned service personnel

rugby 111, 116–20, **119**, 141 *see also* racism & race relations

rūnanga 47, 87

rural *see* agriculture & countryside

Ruthanasia 235, 237

S

Salvation Army 74

Samoa & Samoans 62, 65, 69, 116–17

Sandel, Michael 187, 300

Savage, Michael 166

Schmidt, J. 69

Schneider, Anne 94, 97

School Strike 4 Climate protests 111, 123

Schoon, Theo 135

sculpture 136–38, **137**, 141–42

Seal, Graham 288

The Second Sex 32

Second World War 234, 281

security 152, 215, 236, 299

digital 205, 209

personal & home 31, 154, 159, 167–72, 205

social *see* welfare & benefits

settlement & colonisation 50–54, 230–31, 234, 250–51 *see also* immigration & emigration; Māori; Pākehā

sexuality 68–70 *see also* LGBTQIA+

Sharma, R. 260

Sheppard, Kate 96

Shot Bro - Confessions of a Depressed Bullet 131, 143

Silver Economy 296

Simon Devitt Prize for Photography 161

Six Days in Nelson and Canterbury 133

Skilling, Peter 239

Smith, Rebecca 260

Snow, D. A. 35

social cohesion 13, 145

social identity *see* identity

social media 13, 202, 206, 211–12, 216 *see also* digital; internet; media; specific platforms

& politics 100, 103, 104

& protests 103, 121

social mobility 242

social norms 31, 35, 154, 207, 210, 213, 224

domestic 164–66

& wartime 275, 282, 286

social security *see* welfare & benefits

soils & soil quality 258

Solace in the Wind 141–42

SOUL (Save Our Unique Landscape) 122

South Africa 116–20, 141, 194

South African War 231

Spoonley, P. 290

sport 117–18, 144, 208 *see also* rugby

Springbok tour, 1981 111, 116–20, **119**, 141

Srnicek, Nick 215

Stibbe, Arran 182

Stoker, G. 89–90, 104

stories, national 224–27

Strombom, Simon 285–86

student activism 188, 190

suburbs & ethnoburbs 67–68, 71, **71**

suicide 131, 143

INDEX 317

superannuation & pensions 73, 98, 231, 285
   see also welfare & benefits
superdiversity *see* diversity & superdiversity
Suppression of Rebellion Act 1863 53, 108, 229
Surafend Massacre 278, 288

T

Taihia, Toa Sieke 138–40
Tait, Peter 110, **110**
Takaparawhau 53, 103, 118
takatāpui 69
tall poppy syndrome 213, 232, 276
tāmoko 62, 129
Tāne 42
tangihanga 50
tapu 43, 50, 55, 122
Taringa 201
Tasman, Abel 50
tattoos 62, 129, 135
Tavassoli, Aida 278, **278**
Tāwhiao 48
taxes 94, 186, 231, 235
Te Ātiawa 108
Te Heke Mai Raro 49
Te Ika a Māui 45
Te Korimako o Taranaki 201
Te Kupenga 54
Te Papa 137–38, 285
Te Punga a Māui 45
Te Punga o Te Waka a Māui 45
Te Rangi Hīroa 41, 87
Te Rata 48
Te Raukaramu 130
Te Rauparaha, Tāmihana 87
te reo Māori 35, 36, 53–55, 60, 65, 120, 178, 201, 225
Te Tauihu o Te Waka a Māui 108
Te Tiriti o Waitangi 37, 50–51, 118, 230, 240, 243, 285
Te Ture Whenua Māori Act 1993 108
Te Waipounamu 45, 108
Te Waka a Māui 45, 108
Te Wānanga o Aotearoa 201
Te whaiao ki Te Ao Mārama 40–42
Te Whare Manaakitanga 143
Te Wherowhero, Pōtatau 87
Te Whiti-o-Rongomai 52
Te Whiwhi, Mātene 87
teenagers 28–29 *see also* children; youth
television 32, 254, 255, 287 *see also* media

Thorns, David 167
Thunberg, Greta 123
tiakina 51
tikanga 43–44, 50–51, 60, 178, 201
TikTok 70, 212
tino Rangatiratanga 41, 47, 48, 50–51, 55, 251, 271, 276
Tohu Kākahi 52
Tohunga Suppression Act 1907 229
tōtara tree 42
tourism 235, 252–56, 259, 261, 263, 302–3
Tourism New Zealand 254–55
trade unions 111, 235, 237
transgender 66, 69–70, 112, 116 *see also* LGBTQIA+
Treaty of Waitangi 37, 50–51, 118, 230, 240, 243, 285
'Tribute 08' march 280
Try Revolution 120
Tū 268
Tū Whenua-a-Kura 141–42
Tucker, Corinna 257
Tufekci, Zeynep 124
Tuhoe Never Signed the Fucking Treaty 136
tukutuku 129
tūpāpaku 50
Turner, Brian 136
Turner, Bryan 30
Tutu, Desmond 120
Twitter 121, 203, 212

U

unemployment *see* labour market
UNICEF 123
United Kingdom 63, 118, 140, 167, 230–31, 234–35
United Nations 117, 239, 240, 287
United Nations Declaration on the Rights of Indigenous Peoples 240
United Nations Human Rights Council 239
United States 104, 140, 205, 234–35
United Tribes Flag 47, **47**, 50
universities 15, 83, 154–55, 177–97, 183, 299–300
   see also education
   citizenship 186–87
   expected behaviours 182–85, 188–89
   fees & costs 180, 185–93, 196
University of New Zealand 296
Upham, Charles 276, 277, **277**
urbanisation *see* Māori
urupā 50

V

Vertovec, Steven 63
veterans *see* returned service personnel
Victoria Cross 276–77
video games *see* gaming & games
Vietnam war 271, 280, **280**, 280–82, 281
violence, domestic 171–72
Vive Aramoana 136
voice 34–35, 82–85, 297–98
Voluntary Student Membership (VSM) Act 2011
  188, 190
voting 88–104, **95**, 179 *see also* politics
  Māori 35, 87, 97–98

W

Waikerepuru, Huirangi 42, 50
Waitangi Tribunal 51, 120, 240
Wakefield, Edward Gibbon 232
Walker, R. 44–45
Wallace, Cath 258, 260
Walters, Gordon 133, 135
war *see* First World War; New Zealand Wars;
  Second World War
water & water quality 256–57, 258, 259, 260–62
waterfront strikes, 1951 111
We Will Not Cease 137, 275
wealth 169, 226, 229, 230, 236–38, 239, 242
Web 2.0 211
'Welcome Home' 162
welfare & benefits 73, 168, 232, 234, 237, 242
  see also pensions & superannuation; poverty;
  superannuation & pensions
  disparagement 31, 94
Wellington
  protest, 2022 103, **103**
  sculptures 136–38, **137**
  Springbok tour protests, 1981 119, **119**
Wellington Harbour 233, **233**
Westland goldminers electorate 98
wetlands 258
Whakaako Kia Whakaora / Educate to Liberate
  mural 130, 131, 138–41, **139**
whakapapa 54–55, 157, 160, 229, 251
  familial 46, 49, 60, 62, 248
  of the universe 41–43
whakatauākī 14, 107
whānau *see* hapū; iwi; Māori, social structures;
  whakapapa

whanaungatanga 60
whare wānanga 178, 179
wharenui 49, 129
whenua rangatira 47
Wilde, Fran 114
Wiles, Janine 302
Wilson, E. O. 179
Wilson, H 29
wines 253, 256
wiri 162
women 34, 286
  roles & norms (*see* gender)
  voting & parliament 96, **96**, 98–99, 231
  & work 29, 163, 184, 234, 238
Wood, Aaron 287
World Wildlife Fund for Nature 257–58
Wright, Frank Lloyd 161

Y

Young Māori Party 87
youth 120–23 *see also* children; teenagers

Z

Zakaria, Fareed 179
Zaoui, Ahmed 162
Zoom 158, 183, 195

First published in 2022 by Massey University Press
Private Bag 102904, North Shore Mail Centre
Auckland 0745, New Zealand
www.masseypress.ac.nz

Text copyright © individual contributors, 2022
Images copyright © as credited, 2022

Design by Kate Barraclough
Typesetting by Carolyn Lewis

The moral rights of the authors have been asserted

All rights reserved. Except as provided by the Copyright Act 1994, no part of this book may be reproduced, stored in or introduced into a retrieval system or transmitted in any form or by any means (electronic, mechanical, photocopying, recording or otherwise) without the prior written permission of both the copyright owner(s) and the publisher.

A catalogue record for this book is available from the National Library of New Zealand

Printed and bound in Singapore by Markono Print Media Pte Ltd

ISBN: 978-1-99-101600-3